Members Are Ministers

Members Are Ministers
The Vocation of All Believers

Paul F. Goetting

CASCADE *Books* • Eugene, Oregon

MEMBERS ARE MINISTERS
The Vocation of All Believers

Copyright © 2012 Paul F. Goetting. All rights reserved. Except for brief quotations in critical publications or reviews, no part of this book may be reproduced in any manner without prior written permission from the publisher. Write: Permissions, Wipf and Stock Publishers, 199 W. 8th Ave., Suite 3, Eugene, OR 97401.

Cascade Books
An Imprint of Wipf and Stock Publishers
199 W. 8th Ave., Suite 3
Eugene, OR 97401

www.wipfandstock.com

ISBN 13: 978-1-61097-639-8

Cataloging-in-Publication data:

Goetting, Paul F.

Members are ministers : the vocation of all believers / Paul F. Goetting.

    xxiv + 238 p. 23 cm—Includes bibliographical references.

    ISBN 13: 978-1-61097-639-8

    1. Pastoral Theology—Lutheran Church. 2. Lutheran Church—Clergy. I. Title.

BV4011 G62 2011

Manufactured in the USA.

This book is dedicated to my wife Trudy, who with her faith, counsel, loving criticism, and patience over many years has shaped this work in so many ways, for all of which I am most grateful.

This book is also dedicated to our grandchildren: Jake, Aaron, Haley, Dylan, Catherine, Michael, Elysa, Olivia, Alex, and Andrew. They represent an emerging generation, called to engage now and in the years ahead with unprecedented threats and challenges—political, social, environmental, and religious. In writing this book, I frequently had them in my mind. May the baptism of each, marked by Christ's cross, shape their future and—through them—the lives of many others.

Contents

Foreword by Martin E. Marty / ix
Preface / xiii
Acknowledgments / xxiii
Abbreviations / xxiv

1. Introduction and Overview / 1
2. Ordination and the Office of Public Ministry / 21
3. Baptism: Ordination for Our Common Ministry / 48
4. Our Common Calling and Our Callings / 68
5. The Creation: The Context of Our Callings / 83
6. Discerning Our Callings and Serious Considerations / 104
7. Four "Stand Outs" in Our Discernment / 123
8. The Struggle for a Prophetic Church / 154
9. Working toward an Inverted Church / 180
10. The Art and Science of Inverting the Pyramid / 195
11. The Challenge of Change in a Conflicted Culture / 217

Bibliography / 235

Foreword

PREPARE FOR DISRUPTION IN YOUR WAY OF THINKING ABOUT the organization of life and lives, including your own, as you let author Paul Goetting make his case of "inverting" the life of faith and its organized forms and mission. While writing, he consulted numbers of his friends—he is a consultative and collegial type and his many friends respond when he asks for comment and suggestions. Let's begin at the beginning:

Most authors put great energy into book titles, and Goetting put in greater energy than most. The entertained titles dealt with the main concept of his book, which he wanted encapsulated in a metaphor or an image. We were "present at the Creation," or at least during the gestation of this book. Secretary of State Dean Acheson, major architect of modern diplomatic strategies of the United States after World War II, borrowed the title *Present at the Creation* from a classic reference to King Alphonsus XII of Spain, who was an architect of the modern world.

Pastor Goetting would be embarrassed to find himself in the company of a king and a diplomat, but the comparison fits. The company of Goettingites for some months played games with metaphors proposed to match his plot. He ended up with *The Inverted Church* (see chapter 9). Candidates for an image had been "upside down," "disarranged," "turned over," "bottom up," and "on head": your friendly dictionary of synonyms offers more. Why make so much of one word in one chapter title?

Because, as I read this book and know its author's philosophy, his concept of the inverted church matches his thesis, his main point. If that's the case, I should suggest why it is so important. Philosopher Eugen Rosenstock-Huessy once wrote: "One book is about one thing; at least the good ones are." This good book is about how the vocations of the gathered believers will be enlivened if they have and act upon an exciting image of their community, the church, in all its forms. Now let me venture a second *why* question that I am picturing in readers' minds. Answer: he *wants* to disrupt, invert, overturn conventional ways of thinking about the Christian life. He does so with teasing pen-strokes or, today, in today's church and world, with sequences of taps on keyboard keys.

One more *why* question will help me frame this book. The author would disrupt patterns of thinking which have lulled or bored believers so that they need or they do no more thinking. Last question: where does Goetting get the idea that using the language of disruption, of "topsy-turviness" fits in and can vivify Christian thinking? Simple answer: from Jesus in the gospels and from the authors of New Testament letters or from the prophets in the Hebrew Scriptures. French philosopher Paul Ricoeur argues that you will never understand or be grasped by any parable of Jesus or any narrative about him unless you are jolted by images and the language of disruption and the inversion of the church itself and all its doings and structures.

Think of parables and gospel narratives turning the world upside down: the littlest seed becomes the greatest tree; the lost sheep in the narratives is more important than the never-lost found sheep who, with their complacent shepherds, can sleep while the enemy is near. In other biblical lines, one dies to live; the sinner matters more than the righteous in the economy of salvation; the little flock has power that the powers in Jerusalem can never grasp; the weak and suffering and abandoned figure on the cross is the victor. Try out the Ricoeurean paradox on any text that comes your way and the gospel will be fresh to you. Try out the proposals of Paul Goetting for how the inverted church can embody fresh life and thinking—and action.

I mention action because for the author, the test of all the words in the narratives about Jesus and the church is how they get realized in action. The author knows that such a realization is necessary. He knows how the impulse to *order*, fine in itself—who needs more chaos in church and world?—always becomes a subtle or not so subtle instrument of power. In church life this usually means that order gets in the way of *vocation*, another key word in this book's title. And when vocation gets obscured or neglected or misunderstood, the way believers act and think matches the old, worn way, which was here before the prophetic and gospel messages were heard and read and acted upon.

I have seen the long gestation of this book and its ever fresh and often revised proposals for over half a century, from days when we were almost literally in neighboring fields planting new parishes. I have since seen other themes and theses and suggestions forged in the work by Paul Goetting on the city churches, which were not earlier ready to be inverted, uprooted, and replanted. The Martys have been awed by the energy and wisdom that the Goettings have put to work on several continents. Pastor Goetting has often helped disrupt our mental worlds and inspired us to act out elements of our vocations and help "invert" the church in its many old forms so that new ones can be born. This foreword is my commitment to a vision, a cause, and a strategy that can help change church and vocation in a world of convention, timidity, and torpor until they are reached by the disruptive gospel and the promise of new responses.

Martin E. Marty is the Fairfax M. Cone Distinguished Service Professor Emeritus at the University of Chicago and, like author Goetting, an ordained (by baptism) minister, called to the office of ministry in the Evangelical Lutheran Church in America.

Preface

Thoughts of the Lutheran Church and my dad's labor union, the United Auto Workers, prompt vivid memories from the days of my youth. Like my father I was proud of both, but they seemed to be worlds apart. Growing up in a major industrial city in the 1930s where the Lutheran church was the largest Protestant body, I early sensed a tension within our congregation between the members of the labor union and the church's leadership. My father never talked about the tension, which may have been for him a conflict he could not articulate, especially to his pastor. Nor did he want to talk openly about the apparent conflict because of loyalty to his church. In our congregation it was not difficult to sense that the pastor and the lay leaders were anti-union and anti-labor.[1]

In spite of this tension, our family thought highly of our pastors. Both mom and dad, well indoctrinated by their church, understood that their pastor had a "divine call." In spite of differences with their pastors, they believed their pastors stood in a special place for God and spoke a holy word. They were neither critical nor unkind. In fact, with many of our pastors my parents maintained a close and friendly relationship. Yet what was happening at work was not a subject of conversation between pastor and union families. No one such questions as, "How are you managing without any income during this three-month strike?" The lengthy and bitter strikes that personally pained and financially afflicted my family and many others in our church were off limits in

---

1. My father was one of five children. After his father (my grandfather) and his mule had pulled the last stump from the tract of land he had bought, he died, leaving his wife and young children to survive with few resources. Relatives and members of their local congregation constituted their welfare agency. Before finishing eighth grade my father began working full-time for the family's survival, and at sixteen he joined other boys working in the coal mines of southern Illinois.

church discussion. The silence suggested a judgment upon those who were striking. Those striking clearly recognized gross injustices in the work place. The absence of forums in which to air the issues and to try to understand each other's position exacerbated the problem.

On one occasion, returning from a congregational meeting that was deliberating a call to a prospective pastor, my father explained how an official of the church had instructed the assembly on the "divine call." On being asked when the call becomes divine, the church official replied that the call the congregation was sending to a prospective pastor became a divine call—that is, a call from God—only after the pastor accepted the call. Dad found that humorous. As a very young person I found the explanation confusing.

I was perplexed by all this discussion on the divine call and how so little attention was given to my father's vocation and his very unfair working conditions. If machinery took off your arm, the foreman's consolation was, "Sorry about that. We'll not need you anymore." In many places, you paid your own medical bills for injuries on the job. I early questioned why the church spoke so strongly about the high and holy calling of the pastor, while it seemed to have only a negative attitude toward the difficulties of laboring people and my father's work.

I was startled in my first year at the seminary when my homiletics professor showed an empathetic understanding of the auto workers. On several occasions he challenged us to find ways of relating our sermons to the working man, illustrating his own struggle as a parish pastor while serving a constituency of Chevy workers. That I found refreshing.

For my senior seminary thesis, I inquired of a professor whether I ought to explore the church's official publications, *The Lutheran Witness* and its predecessor *Der Lutheraner*, regarding their editorial positions on labor and unions. His counsel was, "Don't take the lid off the bucket: it stinks!" As a Lutheran in the Missouri Synod and knowing its conservative character, I simply assumed such insensitivity to the plight of the nation's industrial workers was limited to my church body. As years went on, I learned differently. The other Lutheran bodies proved no better. Indeed, the Protestant church's failure to speak meaningfully to the new urban, industrial worker was nearly universal. Unlike the Roman Catholic parishes whose priests were generally closely identified with the urban industrial worker, the Protestant pastors were in most cases identified with management. There were some exceptions, like Reinhold

Niebuhr, who served a Detroit parish in the 1920s. He wrote and spoke openly on behalf of the plight of the laboring man, but he was vilified by most Protestant church leaders at that time. Among Lutherans, A. D. Mattson, a professor of Christian ethics at Augustana Theological Seminary in Rock Island, Illinois, also distinguished himself with his passion and his insight into the social issues relating to unions, labor, and blue-collar workers. Theological leaders like Niebuhr and Mattson were not common among Protestant theologians.

In the 1920s and 1930s there began a massive migration of families from the farms of mid-America to the newly expanding industrial cities of our country, beginning a trend that continues to this day. Committed rural Lutherans were quick to find a Lutheran church in their new urban setting. One person described our churches in this period as increasingly becoming urban congregations while maintaining a rural mentality, though their new urban environment began to isolate pastors from the work life of their members.

While I was a boy, our family regularly visited relatives on their farms in southern Illinois. As I remember those visits, two subjects dominated the family conversations: the weather and the Lutheran church. During several summers spent on an uncle's farm I discovered something missing in our city church. During harvest time, this rural pastor would frequently spend time riding the wheat binder on a member's farm, not for financial gain but to help out those families whose father was ill. The pastor was closely connected to his members' work. My cousins' pastor in Baldwin, Illinois, had it easy relative to his members and their vocations, compared to our pastor in St. Louis. After four hundred years, in many ways the Lutheran churches in rural America were still similar to those in Luther's day. For Luther, as well as for my cousins' pastor, those in the pew represented only a few vocations. The majority were farmers or worked in farm-related jobs; a few people were in business (mostly shopkeepers); and a few were professional people, such as a school teacher. Of course, the most common vocation was that of the family. The pastor would most often be included in this calling. The pastor at St. John's in Horse Prairie, Illinois, where my father grew up could know and understand—indeed be very empathetic to—the stress and struggles of his members. They were nearly all farmers, and most likely the pastor too grew up on a farm.

Many of our city congregations were considerably different. The emerging urban congregations were ill-equipped to adjust to the increasing pluralism of their parishes. While the words "inclusive" and "noninclusive" were not yet in our vocabulary, it was as true then as it is now that urban congregations, especially their leadership, often failed to work toward being inclusive. And the church during this period learned little to prepare itself for the next wave of new arrivals about to swamp the urban scene.

Detroit is the best place to illustrate this next lost opportunity. By 1940, the Auto City had swollen with thousands of one-time rural but now urban laboring men and their families. Vast numbers of Christians had formed huge congregations with massive structures throughout the city. Lutherans had become the largest body among the Protestants. In the 1940s the new wave was made up of African Americans pouring into Detroit from the rural South. If many urban congregations had subtly made the industrial worker feel marginal and abandoned, now the white churches became openly unfriendly, inhospitable toward these newcomers to the American urban scene. Detroit became the tragic setting in 1943 of a major urban race riot, though news reports at the time did not implicate the unions or the churches. The white auto workers had discovered the strike to be their instrument in compelling social change, their means of obtaining recognition of their rightful presence in the newly emerging industrial cities of America. As African Americans attempted to draw attention to the gross injustices afflicting them, they were met with brutal attacks by police and a barrage of hate from shouting crowds. Following World War II, white Christians in Detroit fled to the suburbs in greater numbers and in a shorter time frame than in any other major city in the United States, abandoning many magnificent churches in their flight to the suburbs.

Seminary students in the 1950s, of whom I was one, were excited about the opening of so many new churches in the suburbs, great places for us to begin our ministry. At the same time there was a growing awareness of the church's seeming abandonment of its mission in the nation's inner cities. And an even darker cloud began to appear. Hovering over our studies was an increasing awareness of the Holocaust, including the complicity of many German Lutherans and a good number of well-known theologians, far too many of whom were uncritical and, in some cases, openly supportive of Nazi activities. There were indeed major exceptions. Some bishops, pastors, and Christians were known to protest the rise and practices of the Nazis, but they were in the minority.[2]

Many seminarians, and I was among them, began to take comfort in reports of major efforts at German church renewal following the war. Especially exciting were reports of the development of the German Evangelical Academies. These were organized retreats that gathered groups from many different professions—such as plumbers, lawyers, government officials, and teachers—to study Scripture and to discuss the intersection of the Christian faith with their respective vocations, searching for renewal of faith and ethical direction. Luther, we were told, was being heard in these academies.

Both at Concordia Seminary and Union Theological Seminary I had opportunity to delve into Luther's writings. At Concordia Seminary in St. Louis, Jaroslov Pelikan introduced me to Luther, and at Union Theological Seminary in New York, it was Wilhelm Pauck. Simply reading Luther brought wonderful "ah-ha!" moments, and nothing struck me with greater force than Luther's understanding of the Christian calling with its implications and insights for a compelling social ethic. His sermons spoke directly to people in the context of their vocations and life situations, wonderfully illustrated with earthy, everyday images. So began a career, culminating in this writing, to relate Luther's biblical understanding of the church and the Christian calling to the newly emerging forces in an industrial age, and now an age of computers and the Internet.

As our own family was enlarging through one birth after another, I began sharing Luther's comments on the Christian calling with my wife, especially Luther's references to the calling of a mother and the father. With five children, and three in diapers at the same time, one quote from Luther especially inspired her and challenged me: "the wife

---

2. Lazareth, *Christians in Society*, 9. Pastor Martin Niemoeller led a major protest of Protestant clergy, identified as the Confessing Church, which in 1933 totalled some six thousand of the fourteen thousand ordained German pastors. Many of the movement's leaders would be imprisoned or placed in concentration camps. The most well known were Dietrich Bonhoeffer, Hans Lilje, Heinrich Grueber, and Niemoeller himself.

should consider nursing, bathing and all other care for her baby and all other work . . . as truly golden and precious works [when done in faith] . . . And if a man should wash the diapers and do some other job which is commonly considered unfit for a man, and everybody should ridicule him and consider him a sissy and henpecked, if he does these works . . . in Christian faith—my dear friend, who has any reason to ridicule him? God and all angels . . . smile, not because he washes diapers, but because he does it in faith."[3]

Obviously, with our daughters using disposable diapers and raising their children while working fulltime in various professions, along with a growing culture that assumes the father is a partner in all this, the Luther quote my wife and I found so meaningful may need some updating. The challenge is to regain a conviction of Christ's call for ministry in all the menial demands of the family, along with a fresh understanding that our daily work is permeated with Christ's call for ministry and service. The grandsons and granddaughters of the Chevy workers are those who now are young entrepreneurs in the Silicon Valleys of our nation, computer experts, stockbrokers, government executives, university professors, and company presidents. Not all, but many, have moved up in the world, as judged by today's standards. For many, images of poverty are only seen in distant places; social injustice is seldom thought of as occurring in their own workplace. And for many the church seems even less and less meaningful than it was for their parents and grandparents.

Several years ago I had the pleasure of serving an extended interim ministry as the pastor of a congregation located in one of the country's wealthiest counties. Our members were from varied backgrounds and vocations, though many held positions as senior executives in major corporations. Signs of the distance between us were everywhere. They drove a BMW; I, an old Olds. Not knowing my political position, one member (a retired official of the World Bank) introduced himself to me by saying he was one of the only two Democrats in the congregation (an expression of how he felt; I am sure not statistically true). There was little question of the members' commitment to their church.

One day I happened to meet a member, Ben, walking from his commuter train to his car. "How's it going in The City?" I asked, making small talk. He quickly stopped, saying, "It's been a bad day, Pastor. I had to fire a senior member of our organization, a man with four

---

3. Quoted in Forell. *Faith Active in Love*, 152.

young kids." On a street corner, I found myself a listener to his pain and his obvious feelings of guilt. The exchange on that street corner initiated opportunities later for a deeper exchange regarding vocation, grace, and forgiveness. Ben and the majority of our congregation worked in what is often called The City (Manhattan), forty-five miles away. The location of our church and the place where many of our members lived is known by many as The Village. Beyond The Village's quaint shops, one drives through winding roads and a wooded countryside, a very rural setting, with well-preserved, expensive colonial style homes, colonial churches, and shops. At least visually there are two worlds: the very treasured rural setting where folks live, worship, and sleep; and the urban setting—The City—where they work. At first sight, it symbolized the increasing separation of one's world of work and the place of family, rest, recreation, and worship. Yet this apparent division was not really true, if for no other reason than everyone seemed to bring their work home, and in The Village—as throughout the country—television and the Internet are everywhere.

However, people's work and their politics were clearly distant from our colonial sanctuary. Unlike the rural pastor in my cousins' church who sometimes rode the wheat binder during harvest and could visit his members in their barns amid the manure, the flock I shepherded was, on work days, scattered either in skyscrapers across the island of Manhattan, an hour's train ride away, or in corporate parks along the Connecticut coast—a situation certainly far more complex and varied than the one in the church of my cousins. Yet here was that meaningful encounter with Ben, signaling how much more change is needed. Unity of people and pastor needs to be a genuine objective for pastoral leadership—not merely in appearance but with a strong sense that pastors and people are able to relate meaningfully; that we can show respect for different lifestyles, different incomes, wildly differing political and social positions, certainly gender and ethnicity, and together assist one another in greater realization of our respective vocations and ministries through our shared faith.

My visit with Ben was an accident. I take no credit for being especially effective in relating to members around their vocations. So when Ben's wife and my wife met several years later in another town where they had moved, she mentioned how much Ben appreciated my sensitivities to the difficulties of his job. When my wife told me of her conversation, I was momentarily proud. Then a different feeling entered when she reported that Ben especially felt good about those conversations since, according to Ben, no pastor had ever asked him about his work. If the encounter with Ben was typical, I realized we had not come far from where the church was in my father's day. If, in the past, pastors had difficulty relating to the congregants who were known to be members of a labor union, today I sense many pastors feel uncomfortable in warmly interacting with successful managerial types and those who are wealthy and financially successful.

Several years ago I made a return visit to the place of my family's rural roots in southern Illinois. Leaving the main highway, driving along open fields, passing scattered farm houses, I sensed that everything looked as it did when I was a boy. At a crossing of two country roads, the Lutheran church and adjoining cemetery stood stately and isolated in the open field, just as it did sixty years ago. The only other churches nearby were still Lutheran, and those were some miles in each direction. Late that afternoon, sitting with my elderly aunt Ella on her front veranda, we reminisced about the past. I commented, "Horse Prairie has not changed a bit, has it?" "Ah," she said, "the only thing that has changed is its name. Now we call it 'Prairie,' no longer 'Horse Prairie.'" About that time a car passed, filled with men. "That," said Ella, "is a car pool that leaves Prairie every morning at 5:00 a.m. They're farmers who work at the Chrysler assembly plant in Fenton, Missouri, fifty miles away." A short time after that, a ten-year-old boy pedaled his bicycle past the house. With sadness, she said softly, "He was expelled last month from the Lutheran school for peddling pot." And only the name has changed?

In this preface I have shared some of my life experiences pointing toward specific concerns for a more effective ministry of every baptized Christian. The account of my father's experience may suggest to some that such will be a major focus of this book. It will not be forgotten, but it will be only one of many vocational contexts that I trust you as reader will encounter as we proceed. My intent is to broaden, deepen, and enrich our biblical and historical understanding of the ministry of all Christians, clergy and laity. I will challenge us to review some of our past and present rhetoric and practices, and also suggest that the typical hierarchical structure of the church may no longer lend itself to the best of relationships within Christ's church: that the culture is summoning us to explore less authoritarian interactions, which may today be a more effective channel for the Word in energizing the people—all of us—in our respective ministries.

In writing this book I have assumed that we learn and are able to share most effectively both who we are and what we believe when we examine our personal experiences and our related spiritual struggles. This piece, I trust, sets a tone that will penetrate the chapters that follow. As I write I assume that in order to learn and faithfully practice a Christian ethic we must examine case studies of Christians struggling to bear witness to their faith, sometimes effectively, sometimes not so effectively. In other words, we learn the cognitive side of the faith through recognizing ways in which the faithful struggle experientially. My personal experiences surely are not representative of everyone's; we each have our own stories to tell. Nevertheless, I hope that my personal experiences, my failures and successes and those of others, will help the reader to grow in the Christian faith and to give a stronger witness in daily life.

As is evident, I write from my personal perspective as a Lutheran and with a strong appreciation of Luther. However, it is my intention as we proceed that non-Lutheran readers will find themselves a welcomed participant in every discussion and in no way feel that they are outside, looking over the shoulders of Lutherans. In rereading the manuscript, I have recognized that I frequently employ the word "we." Occasionally, that word may seem to include readers who would not see themselves within the "we." The format of this book commits me to a personal, one-on-one, face-to-face (as it were) style. I think of it as a kind of letter, a bid for conversation in which you could freely cancel out where you don't fit into a particular "we" and feel comfortable in doing so. Luther and his theological insights ought never to be seen as solely owned by Lutherans. His writings have long been treasured by a broad-based ecumenical community, and I trust that this awareness will be evident in what I write. Where there are readers who may disagree with my emphases or my understanding of biblical and historical interpretations, I welcome them into the conversation, and I trust we will have an opportunity to hear each other. I hope we will all feel comfortable and accepted in the discussions that follow.

Acknowledgments

Robert W. Bertram and Timothy F. Lull, both Luther scholars and long-time friends (now deceased), early encouraged me to pursue the subject of this effort. For their early council I am most grateful. A community with whom I have been associated over many years has made this work possible. I have had the benefit of scholars of various disciplines with whom I consulted and from whom I learned so much. Several nonscholars, endowed with faith and rich life experiences, are equally appreciated for their insights and suggestions. Several of those named below devoted considerable time to carefully reading, critiquing, and offering helpful suggestions, often enabling my garbled words to become meaningful and errors to be corrected. For all of these, their work and assistance I am most grateful: Trent P. Alexopoulos, Kenneth B. Bitter, Anne-Marie Bogdan, Daniel R. Borg, Richard R. Burholm, Mary F. Fletcher, Kenneth C. Haugk, Kurt K. Hendel, Beverly A. Hobbs, Everett R. Kalin, Ralph W. Klein, Edgar M. Krentz, F. Dean Lueking, Martin E. Marty, B. Eugene McCarthy, John H. Nieman, Barbara A. Rank, Jochen G. Salfeld, Edward H. Schroeder, Arthur Simon, and Milton E. Stohs. Also, I am most grateful for the work of K. C. Hanson, Editor in Chief, and his associates at Wipf and Stock Publishers. They have been a delight to work with and in a highly professional manner. To each and to all I extend a very public thank you. As is surely understood, in the end only I am responsible for what appears in this book.

—Paul F. Goetting

Abbreviations

In the footnotes, the abbreviations *LW* and *WA* denote, respectively, *Luther's Works* (American edition) in English, and Luther's works in German, commonly called the *Weimar Ausgabe*. In citations for both these works, the abbreviation is followed simply by the volume number and page: *LW* 41, 17. *WA* 34 II, 300.

1

Introduction and an Overview

SEVERAL THEMES WILL REVERBERATE THROUGH THESE PAGes. Each is connected to the others. But one theme, the ministry of all the people of God, should be viewed as central. It is my assumption that since the days of the Reformation the ministry of all the baptized has only causally held the attention of the church, its clergy or the laity. A great deal has been written on the subject; it is often the topic of sermons at Reformation observances. It is, however, difficult to find evidence that the ministry of all the people has been broadly understood and practiced, or that this ministry is fully supported by the clergy and the church's leadership. To be sure, the laity have been challenged to find their ministry in service to the church as institution and to engage in social services and in evangelism, the primary feature often being restricted to inviting the non-Christian to church. There is nothing wrong with this, of course, but it is much too limited. It is important today that the understanding of the ministry of all the baptized includes personal and corporate ministry in the daily life of every baptized person, in and through their unique and varied vocations. Thus living the faith active in love for others entails a lifelong, full-time activity that includes the continuous struggle for faithful ministry by all. Both pastor and people are called and motivated by Christ's love every day, all day, to actively engage the plight of others in service and justice as we witness to the resurrection.

In years past, the ministry for others has usually been expressed within an organizational pyramid, a hierarchy of relationships, even in our Protestant and Lutheran churches. It is assumed that bishops and church leaders, seminary professors and church officials stand at the top; clergy are in some way seen to be near the top, with the laity below or at the bottom; others—directors of Christian education, music, and youth—may be seen above the laity. In the midst of today's societal and cultural changes, many are questioning this traditional hierarchical structure. However, the critical reviews of organizational pyramids are more prevalent outside the church, focused primarily on secular institutions. Available to all are significant studies pointing to new possibilities; these we will explore as we proceed. I will not argue that the emphases and proposals that follow are a panacea for everything that ails today's church. I am, however, convinced that significant change regarding the ministry of the laity will only occur with a return to a paradigm from the early church, one in which the church is without rank. That paradigm of Christian ministry recognizes that ministry necessitates being close to, and on the same level as, those in need in our congregations and families, and among our neighbors. It is as peers, as equals, that we are best able to listen and support.

Now is a crucial time for consideration of a fresh paradigm for the pastoral ministry, one that is the opposite of the model that has evolved in the church over the past centuries. To be sure, our rhetoric has long spoken of pastoral leaders as servant ministers and the church as a servant church. Pastors have long been recognized as significantly demonstrating such leadership, and the church has long distinguished itself through great expressions of service to people in all sorts of conditions. However, the phrases "servant ministry" and "servant church" are an *oxymoron* when expressed in the context of today's hierarchical relationship. In today's culture it is difficult to envision a *servant* ministry that *looks down* from above. From such a position one is unable genuinely to sense and to meet the needs of those below, and thus it is difficult for leaders to be trusted. Recognizing the tremendous cultural shifts taking place among us, our task in all that follows is to pursue a significant change that is both biblically based and, with the Reformation, provides insights that support this fresh paradigm: *a servant church with all the baptized faithfully engaged in Christ's love for others, including involvement against issues of injustices.*

Signs of the current cultural shift have been present among us for some time. Indeed, a shift became obvious already in the early 1960s when a major reform movement was sparked, not by political leaders nor by the church officialdom, but by young, Christian, African American students. They dared to sit and request service at a Greensboro, North Carolina, Woolworth store's soda counter where they were forbidden to sit because of their skin color. The newspapers and especially the new medium of television captured the hate, hostility, and harassments which the students experienced from whites. The evening news placed the repulsive behavior before the nation. The students' action of civil disobedience set in motion a major social protest which, along with other protests of the period, became political movements that brought down Jim Crow. Other grassroots movements followed; some faltered, while others succeeded. Then within the past ten years *social networking* has rapidly developed, made possible by the Internet. Perhaps most evident was the networking effectively empowering Barack Obama's political campaign. Evident also are other grassroots movements—for good or bad—exemplified by the Tea Party's apparent success in generating a significant following of angry people in protest. Many more cultural shifts are emerging among us.

Books and blogs galore have now been written indicating what this new phenomenon means for our daily lives and for the reshaping of our institutions—indeed, for our culture. We need mention only a few specifics helping to shape a new culture: the rise of twenty-four-hour cable news, Google, YouTube, Twitter, and Facebook. They and other electronic phenomena have called into question the future of print media. Newspapers, including church periodicals, are disappearing; the traditional role of journalists is changing. Blogs, whether good or bad, have enabled almost anyone to become a writer and to gain a following. You no longer need to be a trained journalist or represent a public institution to report the news or to provide a particular opinion on a major political or social issue; you simply develop your own blog and look for a following. The historic and traditional role of the professional is thus changing. A computer-savvy mother can quickly connect with the Mayo Clinic's Web page and obtain pertinent information, enabling a nonmedical person to obtain a preliminary diagnosis of an illness. This does not make the professional medical doctor obsolete nor the mother an M.D., but it begins to change relationships. If the diagnosis of the doctor conflicts with Mayo's information, the mother is able to further go online. She reaches countless blogs and Web pages in a search for additional information and other related medical specialties. If her child's medical problem remains conflicted in diagnoses, she may find a chat room of parents with similar problems, sharing their frustrations with a medical practice that seems to them to be uninformed and, in some cases and in their judgment, insensitive to their child's peculiar illness. This illustration, employing a medical problem, can just as easily describe a process already evident within our Christian congregations. When a church member realizes a sharp difference with her pastor, or a group within the congregation differs with the official position taken by their church body, they are able very quickly to be in touch with a large number of people with similar feelings. They may easily find spokespeople who, in their judgment, reflect their personal position and provide the support they covet. Thus the relation of pastor and people is changing. Very quickly new communities are formed with like-minded convictions, often holding positions contrary to positions offered by their church body or local congregation. These groups have been formed, not related to neighborhood or congregation, but focused on special interests, including new communities of care. A 2010 *New York Times* article reported: "A former model who is now chronically ill and struggles just to shower says the people she has met online have become her family . . . , and a woman with multiple sclerosis says her regular Friday night online chats are her lifeline."[1]

This leads us to further evidence of what is signaled as a major shift in organizational experiences: movement from the authority of a professional—once identified as a highly trusted person in our institutions—to a highly egalitarian, democratic experience in new relationships, in part generated by a growing distrust of our major institutions, including the church. The ability of computer programmers to install filters within their systems means a Web search can quickly and almost miraculously bring before you a tremendous amount of information relative to your special interest, whether political, religious, medical, or whatever. The filter may also work against your obtaining alternate, contrary information that may be most important in gaining insight on your special need. Your focus may give you clear and important insight but fail to challenge you with information that refutes or re-colors what you initially obtained. In other words, it may both open your mind to greater

---

1. Miller, "Social Networks."

knowledge and also isolate you in a cyber box, limiting a fuller view and a better understanding of the world in which you live and struggle.

It is generally assumed today that organizations, including the church and its larger judicatories, are or will be undergoing difficulty and stress if they remain insensitive and nonresponsive to this major cultural shift. There is considerable interest within the church to be on top of these new communication devices, especially using Facebook Twitter, and YouTube to advance the traditional programs of the church. While not belittling this endeavor, I am most concerned in these pages with the systemic changes, especially in pastoral leadership and the interrelations between pastor and people, as well as among the people. This will be a constant concern as we proceed through this writing. This emphasis in these pages will have a direct relationship to our concern for the ministry of every Christian and to a church without rank. The ministry of all the people, and an insistence that the authority of the church lies not in the pastor nor in the people but in the Word, has the possibility of significant compatibility with elements of this still-emerging culture. Related to this phenomenon is the need to explore how the people of faith are related these days to issues of justice, and who identifies an injustice and by what means.

Several years ago, our family was to gather in St. Louis for a reunion. Before their arrival, I had an opportunity to spend some time in the library of Concordia Seminary, where I have studied. I was especially interested in obtaining a copy of the student monthly publication, "The Seminarian," for January 1955. I had written an article in that issue only months before graduation, and could no longer find a copy in my household. The librarian quickly retrieved the issue. As I examined the table of contents, I experienced an elevated level of hubris. I was astonished! My article was surrounded by those of fellow seminarians who later went on to distinguished academic careers. I never realized I had been surrounded at that time by persons of such quality! I was thrilled.

On a quick reading of the article, my ego began to deflate: I felt as though I had not grown. The article focused on the Christian faith interacting with politics and government, especially in the life and ministry of the laity. As I read, I asked myself: Am I stuck in the past or was I way ahead of my time? What I had written in 1955 was not much different from what I believe now. The only response to the article that I remember was that of a classmate who told me, "Your article does not belong in a theological journal." Later, however, I realized the article was a factor in leading a faculty committee to recommend that, following graduation, I teach social studies at Concordia College, Milwaukee, which certainly affected my career path.

I joined the Concordia Seminary faculty in 1969. Three years prior to joining the faculty I completed an STM at The Lutheran Theological Seminary in Philadelphia, and spent the next three years in an ecumenical "action/research" program. I was called to the program by The Lutheran Church—Missouri Synod (LCMS) Mission Board; the project was generated by the New Delhi Assembly of the World Council of Churches. Both my STM and the ecumenical think tank were centered on restructuring the local congregation for a more effective ministry by the laity in engaging issues of social justice. My call to the seminary faculty included developing programs that were similar. Much of what I had hoped to accomplish at the seminary had to be placed on hold because of an intense conflict that raged at the time between the leadership of the LCMS church body and the seminary, a conflict that brought major adverse change, affecting every sector of seminary life. Many of my goals were never achieved. However, Professor Robert W. Bertram and I were able to develop an important program, "Theology in Metropolitan Experience" which I still consider a major accomplishment. It was a quarter-long interdisciplinary program with extensive interchange with laity in various vocational settings.

My commitment to this subject has indeed grown through the years since then. I have particularly sought clarity on the necessity of connecting Luther's insistence on faith active in love with the Christian's engagement in issues of justice, especially as carried out in the context of multiple offices and callings. Christian faith reaches deep into God's word for insight, courage, and strength in struggles against evil and corruption. At the same time, we need to learn to pursue justice with reason and our senses, distinguished from the reality of faith, while also maintaining the inseparability of the two in the Christian life.

All this has led me to insist that we need to review our public expressions of the meaning of ordination and clarify for the public that the grounding of all ministry lies in holy baptism, that the call to public ministry is not separate from the common call of all Christians to offer our whole lives to a living sacrifice to God in view of the mercies given in Christ. We may properly teach that the call of the pastor through the congregation (a very human process) should be accepted as a call by God to a specific office, the office of public ministry (though it may not be the pastor's only calling, he or she may also be father or mother, husband or wife, son or daughter, citizen, and so forth). At the same time, we need to teach that such a process is in effect similar to the calls received by each lay person—calls by God through very human channels—to particular ministries: whether that of a garbage collector or an executive or a pastor. For both clergy and laity, this call is a call to witness to Christ's redemption and the promise of the resurrection, and to creatively engage God's world. We are to shape the present world toward the better world that is not yet here, the better world for which God calls us to work even now, hindered as we are amidst the fog of a fallen world, even as we await The End. The church's process of calling a pastor ought to be a public model for the laity in approaching their various callings, offices, and stations in life. We will expand on all of this as we proceed.

Several years ago I was in Berkeley, California, about to teach a seminary course in the January interim for the Graduate Theological Union. A pastor's conference happened to be gathered for lunch on the seminary grounds. Sitting with several pastors, I was asked a question about the course I would soon be teaching. Searching for just the right phrase with which I could succinctly describe the subject, I said it was about "inverting the church's pyramid." At that moment, one pastor frowned, suggesting either that he did not understand or that he disagreed with me. Another pastor smiled as he began to explain his experience as the chaplain in a major facility for the elderly. He indicated that his agency's management and their entire staff had recently completed an intensive training program, working toward what was called just that: inverting the pyramid. He confessed that throughout much of the training he was asking himself why the church was not as concerned about accomplishing this objective as was this for-profit agency. He believed as I do that there are theological grounds for calling the church to actualize much more fully—both in its practice and in its structure—its claim to be a servant church.

To achieve any degree of an inverted church, our attention must first focus on the unique character of leadership, that is, the heart and mind—the soul—of the leader, along with the faith and commitment of the people. With Christ the Christian seeks an emptying of self as one lives and serves in Christ. This is crucial for affecting the bottom-up congregation.

When Martin E. Marty's book *Protestantism* was released in England in 1974, the publisher obtained a sixteenth-century German woodcut for the cover. It depicted a church building standing upside-down with its steeple in the ground, a monk plowing the nearby field, and a farmer preaching inside the church. The woodcut is indeed eye-catching. The upside-down church indicates that the highest among us is the servant of the lowest. In our Lord's own words: "Whoever would be first among you must be slave of all" (Mark 10:43). Unfortunately, the switching of roles between the priest and the farmer is misleading. While the New Testament and the Reformation insist that people are not to be ranked, we are indeed called to offices and roles that are not all the same. However, all offices and roles within the Christian community are callings under the cross, and each must certainly be expressive of servant ministry. Regardless of position, all are without rank, as Luther recognized.[2]

The image in the woodcut is, however, most provocative. It is interesting to discover that elements of the Reformation already perceived that the gospel called the church to demonstrate a posture in its leadership that was radically different from the one it had traditionally experienced. Christ's servant posture, ultimately suffering death on the cross for us and our salvation, calls for an authentic humility as Christians carry on their individual and corporate servant ministries in all aspects of daily life, both in the community of faith and in every other community.

Very simply, inverting the church's pyramid means that the highest office holders among us—the presiding bishop, synodical bishops, pastors, church leaders and officials, theologians—must be seen as the servants of all, including or perhaps especially the lowest, and not just symbolically. Since Christ is our model in this ministry, the highest person among us (from a human perspective) continues that modeling for the rest of us. Indeed, each of us has a similar calling, whether clergy or laity. Whatever our situation, in all our relations with others, the sign of Christ is seen in our care for others in his name, especially in our care for the forgotten, neglected, oppressed, and marginal, as well as for those close to us in our families, churches, and neighborhood (that is,

---

2. Marty, *Martin Luther*, 89–90.

our world). The inverted church is not so much an expression of a new management style as it is a means of allowing the gospel to shape our relationships with one another, especially reshaping our roles in leadership, thereby affecting the public image of the church and its witness.

Pastors, bishops, and parents today would seldom admit to being anything less than serious caregivers. The very nature of being a father, a mother, a pastor, or a bishop means that one's life is dedicated to the lives of others, certainly to those understood to be in our care. Leaders may even speak of being in a partnership with their followers, of sharing a common responsibility for all the issues they face. We may, however, say the right things, while our leadership behavior often conveys a contrary message. The way we see ourselves may be quite different from the way those in our charge see us, especially as they experience us in various religious ceremonies, public pronouncements, and stressful interactions. Followers respond to their leaders, not as these leaders speak of their position and their public posture, but as the followers ultimately perceive the leader through a multiplicity of observations. When we are in a position of authority, we too easily assume that we are seen by others as we see ourselves. The perception of others, however, may be quite different; and failure to be in tune with others' perception can lead to unanticipated conflict or quiet resistance to the will of the leader. Very simply, the perception by the membership of their leader is a reality, which is to be taken seriously, along with other factors. It is the basis of much of the follower's response and the group's behavior. How one views one's own leadership, both in the church community and in the wider world, and how one can sharpen an understanding of one's leadership will be important topics in the pages that follow.

Central to our effort in these pages is the challenge to review the rhetoric relative to ministry. I am convinced that the ministry of all the people will not be fully grasped until the people of the church perceive that the leadership—from across the whole church to synods and conferences to the local congregation—is supportive of ministry in their daily lives. Thus our primary concern in these pages is a greater ministry in full-time service by every baptized member of Christ's church, and that those members feel the support of their pastoral leadership.

There are insightful and very capable people who may be uncomfortable with the topic of an inverted church. It is admittedly not a concept everyone easily accepts. My hope is that we can be in dialogue as we proceed. We need to explore theological grounding and current insights of the behavioral sciences and be sensitive to a clearly seen cultural shift among all of us. Both sound biblical theology and secular literature, especially in view of our changing culture, call the church in these days to a serious review of its public posture and to a re-evaluation of what it means to be committed to the common priesthood of all the baptized.

While speaking of the inverted church, we often also speak with similar meaning of an *inverted pyramid*. For the latter word, we could use the word "hierarchy." But as I will discuss later, "hierarchy" is loaded with medieval theological baggage and relates to a current, specific Roman Catholic dogma. I will, however, refer at times to hierarchy and historic Roman Catholic theology in order to clarify the Reformation's advocacy of evangelical ministry. Secular literature on leadership today speaks a great deal regarding the necessity of change from the traditional models of hierarchical leadership to one that is inverted.

Those in organizational research have identified the basic ingredients that signal the existence of a genuinely inverted community. Here are some of the characteristics often cited.

1. Rank and signs of status are absent or significantly lowered. Though there are identified leaders, they function and are experienced as being below, supporting those above. Those who are identified as leaders are recognized as assistants to all, including to those who appear marginal. Those understood to be of high rank are frequently seen talking with and listening to those in the lower ranks.

2. People are recruited because of their commitment to the central core of the organization's mission.

3. The central mission is understood and shared by all; each assists the other in keeping focused on the mission.

4. Diversity of skills and abilities is valued.

5. Commitment to the central mission is most important, but uniformity, conformity, and rigidity are not appreciated.

6. Creativity is expected from all, augmented by diversity. Bold new ideas are encouraged and are assumed to develop in work groups related to the organization's mission, not necessarily from above.

7. Unusual ideas are honored and allowed to percolate. Failure is not seen as defeat, though critical review of failure is thorough and expected.

8. Loners are encouraged to open up and learn to work with others.

9. Work facilitation is a common activity of all. Each person is willing and quick to assist another when called on or when one sees the opportunity. One frequently hears, "How can I help?"

10. There is a strong commitment to excellence; mediocrity is discouraged.

11. Power to control is discouraged; rather power is encouraged as a means of supporting, enabling others to embrace creatively the group's purpose and goals. What controls the group or organization is its common commitment to its fundamental purpose and reason for being.

12. Finally, leadership committed to this paradigm is a key factor in initiating and sustaining an inverted organization.

These are my compilations developed over time from many sources.

Is this simply idealistic? You might say so, but these characteristics are discernable in an increasing number of organizations, who have come to realize that unless this culture is in place they are unlikely to survive. Indeed, there have long been organizations, including Christian congregations, who have demonstrated these values to various degrees in their life and mission. There have been and there are now congregations, though perhaps not many, who illustrate this relational and organizational structure. It is from both secular and religious organizations that the above characteristics have been extrapolated.

I am confident that in both the New Testament and Luther you will find support for inverting the church's pyramid. Professor Steven Ozment, Harvard historian and internationally known Luther scholar, reports in his book on the history of the German people on the profound social changes affected by the Reformation: "Luther even spoke of the church as a *Gemeinde*, a neighborly community of spiritual equals . . . [who] took moral responsibility for one another's welfare—not a church pyramiding from lowly laity through clergy and the pope to the saints of heaven."[3] This reform movement contrasts with the historic

3. Ozment, *Mighty Fortress*, 68.

medieval character of the church as a hierarchical institution. Biblical scholar Edgar M. Krentz, focusing on the Gospel of Matthew, writes: "There is no respect of persons in the Matthean church. All who respond to the proclamation and become disciples are equal."[4] In a later paragraph he says: "The church is unstructured. It has no distinctions of class or office . . . Matthew 23 is a massive rejection of Jewish leadership models—and it is only the final statement of an argument that runs through the Gospel." Biblical scholar Ken Bailey has spent much of his career living and studying Arab culture in remote, isolated communities. There he listened to their oral histories and observed their long-established customs, which in many cases profoundly deepen our understanding of specific words of Jesus. In his book on the parables of Jesus, he makes the following observation: "If you talk to a king as you would to a street sweeper, you anger him. If you talk to a Pharisee as you would to a shepherd, you would infuriate him. Yet this is exactly what Christ does. He refuses to show deference to their rank, and in the East rank is everything."[5] Consider also St. Paul's words to the divisive congregation in Corinth: "God has so arranged the body [the church], giving the greater honor to the inferior member" (1 Cor 12:24).

I need to be more specific on this subject. A pivotal position of this effort is to challenge our existing paradigm that sees the church as layered, with some—such as bishops, church executives, and theologians—in higher callings, while others are "merely" pastors; lower still are deacons and associates in ministry; and seemingly at the bottom are laypeople. On the contrary, the church is distinctive. It is a living sign of God's Kingdom, God's unique reign of mercy breaking through among humans empowered by the Spirit. The gospel is constantly challenging us to see the church as a community more than an institution, a community in which everyone is a disciple of Christ united in fellowship with God, rather than merely a member of an organization.

This necessitates a careful review of our understanding of the call to ordained ministry and the Christian calling. These are terms we frequently use in our churchly conversations without always being clear about their meanings. We all need clarity and a deeper understanding of our common Christian calling, that is, God's invitation to believe the gospel and its apprehension by faith. With a solid grounding in the

---

4. Krentz, "Egalitarian Church," 336, 337.
5. Bailey, *Cross*, 21.

gospel we are able to distinguish the faith that apprehends the gospel and the freedom to engage our various vocations with reason and our senses. The latter callings are always a summons by God for service in Christ's name. Seeking an inverted church without a solid grounding in the Christian faith and a common insight into our primary calling will lead to chaos and strife. However, the assumption that the faithful church of the future relies solely on a biblically educated clergy will lead us into a similar dead end. What is called for is a deeply spiritual, critical review of our roles as both clergy and laity as we all together proceed in a new and fresh direction.

Another objective, closely related to the experience of an inverted pyramid as a model for our relationships, is to explore the necessity of reshaping the culture of the congregation, indeed, the culture of synods, seminaries, and other jurisdictions too. A culture can be defined in various ways. Here I think of the culture of a congregation or any other Christian entity as the common behavioral pattern, reflecting its basic values and shaped by its core beliefs—often unexamined, yet maintained over an extended period of time and very resistant to change, though certain basic assumptions may be changing or have changed. The fact that the church's cultural pattern is resistant to change should not in itself trouble us. It provides predictability, reducing the unexpected. If a congregation were so undisciplined as to arbitrarily abandon its own culture and be unpredictable in the ordering of its activities, life in its midst would be most stressful and difficult. Disorder, discord, and disintegration would be the order of the day.

It is good that congregations seek consistency and resist substantive change. At the same time, this awareness should sober us in any effort to affect significant congregational change that is both substantive and lasting. And this is true of all ecclesiastical jurisdictions as well. To alter the culture of the congregation we need to proceed carefully and patiently, sensitive to the values that have long undergirded its patterns of behavior and its public witness. Frequently the supporting values and deeply felt assumptions have shifted, while their historic organizational expressions persist. It is also clear that a congregation that is incapable of change, and unwilling to examine its basic values and theological beliefs, will most likely die, especially in the changing conditions of our day. Or it may hang on as a mere artifact of something whose meaning has long passed.

Many of us want immediate gratification. If things are not working well in our churches, we often expect quick fixes. For much of my pastoral career, I have witnessed a great number of church renewal programs that promised so much but delivered so little; to genuinely invert the church's pyramid is neither easy to do nor quick to accomplish. This is especially the case when you consider that the church, both Western and Eastern, has for much of its history seen itself as a hierarchy and often claimed theological justification for such. One can argue whether the early medieval church initiated the hierarchical structure which then was adopted by much of the Western world, or whether the political institutions initiated it and the church copied. Or is resistance to inverting the pyramid reflective of the fallen human condition, with many striving for the top and with those attaining the heights trying to control those below? In any case, in medieval society both the culture of the church and of the state, and later corporate institutions as well as the home, saw hierarchy as their sole organizational structure. Thus admittedly we are going against the historic currents of both church and society.

Currently, many nonreligious organizations have already called the past hierarchical model ineffective. They have seen it to be inappropriate and ineffective, given the major societal and cultural shifts taking place among us. In fact, a significant sector of today's management literature speaks of "servant leadership" related to training its personnel toward inverting the organization. If the change proposed for the church is both necessary, possible, and justified theologically, we ought to commit ourselves to bringing it about, even as we ponder how that change will actually alter the very culture of the congregation.

Central to our task is this: to demonstrate that the struggle for faithfulness as we pursue ministry in our various vocations is always under the cross of Christ. Thus the spiritual condition of the heart and mind of the Christian is crucial in this effort. God's Suffering Servant, Jesus the Christ, shapes the servant ministries of all God's people, which are integral to Christian life and witness. This understanding is central to Luther's theology. He clearly spelled out the character of the Christian life in his essay "Freedom of the Christian," in which he asserts: "A Christian is a perfectly free lord of all, subject to no one; a Christian is a perfectly dutiful servant of all, subject to all."[6] Dietrich Bonhoeffer had a similar understanding. During the summer of 1944, while imprisoned

---

6. *LW* 31, 344.

by the Nazis and shortly before his execution, he had begun an outline for a book. Only his notes have survived. Boldly they state the theme he was working on: "The church is the church only when it exists for others." In the same paragraph, he writes: "The church must share in the secular problems of ordinary human life, not dominating, but helping and serving. It must tell men of every calling what it means to live in Christ, to exist for others. In particular, our own church will have to take the field against the vices of hubris, power-worship."[7]

A church whose pyramid is inverted is one in which—more than in words, and yet through the Word—the masses of the people experience the church's leadership as truly supportive of their struggles in the whole of their lives. The baptized are called to be witnesses to Christ and his resurrection in and through their vocations. All this is in contrast to our traditional assumption that the clergy are those in the forefront of the church's mission and ministry. Here is our needed paradigm: *The people in the pew, pouring out of the church into their various vocations following public worship, should be seen as the front line of the church's ministry and mission. Below them, uplifting and supporting them, there are the bishops and the pastors and leaders of the congregation.* This is the paradigm we should hold in our heads and hearts as we work to express it in our congregation's public and private witness, and as we have a similar heart and posture in our personal and private lives and in all our vocations as Christians. This is a perspective on the relationship of pastors to people that we hope to see implemented far and wide.

Is this talk about the pastor, minister, bishops, and lay leaders being *below* the people in the pew contrary to what I have identified earlier, that the church is a community of people without rank? We are constantly taking on a different frame of reference as we work our way through countless situations and difficulties. In one situation, the pastor as servant is clearly experienced by the people as one who is among them, holding them up in the faith. In another situation, the people—or a few—are ministering to the pastor who gratefully accepts their servant position in their relationship. The phrase "below them" is surely a sign of the servant ministry. However, Christians experiencing "services" from "below" surely are not by such a relationship free to trample on those who give service; nor ought the servant role of the leader lead to patronizing or dependency relations.

7. Bonhoeffer, *Letters and Papers*, 382, 383.

Many of us may agree how difficult or, humanly speaking, impossible it is to achieve an inverted church. Yet not to work at leveling the church's social structure into a more authentic community is an abandonment of Christ's call. In addition, we cannot expect this effort, or others like it, to be magic wands enabling us to awaken one day to a new church community of this kind. We must work for this objective, never for self-justification or self-glory, but simply because it is our calling in Christ, the response to his gift of himself to us. As in all the signs of the kingdom, people of faith struggle to achieve the maximum, not for self-justification but simply because that is God's call to us in Christ. Not to do so means to slip into behavior that belies any testimony to the clear signs of God's reign, fulfilled in Christ's gift of mercy, a reign to be seen and known in the world through the church's witnesses in its multiplicity of ministries by all its people. Inverting the church's pyramid is not a simple answer to the many problems facing today's congregations. But it can greatly assist us in obtaining a greater unity and a clearer witness in the faith, and a more hopeful assurance that conflict and differences can be overcome peacefully. It is also a crucial consideration because of a shift in people's expectations of their lives in organizations and community, especially recognizing that people today generally expect to be active and trusted participants in the life of their community, particularly with issues that affect their life and well-being.

An initial challenge to our existing paradigm is an examination of our use of the word "laity." The word is derived from the Greek word *laos*, which means "people." But not just any people. *Laos* in the New Testament is twice coupled with another Greek word, *theou*, meaning "of God." Thus we should see that behind the word "laity" is the Greek term *laos theou*, "the people of God," a reference to all the baptized, to the Christian Church. In a nonbiblical manner, and in a way that should be offensive to Protestant Christians, we have allowed the word "laity" to identify all those who are not ordained, thus dividing what God has made one. The church ought not separate the people of God from the ordained, suggesting that there are two groups in the church: the laity and the clergy. That people and clergy are one body in Christ is not even debatable, yet the separation in language and practice is deeply imbedded in the life of today's church and in our secular and religious culture. To paraphrase St. Paul: "There is neither Jew nor Greek, . . . there is neither clergy nor laity; for you are all one in Christ Jesus" (Gal 3:28).

When contrasted with the hierarchical priesthood of the Old Testament, the New Testament church is clearly an inverted structure. The early church makes a major break with the Old Testament priesthood, recognizing only one priest, Christ, and his once-and-for-all sacrifice of himself for the world. The church is the body of Christ; all the people together form a royal priesthood. By "royal" it indeed refers to a kingly rule, but this rule of power is a lowly rule. The power of the rule is God's grace, mercy, and forgiveness. Abandoned in the New Testament church is any thought of a rule of the church by a priesthood, a hierarchy (a word derived from the Greek term *hiereus,* meaning "priest," and *archē* meaning "authority" or "rule"—thus, "rule by priests"). Indeed, the New Testament had no equivalent for the word "clergy," as this term is understood today. While the Old Testament knew a rule by the priesthood with dramatic clarity, such a rule is totally absent in the New Testament.

A related, inappropriate connotation has entered into the meaning of the word "laity," as in layman and laywoman—that is, someone who is not professional, who does not fully understand the subject, their knowledge ranging from considerable but not a full understanding of the faith to ignorant and unenlightened. Indeed, by any behavioral science analysis the church has sharp class structure, clergy and laity. The structure has attributes similar to those in a parent-child relationship, one in which a dependency relationship often exists well beyond adolescence. This class structure might arguably have been appropriate through much of church history, when the clergy were the primary educated class. We are in a different time.

What term then should we use for those who are not clergy? Surely not something even worse: "the nonordained." I will attempt to stay with the simple translation of the word *laos,* "the people"; thus, people and pastor. One ought not forget that the pastor is always one among the people, that is, one among the people of God, a member of the "laity" in the biblical sense of the *laos*. Nor ought one to forget the various offices in the church and in the community, as well as what Luther called stations and vocations in life. Others talk about situations of responsibility or places of accountability. As Christians fill offices and stations, those within such are "without rank." And to be sure, faith recognizes that the offices, by their very nature, demand even greater service to others.

Experienced authors insist that a book should clearly identify its audience and that there should be only one audience. With that counsel in mind, some may question whether I have attempted to address two audiences: clergy and laity. I should be clear. The audience I wish to address is the community of baptized Christians. Indeed, within this singular audience there are in reality two unique, historic entities, clergy and laity. It is a premise of this book that these two entities unnecessarily have been socially, religiously, and institutionally separated too long and too often. Clergy meet as a group together frequently for study and growth. A listener coming from outside quickly recognizes that much of the subject under consideration addresses the laity who are not present. This is not healthy in these days. In all that follows, I hope we will be together in an open conversation, each listening to the other. We must learn to struggle together toward a greater common Christian growth. When the subject of the discussion in the following chapters is directed to the clergy, laity in effect should be present and heard. When the subject is directed to the laity, the clergy should be present and involved. We need to learn more from one another, and together we need to ask in what way are we similar and not always ask how are we different. Indeed, what is really meant by the assertion that in Christ we are all one?

Now is the time for a fresh approach. Faith-filled people need to allow God's Holy Spirit to raise all the people of Christ's church—those in the pews, those in the pulpit, and those at the altar—to a higher awareness of the uniqueness of our common calling. From that crucial awareness each of us will unpack our various callings and offices within the one body (the church) and within society (avoiding any ranking) and find our respective callings in our unique daily situations. We will be gathered together as the body of Christ, united as one—all together on an elevator (which incidentally the British call a "lift")—and all raised to a higher awareness of our common calling in ministry through Christ. Together we will learn to honor and assist each other in our respective callings, always in Christ. The church has no place for a seesaw, the practice of putting down one in order to elevate the other.

To be sure, there will be times when I will revert back to "clergy and laity" language, simply because those words represent an ecclesiastical and social reality and an existing separation. We have no other appropriate words with which to describe the situation and the division that has been shaped by history and so often researched by sociologists in great detail. Indeed, the church in its long history of dividing itself into the two entities of clergy and laity inhibits us from so easily discarding the phrase. Yet in substance we must find ways of coupling them as the biblical texts do so clearly, declaring the church to be the people of God.

Our effort, genuinely Trinitarian, is anchored in the three articles of the creed. Two articles are commonly understood to express the Christian calling. The Second Article centers on Christ's activity of redemption, reconciling all the people of the world in a new relationship to God. The Third Article confesses the Spirit's activity of generating and sustaining faith in those living in Christ, that is, in the new life to which we have been called by the Holy Spirit. What about the First Article, creation? We so easily let our Christian calling remain boxed into the Second and Third Articles, but to do so misses the excitement of the journey, as Abraham experienced it: birthing, working, relocating, tilling the soil, shepherding a herd, even fighting and defending family and community, gathering food and preparing meals, caring for children, arguing for justice before kings and courts. All this is enveloped in the First Article of the creed. *For the Christian, the Second and Third Articles of the creed are lived out in the First Article—that is, within God's creation: the world.*

Finally, there must be unity in our approach, not discussion on a number of unrelated subjects. Frequently one hears a great deal about the ordained ministry and, oh yes, there is also the ministry of the laity—a second thought. Our common Christian calling and all our respective ministries flow from the center of the faith, Christ. The Swedish Reformation scholar, Einar Billing, insists that Luther never saw the important aspects of the Christian faith lined up like pearls on a string. Rather, each article of the faith is like a petal that comes together making a whole: the forgiveness of sin seen as a beautiful red rose and, we might add, with a scent of the holy and the eternal. [8] This is as it should be in our understanding of our callings. Our varied callings, our ministries, should not be seen as one more important than another or as disconnected from the center of our Christian faith They are all part of our common calling in Christ to offer ourselves as living sacrifices to God: our reasonable service in response to God's saving grace enveloped in the phrase "servant ministers," inseparable from our baptism (Ephesians 4).

In our next chapter we leap into the ministry that is most familiar: the ordained ministry. Why begin there? The simple answer is that, for the vast majority of Christians, the ordained ministry embodies and

8. Billing, *Our Calling*, 7.

limits our understanding of ministry. For some it is either the sole understanding of ministry or it is the primary form of ministry, all others being secondary. Indeed, among many Christians there is an assumption that the call of the pastor for public ministry is a distinct and unique calling of the Holy Spirit, unlike any other calling. Ordination and the office of the public ministry are indeed most important for the life of the church. We must, however, identify in what way they are important and how they interrelate with the life and ministry of all the baptized.

2

Ordination and the Office of Public Ministry

LET'S SIT IN ON A SUNDAY ADULT FORUM OF A RATHER LARGE Lutheran congregation. There's an excitement among the participants and the subject is: what really is ordination? Five people were ordained into the public ministry of the church in a special worship service the past Friday. It took place as part of the synod's annual assembly held in a nearby town. Two members of the congregation, Erika and Jason, were among the five ordained. Many from the congregation were present. Promotional material for the adult forum on the previous Sunday invited the congregation to gather and discuss what happened in the service of ordination. The forum leader is experienced in gaining group participation with free and open discussion. Standing before a sheet of newsprint, she invites the group to list what they saw in Friday's service of ordination. She asks, "What did you see or think was happening in the service?"

The first respondent says somewhat jokingly, yet with an element of seriousness behind the chuckle, "Erika and Jason were being inducted into the clergy organization." "What," asks the facilitator, "led you to that conclusion?" He replies, "It was only clergy up there in front; and they all seemed to initiate Erika and Jason into their community by placing their hands on Erika and Jason's heads and giving each a stole like only pastors wear in the service." Another agrees, but with a nuance, "Erika and Jason were formally placed into the long line of pastors and priests since the first ordination of the disciples by Jesus 2000 years ago." Again, from the facilitator, "What led you to that?" The reply is, "The bishop spoke something about the historic episcopacy, saying just that. This service tied the present life of the church to the earliest church through the continual laying on of hands." Erika's aunt comments, "The wonderful thing that happened in that service was the prayers for the Holy Spirit, the blessings of Christ on each of the candidates. I found the service awesome, filled with the Holy Spirit as evident in the singing: the church shook; my spine quavered at times." Many in the group nod in agreement. A fourth person, raised a Roman Catholic, feels that something awesome happened in the service, that God placed an indelible mark on Erika and Jason. She says, "The event of their ordination gave them power to change the bread and the wine into Christ's body and blood in the Sacrament of Holy Communion. None of us have been given that power, right? None of you can do that, right?" The next person insists that it was like passing the bar exam or the state medical exam in order to be licensed a clergy person. Thus the service was both a public acknowledgment of their success and a service of thanksgiving. He continues, "Erika and Jason have passed their theological exams and are now publicly qualified to teach us the faith. They are now the professionals." Another person informs the group that his niece in another part of the country had completed her theological education and passed all her exams, but was still awaiting a call to a congregation and therefore could not be ordained until she had a call. "So," he says, "the ordination service had something to do with having a call to the ministry—as both Erika and Jason have?"

Following this sixth comment, the pastor is asked to lead the group in exploring the positions expressed in order for all to gain a better understanding of ordination. Our task is similar. We will attempt a clarification of ordination which I hope will bring a fuller understanding of what many Christians call the ministry of word and sacrament, or sometimes the pastoral ministry, or public ministry. As we explore this important aspect of the church's ministry, I want to connect it with the ministry of the people. The comments of the speakers in the forum will provide references in the effort that follows. So what did happen and in what way is it biblical?

Ordination: Is It Biblical?

First let me share a dramatic moment from a faculty meeting of a major Lutheran seminary that occurred many years ago, yet in my lifetime.

Women's ordination, long overdue, was beginning to be seriously promoted within the Lutheran church. This faculty had been asked to identify its position on the issue. There seemed to be little or no opposition; many of the faculty had lectured and written in favor of women becoming pastors. It was assumed that the faculty would be unanimous in declaring its full support for the ordination of women into the church's pastoral ministry. The chair called the question. "All in favor?" was met with a resounding, "Yea." "Those opposed," he asked, merely as a matter of routine. And a voice strongly replied, "Nay!" A moment of stunned silence fell over the faculty. The negative vote had been cast by one of the faculty's most distinguished biblical scholars. The chair broke the silence by asking the faculty member if he would explain his position. "Yes," said the scholar, "Ordination is not in the New Testament!" The group sighed with relief, knowing that he was correct, but also knowing that it really didn't matter whether or not it could be found in the New Testament. Scripture did not really matter. The issue under consideration was the right of women to be pastors, and on that they knew where their colleague stood. Yet the faculty members' ease at the lack of a biblical basis for a major practice was also telling.

Like many other Protestant bodies, Lutherans insist that all matters of faith be grounded in Holy Scripture: that the biblical record is the primary source and norm for the church's teaching. At the same time, the church insists that there has been a fluid line of faithful witnesses to the gospel of Christ through these many years, down to our day. A secondary—yet very important—persistent, serious consideration is: What has the church learned, taught, and practiced in the past as it sought to be faithful to its own time and place? Seminarians like Erika and Jason and countless other seminarians before them study the Scriptures diligently, but they also study church history and especially the history of Christian doctrine. And, it should be added, so should all of us. We all need to pay particular attention to the great teachers of the church, past and present, and the accounts of their confession and practices.

While church history and biblical grounding are indisputably important, each generation must struggle with its own faithfulness to the gospel in the distinct context of its time and place. So as we proceed, our task is to take seriously the record of the Holy Scriptures while we listen to history, and vigorously consider how we ought faithfully to teach, witness, worship, and serve in our day. Our days in many ways are unlike any days in the past, and yet a good historian will ask: what is really new? Also important to note is that Christians have sought inferences from the Scriptures that could lead to appropriate practices which may not be explicitly stated in the biblical texts, yet are in support of the gospel. Ordination may be one such inference. The word "ordination" first appears in ancient Roman governmental affairs, indicating the appointment of civil servants. By the eleventh century the word principally refers to the admission of a person into the priesthood. In following centuries it takes on special meaning in the Roman Catholic Church, which we will discuss later. Nowhere is the word "ordination" found in the New Testament. In the church's concern to maintain a Christ-centered public ministry and to assure the people that their pastors are properly called, the service of ordination is justified and appropriate. One may rightly *infer* the appropriateness of ordination for the life of the church. While the word "ordination" is never mentioned in the New Testament, in essence people *were* ordained—that is, selected to various leadership roles through various procedures, as we will detail in the following paragraphs.

Many Different Ways of Electing Pastoral Leaders

Early in his ministry Jesus commissioned his twelve disciples to a designated mission and service within the Jewish communities of Palestine, as recorded in Matthew 10, Mark 3, and Luke 6, 9, and 10. Later, following the resurrection, Jesus commissioned the remaining eleven to make disciples of all nations (Matt 28:16–20). The first task confronting the apostles following Jesus' ascension into heaven (Acts 1:20–23) was to fill the vacancy left by Judas's desertion. Using the words of Psalm 109:8, Peter declared: "Let another take his position of overseer" (Acts 1:20). The selection of "the seven" (which included Stephen; Acts 6) to assist the apostles in providing food for the poor in Jerusalem—to "serve tables"—was in essence a form of ordaining. It is often assumed in our day that the seven were lay people. They were to serve tables and thus allow the apostles to focus on preaching. And yet they are also identified as prophets (preachers), a point that is made clear in Stephen's sermon and for which he was stoned to death (and became a martyr). Filled with the Holy Spirit, the seven preached and worked signs and wonders among the people.

How were the seven selected? The Twelve called an assembly of disciples who were told to pick among themselves seven men "of good standing, full of the Spirit and of wisdom" (Acts 6:3). The word translated as "of good standing" (*martyroumenos*) means to have one's actions or character attested to by others. Then the disciples prayed and laid their hands on the seven. The laying on of hands has its roots in the Old Testament as part of the "ordination" of priests, and is seen in the transfer of authority from Moses to Joshua (Numbers 27:18–23). In the New Testament, the laying on of hands accompanies the gift of the Spirit (Acts 8:17, 19) and also healing (9:12; 17; and 28:8). Following the Holy Spirit's call of Barnabas and Saul, "after fasting and praying they laid their hands on them and sent them off" (Acts 13:3).

Unlike the call of the twelve apostles (who were called directly by Jesus, without the laying on of hands), Paul's call was exceptional. Ananias informed Paul that God willed him to be God's instrument to bring the gospel to the Gentiles (Acts 9, 15) even before he was baptized; then he received a thorough training before embarking on his missionary work. At the end of his first journey, Paul and Barnabas revisited the churches that they had established (Acts 14:21–23), strengthening the disciples and encouraging them to remain faithful. Then it is said that they appointed elders in every church (Acts 14:23). (The Greek word translated as "appointed" literally means to "extend or stretch out the hand.")

The New Testament is clear: In various ways, people were selected for leadership in the emerging church. There was no one pattern. Neither Christ nor the New Testament dictated the process of calling leaders for the emerging church. Church historian Carl Volz writes: "You'll find some churches having bishops and deacons while others are not known to have identified such. In Ephesians 4:11, 12 church officials are called prophets, teachers, pastors and evangelists. Paul and Barnabas are identified as apostles. According to Acts 13ff, they are commissioned by prophets and teachers in Antioch. According to Titus (1:5–7) bishops appear to be synonymous with elders."[1]

In the Old Testament there are 672 occurrences of the words "priest" and "priesthood," while in the New Testament there are really only a few. The important New Testament references (in Hebrews and Revelation) identify "priest" with Christ, his "sacrifice once and for all

---

1. Volz, *Pastoral Life*, 13.

time." In 1 Peter, priesthood is an expression of the life of the whole community of believers. In reading the book of Revelation, one finds that the passages using the word "priest" (1:6, 5:10, 20:6) refer to the believers as a whole. When the Apostle Paul lists Christ's gifts to the church, noticeably absent are priests (Eph 4:11).

If the New Testament church carefully avoided the title of priest as it was used in the Old Testament for rulers of the people, it must also be said that by the early years of the second century and thereafter, the title of priest became increasingly popular as the church expanded in territory and in number of adherents. This occurred at the same time that the church (in many places) became increasingly attracted to the Old Testament. Beginning already in the Gospel of Matthew and central in the book of Hebrews, the word spoken by the prophets in the Old Testament was crucial for the early church in its understanding of God's unique movement through history toward the birth, life, and death of Christ. However, New Testament references to the Old Testament, including Jesus's own words, provide no grounds for reinstating the title "priest." The late (ca. 300 CE) early church, however, did use the title "priest." One explanation for this is their desire to the reach for extraordinary power by claiming for the clergy an authority similar to the Levitical priesthood. It was a time of bitter strife and of considerable encroachment of assumed heretical dogmas upon the life and witness to the New Testament church. Many found greater authority in identifying with the Old Testament Levitical model of leadership to stand against the threatening theological controversies afflicting the church. In addition, in this period (under Constantine, 313–337 CE) the position and office of the clergy took on greater formality and liturgical adornment. This is a time when relations between church and state became blurred. Paintings depicting court scenes late in Constantine's reign show clergy dressed in royal robes, hardly distinguishable from the state officials.

Thus from the third century onward "priest" is the title of choice for clergy in both the East and West. Luther and the Reformation strongly objected. Luther's assertions were clearly a return to the New Testament insight: "All Christians are priests." He also wrote: "It is pure invention that pope, bishop, priests, and monks are called the spiritual estate while princes, lords, artisans, and farmers are called the temporal estate. This is indeed a piece of deceit and hypocrisy . . . All Christians are truly of the spiritual estate, and there is no difference among them except that of office . . . for baptism, gospel, and faith alone make us spiritual and a Christian people."[2] An important phrase in this Luther quote is "except that of office." The Lutheran Confessions makes much of the office of the public ministry, especially the ministry of word and sacrament, which is indispensable for the public proclamation of the gospel and the spiritual well-being of the people. The ministry of the ordained is recognized as an indispensible and treasured office of the historic Christian Church and is to be strongly supported by all the people in today's church, genuinely respected and honored. At the same time, a sound theology recognizes that there are additional offices, vocations, and callings in and through which the Christian witnesses to Christ and struggles for faithfulness. The office of public ministry ought never to be thought of as the only office or vocation to which a Christian is called for ministry.

The Lutheran service of ordination declares publicly that the ordinands have been duly and properly called to the *office* of the ministry of word and sacrament—that is, that a Christian congregation stands ready to receive the ordinand as its pastor, and that a larger entity of the church affirms the qualifications of the candidate. The service declares them certified and thereby authorized to preach, celebrate the sacraments, and teach the Christian faith in a local congregation as the church's public spokesperson. The actual call is to the *public* office of word and sacrament. The adult forum speaker above was correct when he spoke of his niece awaiting a call. Following traditional church polity, a candidate must have a call to a congregation before approval is granted for ordination.

Ordination: The Center of the Sixteenth-Century Controversy

With the laying on of hands, what do the ordinands receive? Is there something indelibly imprinted on their lives as a result of what happens in this service? If the service of ordination is not an induction into a Protestant or Lutheran priesthood, is it an induction into a professional organization called the "clergy"? And in what way do we speak of the "holy ministry" when referring to clergy? How is the public ministry "holy" in contrast to the ministry of the people? By engaging these questions we are drawn directly into the protests and struggles of the

---

2. *LW* 40, 19.

sixteenth-century reformers, Luther and others. By the time Luther posted his ninety-five theses, the late-medieval Western church considered ordination a miraculous event—indeed, a sacramental event. Though poorly trained and often lacking any spiritual discipline, candidates were *charismatically* separated from the people by the event of their ordination. They were mysteriously inducted into the holy priesthood of the church, a body not unlike the priestly caste of the Levites in Old Testament times.

The word "charisma" is intentionally chosen. In the laying on of hands through the person of the bishop, the ordinand is given a charisma, according to medieval Roman Catholic teaching. This charisma is a gift, given by God through the bishop, granted to the ordinand by the ordination. The word in Greek means simply "gift," and in the church it was understood to be a very special gift, an indelible mark upon the priest that conveyed an authority and a power to officiate at the altar. Through this unique gift the priest offers the very body of Christ to God as a "non-bloody sacrifice" for the sins of the people. The body is the body of Christ who suffered and died on the cross. The ritual is called the Sacrifice of the Mass, a repeat of Calvary. The charisma given in ordination was seen to be indelible, marking the priest as a member of the priesthood and thus a member of the church's hierarchy for a lifetime. By ordination the priest is brought into a holy body, an institution whose members are seen to have been consecrated, made holy in a way different from the people. Thus Roman Catholics speak of the "holy priesthood." Its members form a hierarchy, from His Holiness the pope down to the local priest—a unique, holy body that alone has the call and authority to dispense God's grace to the people. When one within the hierarchy is called from the ranks of the clergy to become a bishop, or called from among the bishops to become the pope, the process is referred to an "elevation," a move not just to a higher office but to a level of greater holiness, and not just of the office but of the person who holds the office. He is elevated to a "higher calling."

What do we mean by "holy ministry," or, in what way are both clergy and laity understood to be holy? In the medieval tradition, the clergy were seen as having been made holy through their ordination. The pope, holding the highest office of the hierarchy, was known as "The Most Holy." At the lowest level of the hierarchy were the parish priests often identified as the secular clergy, who moved back and forth between the holy sanctuary before the altar to the worldly context of the laity. At one time they would officiate at the Mass and at a later time they would participate in the distribution of food to the poor. They were known as "holy men" but were not considered to be as holy as those who took an oath of poverty and strict discipline, called "holy orders" within the hierarchy. The laity, however, were outside the hierarchy, so they were not considered holy.

Lutherans and Protestants have formally repudiated this tradition and practice, insisting that all the baptized are holy by God's grace through faith. Yet Protestant and Lutheran laity often object to being identified as holy people. In spite of St. Paul's insisting that all the members of the body of Christ are holy, many of the laity will often "humbly" deny that they are such. "No, pastor, not me. A saint? No!" Yet we would do well to grasp the full dimension of holiness: that through faith we are all holy people and without rank. Clergy are surely recognized as sinners, no different than all the people. Clergy and laity are both equally made one with God through faith in Christ. There is a clear recognition of the consistent biblical judgment: all have sinned and come short of the glory of God; all are made right with God through faith in Christ; all are, as Luther said, beggars before God. Thus the medieval church's act of ascribing holiness solely to the clergy is contrary to the clarity of the Scriptures. Faith both hears and accepts what God declares in Christ: your sins are forgiven! Through the redeeming work of the Son, God gives forgiveness. God bestows the righteousness of Christ through the declaration of forgiveness. This is the bittersweet exchange: God gives us holiness through the power and presence of the Spirit; in exchange, we confess and surrender self and all sin to God in faith. The sign and nature of that gift of forgiveness is that we are named "saint," a holy person. That's the title St. Paul bestows on the faithful, even to those Christians scrapping within the congregation at Corinth.

In addition, whether intended or not, we continue to envelop the clergy with an aura of "holiness," and we have failed to convince the people they too are holy and their work too is a holy work when they live and serve by faith. In one of Luther sermons (July 26, 1534) he clearly illustrates "holy" being similar for both pastors and people. His preaching is an example of what is needed today: "See to it first of all that you believe in Christ and are baptized. Afterward, see to your vocation. I am called to be a preacher. Now when I preach I perform a holy work that is pleasing to God. If you are a father or mother, believe in Jesus Christ and so you will be a holy father or mother . . . Oversee the running of the household and the preparation of meals. These things are none other than holy works to which you have been called. That means they are your holy life and are a part of God's Word and your vocation."[3]

The word "holy" has a root meaning that identifies what it modifies as being "set apart" for something. Thus you may speak of the "holy church" as the community both declared by God to be righteous through faith in Christ and set apart for God (while still being in the world). In the biblical sense of being made holy by God, one understands that one is set apart with Christ and thus made like Christ, holy and free from the guilt of sin and free from this world's demands; no longer in bondage to sin but freed from God's judgment on us humans. Thus with this definition of "holy" in mind, we may and do speak of the "holy ministry" of those in a pastoral office. This office should be seen as similar to the various other offices and stations in life where we find ourselves as Christians, but here the phrase means to be "set apart." Thus those called to the pastoral ministry are indeed set apart, yet the oneness in Christ envelopes all of us. Because of the "holy work" identified with the pastoral office, it is to be honored, and the prayers of the church are sought for it. Never, however, should being set apart in an office in any way suggest being ranked, elevated, or spiritually separated from the people. All Christians—including pastors and bishops—are at one and the same time sinners and saints, and all—individually and corporately—holy and righteous through Christ. In St. Peter's words, we are together "a peculiar nation, a holy people, a royal priesthood" (1 Pet 2:9). So indeed there is a way in which we may speak of the pastor's work and ministry as a holy work, when it is done in faith. So also is the work of every Christian: whatever one's calling, when it too is done in faith it is a "holy ministry." We will expand on this subject as we proceed.

The reformer's most serious charge was against the idea that the priesthood (read also hierarchy) was the sole dispenser of grace and forgiveness to the people. The reformers rejected the notion that since the people were not priests and lacked the gift (the charisma), and since they also were not within the hierarchy, they could not dispense God's grace nor receive God's grace from any person other than a priest. Indeed, it was taught that by means of a designated Mass, through the

3. WA 37, 489.

priest's officiating, special measures of forgiveness and absolution could be obtained for oneself, for others, and for the deceased. The reformers saw this as a crass example of human effort to obtain God's mercy and forgiveness. That a priest performed a human task by which he claimed to sacrifice Christ for the sins of the people was a teaching and a practice totally unsupported by Scripture and, even worse, "contrary to the gospel" in the view of the reformers.

Our intention here is to enable us to understand what is central to the evangelical tradition, especially as it relates to the life and ministry of the people of God. In denying any assertion that the hierarchy was God's sole means of dispensing grace, the reformers simply discarded any justification for recognizing the hierarchy as the cornerstone for the church's practice. The reformers did this on theological grounds with the clear texts of Scripture and, even more, "according to the gospel."

The Word of Christ Is the Important Factor

The primary objection of Luther against these sixteenth-century practices was the Roman Catholic Church's denial of the authority of the gospel as given in Holy Scripture. Luther charged that his church, the Western Roman Catholic Church, had allowed human traditions, human power, and human authority to usurp the power and authority of God, God's word in Christ. The resounding cry is heard in the words of St. Paul to the Romans: you are saved by grace through faith in Christ, not by human efforts. The words of institution of the eucharist in Matthew, Mark, Luke, and in 1 Corinthians are forceful and brief: *Take and eat, take and drink; given and shed for you, for the forgiveness of sin.* To those words alone the repentant sinner should cling with faith and thereby have full assurance of what is promised: God's full and complete acceptance and God's entire forgiveness of all sin. We need not trust anything else.

Regarding the sacrifice of the Mass, the reformers pointed to Romans 6:9–10: "We know that Christ . . . will never die again; . . . The death he died, he died to sin, once for all." They also referred to three passages from Hebrews 10:12, "Christ . . . offered for all time a single sacrifice for sins"; 10:14, "For by a single offering he has perfected for all time those who are sanctified"; and 10:18, "Where there is forgiveness of these [sins and lawless deeds], there is no longer any offering for sin." All these verses must be understood in light of the resurrection of Christ, whom faith recognizes to be very much alive and present in the sacrament of Holy Communion and indeed in the word, the gospel.

The one sacrifice of Christ does not eliminate Christ's call for living a life of sacrifice for others. The character and purpose of sacrifice, however, radically changes. Hebrews 13:15–16 concludes the discussion by making the distinction very clear: "Through him, then, let us continually offer a sacrifice of praise to God, that is, the fruit of lips that confess his name. Do not neglect to do good and to share what you have, for such sacrifices are pleasing to God."

Luther took seriously that in Christ all things are new, as the New Testament asserts: "So if anyone is in Christ, there is a new creation: everything old has passed away; see, everything has become new!" (2 Cor 5:17). Laws of the Old Testament supporting the priesthood after the manner of the Levites no longer had any authority and should not be followed. The reformers could not tolerate humanly devised traditions that were contrary both to the authority of Christ and to the gospel. The Old Testament Laws of Moses and the ceremonial laws (exemplified by the mark of circumcision) were not given authority, nor were they to be placed on the conscience of believing Christians. Therefore, the practice of circumcision was discontinued. As St. Paul wrote: "For in Christ Jesus neither circumcision nor uncircumcision counts for anything; the only thing that counts is faith working through love" (Gal 5:6). For the reformers, the basis on which reform was maintained was the clear word of Scripture, in concert with agreeing voices of the great teachers of the church, especially Augustine. The word spoken by the pastor, both in the sermon and in the words of the liturgy of Holy Communion, is itself the authority of the public ministry, and it is the power of God to ignite faith and to sustain faith active in love for others.

The Common Priesthood of the Baptized

Consequently, and very simply, with biblical grounding the reformers moved from the conveyance of God's grace through the ministry of a few (that is, the clergy) to the authority to convey grace and forgiveness both to and through the many (the baptized). In so doing, it repudiated the historic Roman Catholic hierarchy, and with it went all its related religious and political authority and power. What the Roman Catholic Church saw as biblical texts restricted to the "clergy" and thus supporting the hierarchy, the reformers saw directed toward all Christians. The foundation for the bold assertion of the common priesthood of believers was the clear witness of Scripture. Luther wrote:

> The first office, that of the ministry of the Word, is common to all Christians. This is clear . . . from 1 Pet. 2:9. 'You are a royal priesthood that you may declare the wonderful deeds of him who called you out of darkness into his marvelous light.' I ask who are those who are called out of darkness into marvelous light . . . ? Is it not all Christians? And Peter not only gives them the right, but the command, to declare the wonderful deeds of God . . . So, there is no other proclamation in the ministry of the Word than that which is common to all, that of the wonderful deed of God, so there is no other priesthood than that which is spiritual and universal, as Peter here defines.[4]

Theologian William H. Lazareth adds clarity: "All the Bible is addressed to all . . . This, then, is the key distinction for Luther: not Christian clergymen vs. Christian laymen, but all Christians vs. all non-Christians. Scripture does not make divisions among Christians."[5] Renowned early church historian James D. G. Dunn writes: "In short, ministry in the Pauline churches belonged to all, and each depended for his life within the body of the Christ, not on some special ministry of a few, but on the diverse ministries of all his fellow members."[6] "There is no longer Jew or Greek, there is no longer slave or free, there is no longer male and female; for all of you are one in Christ Jesus" (Gal 3:28).

German Lutheran theologian Paul Althaus, writing in the middle of the twentieth century, needs to be heard here:

> Preaching dare not be taken by itself and removed from the context of the total witness of the church. The Reformation appreciation of the ministry of preaching does not justify making it an absolute and isolating it . . . Preaching lives by its connection with the Word spoken from person to person and only so will it be constantly refreshed and gain authority and credibility . . . Thus, we are led to this further statement: preaching must be framed within the witness of the fellowship, the priesthood of all believers. Preaching does its work in us because fathers and mothers, teachers, and friends have preached to us in their way and continue to preach to us . . . The witness within the fellowship, to

---

4. *LW* 40, 21–22.
5. Forell and Lazareth, *Crisis in Marriage*, 111, 112.
6. Dunn, *Unity and Diversity*, 111.

which we owe our being as Christians, went forth and continues to go forth, not merely in words, but through the whole Christian life of those with whom we live." [7]

It is for these reasons that the selection and role of sponsors at a child's baptism is so important.

Every Christian can in his prayers and devotions hear clearly the word spoken by Christ, "your sins are forgiven." Indeed, Christians are not merely able but ought to speak Christ's word of forgiveness to another who acknowledges sorrow for sin and seeks God's grace: "If you forgive the sins of any, they are forgiven them" (John 20:23). The text here clearly assumes this is addressed to the people, not solely to the chosen leaders of the early church. The rhythm of the Christian life entails both personal hearing and personal sharing of the Word *and* the coming together publicly around the word and the sacraments. Personal and family devotions, private and group prayers with lay leaders, and openness to the thrilling assertions from the Scriptures are encouraged. Indeed, mutual conversation among Christians regarding matters of faith and faith's practices are expected. At the same time, private devotions and mutual conversations with fellow Christians on matters of faith and life ought not to be a substitute, nor should they be an excuse, for avoiding weekly gatherings to hear the same word in the church's corporate, public worship.

The Reformation united the shared ministry of all the people with every Christian's ministry "under the cross." This means that the shared, common ministry of confessing Christ must be exercised with a faith-filled awareness that one has been redeemed by Christ's death and that one anticipates with certainty the resurrection. Therefore, the ministry of all the baptized is in Christ and in his presence always as a servant ministry under the cross, often invoking suffering, and never limited to clergy.

Are Pastors Professionals?

Even if we accept the universal nature of Christian ministry, might we still want to recognize pastors as professionals, and thus different from the nonordained? If not into a priesthood, were Erika and Jason inducted into a professional organization? The US Federal Tax Code

---

7. Quoted in Doberstein, *Minister's Prayer Book*, 433.

recognizes the clergy as a special class of people, deserving tax benefits not applicable to the general public. Does the church recognize this? Protestant churches, especially Lutherans, have generally been reluctant to identify their clergy as constituting a profession like that of medical doctors, lawyers, engineers, and so forth.

Consider civil engineers, to use one group as an illustration of a profession. A civil engineer can jeopardize the health and well being of the public by unprofessional practices. Therefore, civil engineering organizations and the government agree to codes and standards that must be known and skillfully practiced by the engineer to assure the public that civil and criminal infractions will not be made, that in the civil engineer's work the public's health and human life will be protected. With regard to civil engineers—as to medical doctors, lawyers, and similar professions—it is assumed that the professional has acquired a body of knowledge not expected of the general public but which must be known and practiced by the professional for the well-being of the general public. We could call up similar illustrations for each profession. All assume a degree of knowledge and skill without which serious problems and illnesses might be inflicted upon the public. Certainly there is public trust of the professional, but such trust is enhanced by the awareness that appropriate oversight is maintained by both the profession and the government.

Is this true of pastors ordained to the public office of ministry? It is, but only in part.[8] While the church does not expect nor allow the state to participate in the determination of who is admitted to ordination, Protestant churches have long shown a concern that their clergy are properly prepared to preach, teach, and live in accord with the gospel, and to have the skills, the integrity, and the psychological wholeness the office requires. In the process of seminary education and in a parallel review of the candidates by a candidacy committee (generally an examining board consisting of both lay and clergy members), the church seeks assurance that those who are then selected for public ministry are sound, faithful ministers of the gospel. The church thereby wants

8. The one exception: At the federal level, Megan's Law (enacted in 1994) requires people convicted of sex crimes against children to be placed on a national public registry. Generally, states require agencies within their jurisdiction to screen personnel who relate to children against this database and to forbid such people from having contact with children. Church authorities generally clear all candidates through the Megan data bank before offering any person a position wherein one relates to children.

publicly to certify that candidates for ordination are representative of the long line of public spokespeople of the historic Christian church. Following a candidate's installation, it is assumed that the bishop also is responsible for oversight of the faith and practices of both pastors and congregations in the bishop's charge.

Many of us as pastors have given the impression, at times—especially in conflicts—that in our education we have gained theological insights not available to the general membership, the laity. To the contrary, it is difficult to identify a subject or an insight learned in ones' theological education that ought not to be freely shared with the people. There may be subjects explored in seminary education that need not be passed on to the people for the simple reason it would not be supportive of the life and ministry of the people. However, unlike the medical doctor's education or that of the lawyer, the pastor's formal education entails all that ultimately has reason to be shared with the people. The pastor has not been entrusted with insights by God in a seminary education that should not be understood by the people of the church.

While pastors are not professionals in the usual sense of that word, they must indeed practice ministry in a highly professional manner. If they fail to do so, the pastoral ministry easily degenerates to an ineffective and often offensive witness to the gospel, thereby thwarting the congregation's growth in faith. What does it mean to be professional as a clergy person? It means being open to change and growth, to be open to proper, critical review by both bishop and congregation, and to be a model of the godly life. Being professional as a pastor here means being committed to excellence, to a high standard of integrity, being knowledgeable of and faithful to the Scriptures, diligent in preparation, and (for Lutherans) to be true to the Confessions, while at the same time being open to the life of the people with all their difficulties, learning from them as they learn from their pastor. That same commitment to excellence may also be expected of the people, both in their life and roles within the congregation, and in their life in family, community, and work. However, in being a called, *public* minister of the gospel, the bar of professional behavior is understood to be on a higher level. By virtue of the office which he or she occupies, the pastor is very much a public person, a model (for good or bad) and therefore judged in a human manner by a higher standard.

While celebrating the importance of the pastoral office, the common priesthood of believers insists that all need to know and trust the Word, to confess to one another, and in love to keep our brothers and sisters in the faith. Thus the pastor's teaching ministry is one in which he or she shares all the depths of the Scripture's word for the church, while at the same time being open to hear and discuss with integrity the questions and challenges the members bring, however "off the wall" or troubling these questions may seem to be.

The Role of the People in Congregational Oversight

Do the people in the pew have any responsibility for oversight of the teaching and practices of their pastoral leaders? Within the medieval Roman Catholic Church, the bishop held sole power and authority over the clergy in his charge. Today, what positive role can congregational members play, with the bishop, in pastoral oversight?

Inverting the church should not suggest the elevation of the laity to the level of judge over the teaching and ministry of their pastors; a pastor dare not be the object of harsh and unfair attacks by members of the congregation. However, an inverted church does suggest that all are mutually responsible for their shared faith and should be mutually concerned for faithful proclamation and practices of both pastor and congregation. No pastor or bishop should ever assume he or she is above or beyond review, nor should any congregation. At the same time, proper procedures should be in place both to protect people from inappropriate criticism and to enhance the quality of the life and ministry of the pastor and all the people. Every bishop, in a faithful exercise of his or her office, does have considerable responsibility for the faithful teaching and practices of a congregation's leadership. The call to the office of bishop is clearly one of oversight, with particular attention to the faith life of the congregations for which the bishop is responsible. For this reason, bishops regularly schedule visitations to congregations; they meet with pastors and church councils, and carefully read church newsletters and reports of council and congregational meetings.

However, the church members—especially those who are regularly in church and are active participants in the life and activities of their congregation—surely have an important perspective on the quality and difficulties of the congregation. For various reasons, some members may hold sharply different perspectives on the quality and practices of their pastor. These strongly held critical concerns, when they seem to find no listening ear from those in leadership, will often lead to an unholy triangle of communication. The bishop's office may receive a telephone call from a lay leader of a congregation. The caller wants to let the bishop know of a certain problem he or she is having with the pastor and often implies that everyone in the congregation shares the problem. The question is asked, "Have you met with your pastor and discussed this matter?" The caller may respond in one of two ways. She may say, "Yes, I have spoken with him, but he really is not hearing what I am saying; he is not listening." Or the caller may say, "No, I don't feel comfortable talking with her." The next question is, "What do you want the bishop to do?" And the answer is usually, "You or the bishop should speak to our pastor about this matter." This is a no-win situation; it is an unholy triangle. It is something like the old telephone game: member to bishop's associate, to bishop, to pastor, and back to member. Surely this is clearly an unacceptable procedure.

These concerns, valid or invalid, when not shared responsibly or when pursued with devious intent are often the seeds that grow into outbursts of disagreement and sometimes rage, resulting in either covert or open conflict. Some concerns may be legitimate; many may not be. In any case, today's congregations need structured processes by which a person's concerns may be civilly engaged with the hope of amelioration and perhaps even thereby reducing the need for those calls to the bishop's office. One problem that often frustrates people is the absence of any effective entity within a congregation to whom leaders may address concerns in a confidential manner. Within my church body, the Evangelical Lutheran Church in America (ELCA), there is the expectation that a mutual ministry committee is established and is functioning within every congregation (though in many cases it is not in place). The committee should be structured as "trusted space" where a member or members of the congregation might air their concerns constructively (following failed efforts in one-on-one conversations) and do so with a high level of confidentiality and mutual trust. In every parish there needs to be a door open to a safe space for civil dialogue with the pastor and with others regarding personal or group concerns. Such a committee is crucial to avoid the suppression of strong concerns among members as well as to avoid the all too frequent outbursts of conflict that demoralize both people and pastor and do serious harm to the church's public witness.

Such settings of conflict resolution are generally not focused on theological issues (though such should never be excluded), but on a pastor's effectiveness or failures as perceived by some within the congregation. Perhaps the most common concern within congregations today is a growing awareness that an increasing number of members are quietly leaving with apparently little attention by the leadership to the problem. In the parking lot and in parishioner conversations about town, the subject is discussed frequently; and among some a strong feeling emerges, namely, that nothing can be done about the problem and that the pastoral staff seems closed-minded and distant from the problem. Where there is a standing mutual ministry committee, a formal yet confidential request by a few members could be made for a discussion of the problem in the presence of the pastor, and under leadership skilled in maintaining a civil and constructive discussion. One would hope that such a meeting might initiate a fresh understanding on the part of all parties and result in agreements on what new steps or approaches might be undertaken by the leadership with the support of the congregation. Such a conversation might also reveal that the pastoral staff have given this problem a great deal of attention, yet have had little obvious success and perhaps have not adequately involved the congregation. This approach might provide an opportunity for both pastor and people together to own the problem and to grow.

Here is another approach for consideration within a congregation. A new development within many synods is the encouragement to congregations that their pastors be given a sabbatical following a certain number of years with the congregation. The pastor is granted a paid leave for several months, during which time he or she is away from the parish and is in retreat, studying, learning and spiritually growing in order to return refreshed and a better pastor. This practice has been growing and should be continued, as finances are available. However, in my observation, all too often pastors design and plan their sabbatical in a manner that pursues studies related to their primary, favorite interests. A pastor strong in Christian education may focus the sabbatical solely on studying new educational materials and methodologies for use in the parish. Another pastor who enjoys community services plans a sabbatical to study a variety of congregations across the country famous for such work. There is certainly nothing wrong with building on and strengthening an area of special interest, but it is questionable when it ignores an opportunity to spend time engaging areas of weakness. In one case, a congregation's review process clearly indicated a need for the pastor to retool in the area of evangelism and to discover ways to draw the congregation into an evangelism ministry—an area known by pastor and people not to be his strength. Before agreeing to grant the pastor a sabbatical, would it not be appropriate to agree that the sabbatical will focus on an area of weakness, while also assuring opportunities to enhance the pastor's special interests? The same practice would apply to bishops anticipating a sabbatical. Indeed, the sabbatical should also be a time for relaxation from the usual stressful routines. While never ceasing to learn, the sabbatical is also a time for slowing down.

Common in many congregations today are annual performance reviews by an authorized committee of the congregation, and the same is done by the synod's executive committee and bishop. When a bishop annually undertakes a performance review within the synod's structure, he or she is surely appropriately modeling what is expected of pastors within their congregations. This review is not the work of the committee responsible for reviewing salaries. Instead, modeled after reviews practiced today in many institutions, the performance review is an annual opportunity for a give-and-take conversation about what the pastor is doing well and where there may be areas for growth and improvement. Often the evaluation is conducted by reviewing the goals agreed to by pastor and committee from the previous year's evaluation. The session should conclude with an agreement on what goals the pastor will work on during the coming year. When a pastor is planning a sabbatical, would it not be appropriate to relate the most recent agreement in a performance review session with what the pastor proposes to pursue programmatically during the sabbatical?

Preaching and liturgical practices are other areas that need special review within a congregation. A properly conducted review may greatly improve the quality and effectiveness of the pastor's ministry in these two areas. How might such reviews be annually structured? Here is one approach with which I am acquainted and which provides considerable assistance to a pastor's growth. When a pastor gives full and unreserved agreement to the process, the council chair appoints a committee of perhaps five people. It is always appropriate for the chair to consult with the pastor, allowing him to eliminate from the list anyone who would not be helpful. In addition, any who are so enamored of the pastor that they feel he or she is perfect in everything should also be eliminated. Such is an acceptable practice in a sensitive review process; it eliminates those people whose feelings toward the pastor are overly negative or overly positive. By being randomly selected by the council chair, the group is able to be reasonably objective and representative of the congregation. The committee then is assembled, agreeing to meet with the pastor either following one Sunday service each month for five months, or after each Sunday for perhaps five consecutive weeks. Guidelines regarding expectations and proper methods of feedback are given in writing and discussed at the beginning of the committee's work. Such is most effective if it is convened and presented by a third party, ideally one specially trained for the role. The purpose of each hour long gathering is to provide feedback—that is, to share with the pastor what each had heard in the sermon, what was clearly grasped in the proclamation and what might not have been understood, and what was confusing or unclear. The openness of the pastor to feedback is all-important. Assuming the pastor preaches from the biblical texts for the day, a portion of the feedback relates to how well the hearers recognized the sermon's relationship to the Scriptures and what might have been missing. Also, how well did the sermon connect with what is in the life and times of the hearers: their pains and sicknesses, their hopes and their fears? If a synod were to encourage such a review procedure, they could offer a common set of instructions for these committees and possibly identify trained personnel available in the synod to help the committees in initiating the process. The set of instructions might include a brief essay that identifies from a theological perspective what is generally assumed important in preaching, especially an understanding of law and gospel, demand and promise, and the centrality of the gospel: these would be criteria in the review.

In all that I have said above, one may assume everyone in the congregation is committed to decency and that everyone works toward civility in all manners of Christian interaction. Many, however, have experienced that such is seldom the case. All too often there are those who seem to enjoy disrupting reasonable efforts by the membership in conducting the ministry and mission of the congregation. Kenneth Haugk, a theologian and also a trained psychologist, has written a fine, easy-to-read popular book, *Antagonists in the Church*. It is an excellent resource in recognizing this frequent, troublesome problem. The book leads congregations and leaders in a process of responsible and caring engagement of such people. It also deals most effectively with a dimension of today's congregational struggle which has not been accented in these pages, but the reality dare never be overlooked. We might, however, rightly assume that the development and growth of a different quality of human/Christian relationship within the congregation will over time reduce the frequency and intensity of interpersonal conflict.

A faithful clergyperson needs to establish a reputation as one who indeed behaves professionally, yet whose primary public witness is a sign of the presence of God's gospel, a voice of God's word to be heard, a model of the godly life, and a sharer of ministry. The biblical title "pastor" would seem to be all that is needed for the enhancement of this public ministry.

The Role of the Bishop

What does the title "bishop" mean, and how did it become the exclusive title of the pastor who is called to the leadership of clergy and a cluster of congregations? Let me illustrate from my experience. When my synod bishop announced his retirement, the lay members of the Synod Council proposed a plan to assist the synod in preparation for the election of a new bishop. Their approved plan undertook a process that would enable pastors and people of the synod to gather in forums throughout the synod to discuss the role of a bishop and the criteria that point to a candidate's qualifications for the office of bishop. The process was well received and provided a high level of mental and spiritual preparation for an informed balloting at the coming assembly. It also deflected inappropriate, covert lobbying for and by candidates. An excellent information piece was prepared by the lay officers of the council, lifting up applicable biblical material, especially passages from 1 Timothy and Titus. A different lay officer of the council led each of these forums. In the one I attended, the lay leader began by taking the gathering through the passages from Timothy and Titus in which, in our English translations, the apostle used the word "bishop" three times (1 Tim 3:2 [twice] and Titus 1:7). A very talented laywoman, very conscientious and well prepared, led our session. Shortly after reading the passages in question she asked for discussion on St. Paul's words. One pastor, casual but serious, commented that we should all remember that the word "bishop" in Timothy and in Titus is the same word used for "pastor," that the New Testament knew nothing of bishops as we now experience them. The lay leader was obviously shaken and understandably defensive. But the pastor was right. And no one should fault the group leader. We all have taken the Greek word for "bishop" and assigned it to mean the one who is elected to be the overseer of clergy and of a group of congregations. And in our day, as in many past years, we have generally identified the minister of a congregation as a pastor and not a bishop. The Greek word that is translated "bishop" is *episcopos*. Its origin is a secular term, used in the military. Its simplest translation is "over-see-er." It is where we get the word "episcopal," as in the *Episcopal* Church; or a variant, as in the historic *episcopate*. However one defines the roles of pastors and bishops, if one looks to the New Testament, their roles in the church are similar to the pastor: over-see-er of the flock, very pastoral.

The title for the leaders of the church in Acts, the Epistles, and the Pastoral Letters are so varied and so inconsistently employed that one cannot make a definitive statement on what ought to be taken as a biblical understanding of titles for our day; this we have discussed at length earlier in this chapter. The Lutheran Confessions insist that the distinction between pastor and bishop is of human origin. Pastor functions like bishop, bishop functions like pastor. Neither has been given a *unique* gift (charisma) that validates their respective ministries. We will do well to speak of only one public office of the ministry of word and sacrament to which both pastors and bishops are called by God through the church. Among Lutherans, a bishop is not *ordained* to the office of bishop; the bishop is *installed* into the office, and no special (unique) gift is given. The prayers of, say, the church custodian are as genuine and as valid when prayed in faith as those of the bishop. Indeed, a bishop's prayers are spoken in an ordination service on behalf of the church. She or he is the voice of all the people, appealing to God for the gifts for the Spirit to those being ordained. This is no different than when a pastor prays with the whole church for the gifts of the Spirit for those who are being confirmed, baptized, or married, or when a pastor prays for the Holy Spirit in the communion liturgy.

Today, when conducting public worship, bishops will generally *follow* the procession of clergy, walking with a replica of a shepherd's crook to clearly accent the bishop as shepherd. While the English word "bishop" only appears three times in the New Testament, the word "shepherd" appears 17 times, and always as Christ the good shepherd of his flock. Those whom the church appoints to be shepherds of a congregation are sometimes called the "under-shepherds." In many settings, today's church has limited the symbol of the shepherd to the role of the bishop and seldom identifies the pastor as also being a shepherd of a flock. There are, however, some bishops who actively promote the pastor's role of being a shepherd. One bishop whom I knew gave a small gold shepherd's crook to newly ordained pastors, suggesting that they keep the symbol before them as they carry out their ministry. Might we need fresh, public expressions and symbols of the important role of the pastor as a shepherd? The title "shepherd" is important because it points to the intimate relationship of the pastor and bishop to the people. The pastor and bishop like shepherds call the people together and continually recall the wanderers, serve the special Meal, and invite others to participate—the calling centered on the Word, Christ.

Earlier I asked, does the ordination service limit an understanding of the ministry of the whole people of Christ's church? I answer yes. I believe our present symbols in the service fail to connect the ordinands with the daily life of the faithful in a meaningful way. Christians in their public worship articulate their deepest convictions of the faith and in their liturgical actions give further meaning to what they believe. The service itself is a symbol and a sign. Perhaps most clearly read by all is the sign of unity: the whole church gathered around the table of the Lord. The bishop or pastor, as a public sign of the church's unity, consecrates the bread and the wine and leads in serving the church as one body, the Body of our Lord. Indeed, the procession of those reaching for the gift of the Spirit in the shared meal, certainly in the sermon and the singing—all reflect a joyful oneness with the church of all ages and the age to come, a foretaste of the feast that lies ahead. For many the service evokes profound emotions and rich spiritual experiences, as expressed earlier in this chapter by the aunt of one of the ordinands. Such a service brings tears or near-tears to pastors and others.

However, is there something missing in the service? Are there symbols missing? Or were words not spoken that continue to show disregard for the daily ministry of the whole people of God? While the ordination service is centered on the ordaining of men and women for public ministry, where are the symbols that shout that this ministry to which they are ordained is for the equipping of all the saints for their ministry? St. Paul reminds us: we are "to equip the saints for the work of ministry, for building up the body of Christ" (Ephesians 4:11–13). Unless the bishop or the designated preacher of the ordination service makes a point of clarification, the liturgical words speak little if anything in this regard. The service in some respects might be similar to what Hendrik Kraemer has to say about the important research conducted by H. Richard Niebuhr in *The Purpose of the Church and Its Ministry* (1966): it is entirely limited to the ordained ministry without reference to the ministry of the people.[9] In the Lutheran ordination service there is a place where the bishop asks questions of the congregation (the words in italics indicate items that should be changed to apply to each situation): "Will you, assembled as the people of God and speaking for the whole church, receive *name/s* as *a messenger* of Jesus Christ, sent by God to serve all people with the gospel of hope and salvation . . . and in all things strive to live together in the peace and unity of Christ?" The congregation responds, "We will, and we ask God to help us."[10] Following these appropriate questions directed to the congregation, however, there is an absence of any question to the ordinand asking if he or she will receive the people as joint ministers of Christ in their various vocations. However, in the Episcopal Church's order of ordination of a bishop, the bishop-elect is asked specifically: "Will you encourage and support all baptized people in their gifts and ministries?"[11]

To what end is the Word to be preached and the sacraments administered? Certainly, so that faith may be ignited by the Spirit, and so that faith may be sustained through life unto eternity. This is an awesome ministry entrusted by God and by the church to the ordained. But why is there no mention of the whole church's lifelong offering of all the people of God, speaking the same word, carried by the same Holy Spirit? What signs are there in the ordination service that point to the ministry of all the people? Some may point to the Thankoffering at the opening of the communion liturgy: in a Sunday service, the gifts are brought forward by laypeople, perhaps a family, carrying the bread and the wine as a token (indeed a sign) of the total and complete service of all the people. Yes, but! Since the ordination is all about ministry, why not use signs

---

9. Kraemer, *Theology of the Laity*, 83.
10. *Occasional Services*, 193.
11. *Book of Common Prayer*, 518.

and symbols of the ministry of the people as they live in concert with the ministry of the ordained? Only clergy offer God's blessing on the ordinand in the ordination service. Why not, say, an officer from the ordinand's home parish? The Episcopal order of ordination of a priest states, at the beginning of the service: "A Priest and a Lay Person, and additional presenters if desired ... present the ordinand."[12]

With only clergy laying on hands in the ordaining of pastors, does this give a narrow signal about ministry? Again some will answer, "the clergy are the public sign of the church." Certainly. Yet where is the sign of the all-inclusiveness of the church in seeking and speaking the blessing of God upon the newly ordained? Why cannot we include lay leaders from the congregations to which those being ordained are called? Why not also include them in the laying on of hands and in speaking a blessing of the Spirit upon the ordinand? In *Lutheran Book of Worship* and the newer *Evangelical Lutheran Worship*, the wedding liturgy invites the parents of the bride and groom to rise and declare a Christian blessing upon their children along with the blessings the pastor speaks. If the people may speak a blessing in Christ's name in the wedding service, why not in the service of ordination? Indeed, since the earliest records of the Christian liturgy there has been an important though often misunderstood exchange of blessings between pastor and people. In each crucial section of the liturgy, the pastor begins with the word to the people, "The Lord be with you." The people respond, "And also with you." The people speak an important blessing upon their pastor, saying, "May God's Holy Spirit be with you in your ministry," just as the pastor says the same for the people.

In some of the Lutheran church bodies preceding the formation of the ELCA, the ordination of a candidate for public ministry was held in the candidate's home parish. With the beginning of the ELCA, ordination was moved from the local congregation to a special service as part of the synod's annual assembly. The purpose of this move was to demonstrate that the ordination was not merely a local event but an expression of the larger church. A deficit of this move is that it gathers the "elite"— the primary lay and clergy leaders of the synod—with the families of the ordinand, thus locating the event apart from the people. Those who with the church leadership should be caught up also in the drama of the service and be an integral part of the celebration and commitment.

12. Ibid., 526.

Ordination is about ministry: the ministry of all, not just the ordained! The ordained are known to be necessary for the public means of conveying the gospel and for the support of the life and ministry of the church, the whole people of God. The sermon in an ordination service, as in other teaching opportunities of bishops, is surely a time to connect the public ministry with the ministry of the baptized. In the liturgy of baptism we are told to "let your light shine before others, so that they may see your good works and give glory to your Father in heaven" (Matthew 5:16). Is it only the ordained who are called to do the "shining?" Indeed, the pastor's "shining" is a public illuminating of the Word in and through his or her office. However, the call is for the whole people of God to shine forth with praises of thanksgiving and a lifelong, daily witness and service in Christ's name in and through their varied vocations.

3

Baptism

Ordination for Our Common Ministry

In this chapter I want to demonstrate that the sacrament of Holy Baptism initiates faith and—through faith—a lifelong, total commitment of witness and service to all manners of human need, which is, in fact, the activity identified as "ministry." First, however, we need to review baptism in the early church and then look at how the rite often appears to have become a hollow ritual for so many. Our objective is to regain for one another a deeper, more extensive understanding and commitment to the spiritual realities inherent in the gift of Christ through the water and the word, especially how that gift initiates the common ministry of all the baptized.

Let's begin with church historian Martin E. Marty's description of a service of baptism in the early church.

> It is dark.
>
> A shivering band of people has commandeered a cistern. In the depths of the earth the sound of moving water is heard. The slightest shuffling of feet echoes through the chamber. Most of the band are quiet, though a few whisper. Above the ground, heard only faintly from below, a rooster crows, marking the day's beginning. Soon farmers and merchants will be rising from sleep to take up their daily occupations, unaware of the activity underground. They would not understand the quiet rites, nor approve, and might even take action against the participants if they had knowledge and opportunity. Meanwhile, below, a

leader has come to the fore, a man of serene but slightly severe appearance. He whispers some words in the almost eerie setting. Some of the people begin to take off their clothes, folding them and setting them aside. With great solemnity and in many cases no little fear they approach the bowl of the cistern where water bubbles and flows. The children are put forward and dipped in first, after some questions which in many cases are answered for them. Then come the older children and the men. They are asked a number of very serious questions; after answering, and being placed under the water, they come out struck dumb by an experience of both physical and spiritual shock. Finally the women remove all their ornaments, and loosen their hair. They are to have no alien objects, no rings or jewelry or bandages on them. Warily they step into the water and come out, dressing again in the now brightening glow of candles and torches. The leader is very busy with various kinds of oil which he seems to be blessing and pouring on the people. He is asking questions and hearing answers and repeating formulas. Somehow his magisterial appearance and manner assuage the fright of the people near him. He seems satisfied with the proceedings, and gives orders for an exit to be prepared. The group makes its way through some passageways into a larger room. Here others who have themselves undergone the experience on an earlier occasion greet them warmly and invite them to a meal of bread and wine at which sacred words are spoken and hymns are sung. The people now seem relieved and are obviously happy. They have been baptized.[1]

And now let's look in on a service of baptism in a local congregation. It's 9:30 a.m. on a Sunday in the twenty-first century. The Wilton family of five is sliding into their traditional pew at St. Peter's, a typical suburban congregation. Dad immediately recognizes a larger-than-usual group seated on the left side of the nave in front of the baptismal font. He recognizes only a few among the many gathered there. Next he looks at the bulletin for the day's service. He sees the details of the baptismal service—not a common feature of their Sunday worship. He motions to his wife, letting her in on his anxiety. "We're in trouble," he says to himself. "This service will be at least fifteen minutes longer than we expected. Jimmy must be on the soccer field for a big game by 11:00 a.m. and little Janie has a birthday party across town that begins at

---

1. Marty, *Baptism*, 1–2. The ceremony is described by the author as "more or less after the manner of the *traditio apostolica*, the apostolic tradition of Hippolytus in the earliest centuries."

11:30." So he whispers to his wife, "We'll have to scoot out right after the benediction." And once again the children will be absent from Sunday school following the service; and as happens so often, Mom and Dad will miss the adult Christian educational forum. So also Tommy will miss the confirmation class that meets for an extended time with pizza at noon. As the family leaves the service, old Mr. Schmidt (a member of the congregation since its formation years ago) walks out of church beside the father, commenting, "Great to have those children baptized, but we see so few of those families and their children after they're baptized."

The Wiltons have been active at St. Peter's for the past five years. They are typical of many in the parish: grew up in another part of the country, got married there after college, and have moved around the country three times since. They are rooted in the community and involved with many activities, church being only one of the many. They are dedicated and active members of their church, yet are often troubled by an awareness that their schedules conflict with their presence at church and feel somewhat guilty that their children are not "getting it."

Congregations today are too diverse to call any family typical. There is in this account, however, something commonly experienced among today's historic Christian churches: the lightheartedness with which baptism is pursued and the conflict between the family's faith commitment and the social and recreational activities of the community. In so many ways our congregations today are failing to instill in their children and youth the basic understanding of the simple and yet profound meaning of our baptism.

During the Communist rule in Eastern Europe, we often read reports of atheistic Marxists' sinister efforts to enlist youth to participate in sporting events and political rallies on Sunday morning in close proximity to Christian churches. Their objective was clear: obstructing the church's worship and frustrating the efforts of Christian education. At that time most North American Christians thought such was evil and expressive of the demonic nature of communism. Today it seems we Christians have unwittingly accepted something similar and have in many ways been party to its growth and practice. As in once-Communist Eastern Europe, so today: it is not easy to restrict our children from being involved in something other than church when multiple choices are put before them. Parents too may find community activity apart from the church much more satisfying than their experiences in their local congregation. With the excitement of iPods, video games, and varied television programs, the church's social and educational programs are an apparent bore to many, especially the young.

How are we to address this dilemma? One, we can move our families to a remote place where one does not expect to find encroachment into the life and ministry of the church. But a phrase I learned from a friend fifty years ago sums it up: "Hell is portable," and then said more softly, "we carry our problems with us." Here is a current example. A few years ago, while I was a guest preacher in a small congregation in northern Vermont, a member shared with me her family's plight. They had intentionally located to this remote part of our country to escape the frenzy of urban life as they had known it, especially for their children. To their horror and sorrow, they soon discovered a serious conflict, not unlike the problem back home. Here in Vermont the local ski resort, in an effort to generate the good will of the community, offered free ski passes to all the children in the area. This was seen as a great gesture, but the passes were useable only on Sunday mornings. Next community youth leaders followed, organizing competitive skiing events on Sunday mornings for children in various age groups, all of which played havoc with the Sunday worship and educational programs of the churches. Efforts by the local clergy association were of no avail; the ski resort realized the community was on their side, not on the side of the churches.

No Escape

Until death there is no escape for the Christian from the world. Every attempt to separate the Christian life from the world has ended in failure. Consider the pious and devout—indeed learned—Christians who thought they could escape the world and all evil by becoming hermits and living in caves in the Sinai, as many did in early church history. Later, in the medieval era, many men and women sought refuge from the world by forming monasteries and convents. Consider also the Christian sects in early North America, the Shakers among others: awesome in their Christian devotion and spiritual discipline, insulated in their own unique villages. Though many of these groups flourished, developing simple and beautiful architecture, furniture, and delightful music, their communities all eventually vanished. Many Christians, deeply troubled by today's culture, attempt to insulate their church from the bad world outside, but all sooner or later discover that the devil is within the congregation as well as outside. There is no escape from the world this side of death, and anyone who thinks they have escaped lives an illusion. With Christian baptism we confront a reality. The rite declares that through Christ's death and resurrection and the gift of the Spirit we are no longer *enslaved to this world*, while insisting that we are still very much *in the world*. In Christ we recognize our own dying and rising in baptism to a new life now and the promise of life eternal. Our temporal citizenship is recognized as valid by God—until death. The Word and the liturgy speak of baptism as dying to this world and rising to a new life in Christ in the thick of this world. There is no suggestion or hint that baptism removes us from this world with all its troubles, pains, hates, wars, and suffering. This world is the context in which the Christian life is to be lived and in which the Christian both bears witness to God's protection, love, and forgiveness and holds a vision of a better world, even here and now.

The Word made flesh—the embodiment of the promises of God made real in Christ Jesus—is given to those who come to be baptized. Whether you are baptized in the Jordan River or at a huge, stone baptismal font or from a simple washbasin, in every case, you will find in the water of your baptism all that God obtained for us earthly creatures by his coming among us. The water and the word of Christ ignite faith and sustain the faith amid the prayers and teaching of the faithful who surround the life of the baptized. As Luther reminds us in the Small Catechism: "[It] is not simply plain water. Instead, it is water used according to God's command and connected with God's word."[2] The church, in faithfully baptizing the young and the old who come into her midst, is the mother who gives us our spiritual birth. Christian faith insists the baptismal rite is a life-changing event. But truth be told, and illustrated earlier by the preoccupations of the Wiltons, the service of baptism for many is merely an occasional intrusion, something that we observe. For others it is the opportunity to recognize the cuteness of a baby and to share the joy and delight of a family's newborn.

But for biblical truth to be told, the event is God's offer of all that Christ won for humankind by his entry into world history. This gift of Christ is what the Christian community clings to and celebrates in both public worship and in private praise to God. It is a grand celebration

---

2. Luther, "Small Catechism," 1164.

of the resurrection and of the eternal hope that Christ instills in all the baptized. Christian baptism is, very simply, the gospel.

Baptism is indeed a communal act, that is, it is God placing the newborn into the most spiritual family, the church. Yet it is also a highly individualized event. The person is named as the water of grace is poured over the baptized. No matter how many are baptized in a worship service, each candidate is baptized individually, thus allowing one to confess throughout one's lifetime, "I have been baptized." Not only does my baptismal certificate attest to the event, my sponsors, godparents, and parents have frequently and regularly reminded me of that day. God makes us his own, giving us Christ's reign of love, grace, and peace within us through faith.

God calls each of us through holy baptism to live the life to which Christ calls us in the center of this fallen world. In our baptism we have been mightily called to faith and enabled to trust in God through the mercies of Christ. In and through that gift, we are called by God's grace to love others. In our baptism we learn God's pure gift of acceptance, since we are fully accepted by God. Appeals that our good deeds should gain God's good favor are offensive to God, belittling what God has already accomplished for us in Christ. We need only to trust God's mighty deed in Christ, received in the word in and with the water of our baptism. In the midst of the good life, including days of pain, suffering, and despair, the Christian community asserts Christ's resurrection. The faith of our baptism daily breathes hope for the future. Christian baptism is a declaration of God's victory over death and the gift of that victory to the community of faith, even in this life. The victory is Christ's overcoming death through the cross; it is certified and guaranteed with his resurrection. On the cross God's Son stoops to the lowest level of human existence, becoming the servant for a fallen world, and suffers, bleeds, and dies for the sins of humanity—our sins and all sins—to give us life now and eternally.

Christ empties himself in going to the cross for the world's dire need. Bathed in our baptismal water we too, by the power of the Spirit and in confession, are emptied of our sins and our self-service and are turned to our neighbor. Because of the power of the Word, and the word of our baptism, we dare never rise to such heights in this life that we cannot bow lowly before the Christ child and our neighbor's needs. Thus baptism initiates a lifelong ministry not only within each of us but also together with all Christians. Luther insists, "Although the Christian is thus free from all [self-righteous] work, he ought in this liberty to empty himself, take upon himself the form of a servant, be made in the likeness of men, be found in human form, and to serve, help, and in every way deal with his neighbor as he sees that God through Christ has dealt and still deals with him. This he should do freely, having regard for nothing but divine approval."[3]

One may say with Luther that in our baptism we receive the common call of all Christians, that is, to be faith-filled, to truly trust God and genuinely to believe—not just anything but very specifically the gospel, the good word in Christ. Inherent in our common calling is the call to serve our neighbor. Thus we find our calling in our baptism. And thus our calling is a summons to faith that is active in ministry, *service in word and deed, to all in need*. Luther reminds us: "We have a double vocation, a spiritual and an external. The spiritual vocation is that we [Christians] have all been called through the gospel to baptism and the Christian faith . . . That calling is common and similar for all . . . The other contains a differentiation: It is earthly, though also divine."[4] By "spiritual" here Luther thinks of the word of faith engendered within one, a new heart and a new mind, all in and from Christ and his Word. The faith within becomes audible and visible in the word spoken as a Christian and by the life of love, Christ's love active through us. This is especially expressed in our vocations, as Luther said above, which are earthly though divine. Within our various earthly ministries the power of God's love is effective through us. The very focus of ministry is the neighbor's needs. Always connected to—never hidden—is the word, the gospel, which envelops the whole of God's redemption in Christ. Luther marvels: "This, then, is the great glory with which the divine majesty honors us: It works through us in such manner that It says that our words are Its Words and that our actions are Its actions, so that one can truthfully say the mouth of a godly teacher is God's mouth and that the hand which you extend to alleviate the want of the brother is God's hand."[5]

The sharing of the gospel is—without question—central to this ministry in concert with service. St. Paul tells his young associate,

---

3. Lull, *Martin Luther's Basic Theological Writings*, 405.
4. WA 34 II, 300, 306.
5. LW 3, 272.

Timothy: "What you have heard from me through many witnesses entrust to faithful people who will be able to teach others" (2 Tim 2:2). God calls the sinner to redemption in Christ—to become calling ones for Christ. Throughout the next chapters I will speak often of identifying our earthly calling as ministry, a divine ministry. As Christians we dare to say that the call to preach the Word, as well as the call to be witnesses to the gospel, is the call of the Spirit to all the people, initiated through the water and the word of Holy Baptism. To be sure, pastors who are called to fill the office of public ministry share with all the people both an earthly and a divine calling, a common holy calling to be Christian as well as earthly callings. Recall again Luther's words quoted above: all have both the interior working of the Spirit and the external witness to the Word, including social service; one's own hand becomes the hand of God in giving aid to the person in need. Christ's word and the Spirit's gift of generating faith within us are expressed through us earthy creatures to each other and to the world.

Baptism envelops the whole of our Christian witness and ministry. Recognize the fullness of baptism's testimony: It spans God's judgment on all humans of the complete, total acceptance of the baptized and of the life to be lived in God's grace for others, from the often assumed innocent infant to the most pious person to the publicly disgraced hypocrite. Observe carefully what the sin of all is: People of all nations and races are separated from a knowledge of and trust in God. And the common sign of our separation is making ourselves like God, cleverly and persistently attempting to justify ourselves, saving ourselves with claims of self-righteousness. The divine solution, known by faith, is God breaking through to humanity with the incarnation (God in the flesh); God's Son, the Christ, being put to death; and God declaring the forgiveness of sin and certifying the divine activity with the raising of Christ from the dead. Faith receives the Holy One who broke through to us personally in our baptism. God with the water of baptism joins us to this Christ event and enters our lives in a personal and unique manner. As sin is removed, we are joined with God in Christ. The Holy Spirit is within us and quietly leads us on. Thus among, within, and from the people of God we hear the call for consistent care of the world and its people.

Having been centered on ourselves by our common fallen condition, we are converted. We are turned to God both through Christ's love and by the power of the Spirit. In being turned to God, we are called simultaneously to minister to our neighbor; by "neighbor" is meant all within our reach who are in need of help. The nature of our ministry is always one of support—offering up to people in need—from a humble and lowly posture, not from a position of superiority and authority. When converted we face up to God as we live below, supporting those above us—an inverted lifestyle. As Bonhoeffer accepted circumstances among the lowly and marginalized, especially during his days in prison, he could speak, in his words, "of an experience of incomparable value. We have for once learnt to see the great events of world history from below, from the perspective of the outcast, the suspects, the maltreated, the powerless, the oppressed, the reviled—in short from the perspective of those who suffer . . . We have to learn that personal suffering is a more effective key, a more rewarding principle for exploring the world in thought and action than personal good fortune."[6]

For those who bring their children to baptism, for those who elect baptism as an adult, and for those of us who gather on Sunday to witness again the baptismal service, all should be conscious of the great act God is performing through the water and the word. The profound importance of baptism in the life and faith of the church should be on our mind and in our heart. Baptism should not become merely a social celebration of the birth of a new child, or a hollow religious effort. Baptism is the gift of the redemption: Christ's death, resurrection, forgiveness, and the empowerment of Spirit. Obviously we ought not to be in a hurry to get through those baptismal services in Sunday worship.

God not only breaks into our lives through our baptism with love and acceptance, God also in that very act ordains us for ministry. God places us into the unique community of ministers, called "a royal priesthood." Accordingly, through baptism all of us are consecrated to the priesthood. Luther adds clarity: "Consequently every baptized Christian is a priest already, not by appointment or ordination from the pope or any other man, but because Christ Himself has begotten him as a priest and has given birth to him in Baptism."[7]

Listen to the words of St. Peter: "You are . . . a royal priesthood, a holy nation, God's own people, in order that you may proclaim the mighty acts of him who called you out of darkness into his marvelous light" (1 Pet 2:9).

---

6. Bonhoeffer, *Letters and Papers*, 17.
7. *LW* 13, 329.

The Model for Christian Ministry

Christ is the power and the model for Christian ministry. The record of Scripture is paramount in this effort, and no one exemplifies ministry in Scripture better than Jesus, summarized by his announcement that he came "not to be served but to serve" (Mark 10:45). His coming and his ministry sets an example for the whole church. Following Jesus's washing the feet of the disciples he startles them by insisting that they too should wash one another's feet. Then he says: "For I have set you an example, that you also should do as I have done to you. Very truly, I tell you, servants are not greater than their master, nor are messengers greater than the one who sent them. If you know these things, you are blessed if you do them" (John 13:15–17). Our Christian life today may not be recognized in "foot washing," but the Christian surely needs to express—as Christ did—genuine humility, an emptying of one's self, to meet specific needs of another. This is the unique character and the model of Christian ministry for all the people, both pastors in their office and the people in the pew and in all vocations and offices. In Christian ministry the unselfish service is powered by Christ, who is the divine embodiment of God's love. In addition, the focus of his love and mercy is revealed, certainly to everyone but especially the outcast, the lowly, the grief- and-guilt stricken. The same character and model of ministry is (or should be) identified with the followers of Christ. Clearly, in our various ministries, the primary direction of our service must be others and especially those in various needs. The presence and love of Christ with the power of the Holy Spirit within us sustains us in the faith and in our various services. Indeed, the "new life" is identified as having faith, love, and patient endurance, up-building the body of Christ; and doing the work of reconciliation (2 Cor 5:18; Eph 4:11–12; Rev 2:19).

At the same time, the Christian "caregiver" must be cared for by the church and by one's immediate family, as Christ's Father cared for his son. Ministering to others is never an excuse for neglecting one's personal care, physical and spiritual. If we have not fully realized God's love personally, genuinely confessed sin, and sincerely received his word of forgiveness, we will be an empty shell, perhaps a loud sound, doing good but empty in Spirit. The instruction of the airline flight attendant is a good lesson. As the plane is about to take off, she or he instructs the passengers on the use of the emergency oxygen, saying, "Parents should place the mask on themselves first, then on their children." The lesson is obvious: If the mother passes out because of a lack of oxygen, there is little hope for the children. The parents who neglect their own spiritual health are not in a position of sustaining the spiritual health of their family.

Service is our common calling—that is, to be in Christ is to be in service to others with the word and acts of goodness, and should not be seen as competition with ordination to public ministry. Both rites in their respective liturgies—baptism and pastoral ordination—remind us of God having marked us with the gift of the Spirit in the word in our respective baptisms. Yet it must be said: The ordination of pastors for the public ministry of word and sacrament finds its basis and grounding in our common baptism—our common initiation into the "priesthood of believers." There is only one ultimate gift of God: the gift of Christ to us, lasting a lifetime. This mark of Christ on our forehead in our baptism is the indelible marking. Coupled with the initial gift in baptism is the daily remembering of that gift throughout our life. Luther suggests that as we wash our face in the morning we should recall God's washing us in our baptism. The message is weekly brought to mind most clearly in the pastor's sermon and in the word of the eucharist, "given and shed for you for the forgiveness of sins." Yet that same word has been entrusted to parents and to the entire congregation, to be said again and again in various and countless ways—to all within hearing, to each other, young and old. And wherever possible and appropriate it should be climaxed—not just at Easter—with the bold declaration, "Christ is risen!" The reply of the faithful is, "He is risen indeed!" Paraphrasing St. Paul: If Christ be not risen, our baptism is in vain. But Christ has risen. He is the power of God for our salvation and for our services to others.

Five-Hundred-Year Conflict: The Ordained Ministry vs. the Ministry of All

Here I must address a significant tension that has run through the history of both the Lutheran and the wider Protestant church, a tension still very much alive among us today. It is the insistence of many that a unique and very clear distinction must be recognized between the call to the ordained ministry and the various callings to ministry of the baptized. While respecting their commitment to a unique calling of the clergy by the Holy Spirit—different from the callings of the baptized—I disagree, for reasons I will explain as we proceed.

Luther's writings between 1520 and 1525 reveal a strong emphasis on the common priesthood of believers. In his writing in following years it can be shown that his attention focuses much more on the authority and importance of the ordained ministry. At the same time, one will not find any rejection, retreat, or critical review of what was said in the earlier period. If there is a tension between the two, Luther never resolved the tension.[8]

A review of the two timeframes as described above will be helpful. Above all, one must recognize the context in which Luther struggles in both periods. What were the dominant circumstances confronting him in each of these periods that provoked a particular emphasis? A critical review of Luther's various historical contexts may also suggest a critical review of our own historical contexts and a questioning of how our own circumstances color our respective callings. Between 1520 and 1525 Luther's enemies are quite simply the pope and those bishops loyal to the pope. The pope was the nemesis because of his manufacturing and maintaining teachings clearly contrary to the historic church and the biblical witness, including oppression of reform efforts. The bishops were a problem because they preferred to hold on to their political and economic power, their wealth, and their social status, thus resisting the call for reform while enforcing blatant unbiblical teachings. Together they clearly represented the hierarchy and the political and religious power obstructing biblically grounded reform. In Luther's judgment, they simply opposed and oppressed God's word in Scripture. During the same period, a growing number of priests and congregations were joining the reforming movement, including many of the princes in Northern Germany and other parts of Europe.

In the years following 1525 Luther was confronted with several major challenges. A large number of congregations and their priests had abandoned Rome, resulting in a growing motley crowd of evangelical churches. By necessity Luther had to bring about some form of ecclesiastical order. There was clearly a need for pastoral leadership within clusters of these congregations. But an even more acute concern was

---

8. Kurt Hendel, a Luther scholar with whom I discussed this problem, wrote: "It is likely that he [Luther] did not resolve it because he did not consider it to be a tension but rather another example of his dialectical perspective. It does not have to be a matter of either/or. It can be a matter of both/and. Lutherans considered this to be a tension later on, perhaps because they have a difficult time with a dialectical perspective. It remains with us to this day." In correspondence with the author, June 2008.

how to ensure that those who had left Rome were now truly evangelical, biblically grounded pastors. To meet the latter need, the Saxon Visitation of congregations was conducted in 1528. Its findings were disturbing. Evangelical preaching and teaching were generally absent. The laity's financial support of their pastors was abominable. Many priests had little understanding of the very heart and center of the Reformation, though they and their congregations were identifying with the Reformation. A traditional Roman Catholic theology still prevailed. Absent in many quarters was any clear proclamation of the gospel; absent were biblical texts in the administration of the Holy Communion. Luther had to conclude (though he does not seem to write it), that with such conditions among the pastors in these congregations, one surely could not expect to find the presence of an informed laity. Pastors were simply not leading the people to faith and to a practice of ministry to which the gospel called them. Thus he began to give intense attention to the theological education of the clergy, as evidenced in the publication of his Large Catechism (1528). This was an effort to educate priests (pastors) in the evangelical, biblical word for an appropriate and faithful pastoral leadership. Being preoccupied with the theological education of the clergy, issues related to the ministry of the people in general appear to take a back seat.

At the same time, both a civil revolt took place and a religious movement began. Both appeared to be heretical off-shoots of Luther's assertion of the common priesthood. The civil event was the Peasant's Revolt. The movement was the rise of the Anabaptists, who refused infant baptism and resisted the rule of the state; the Reformers identified them as "fanatics." Luther responded to these two challenges with bitter indictments and harsh condemnation. Regarding the Peasants War, according to Kurt Hendel, "Luther was informed, and he showed sympathy in his communications with the princes. At the same time, he refused to support the peasants because they revolted against constituted authorities, used force and pointed to the gospel as a justification for their actions. He also believed that the gospel could not be preached effectively during a time of social unrest. Luther's response to the Peasants' War must be nuanced and viewed carefully, although his stance should never be defended."[9]

The Peasant's Revolt grew out of serious, unjust economic and social conditions experienced under the oppressive leadership of some

---

9. Hendel, in correspondence with the author, June 2008.

princes and landowners. Luther must have recognized two factors that led to his rage and denunciation of the Peasants' Revolt. One, they were extremely violent, severely vandalizing the property of their "masters," and there were killings. The peasants—Luther surely saw this—were motivated by a new sense of freedom gained from Luther's own teaching: they had caught from Luther the freedom to question authority, something unheard of until then. Two, Luther surely felt threatened personally as well as organizationally by their revolt. The princes and landowners were major economic and political powers that had strongly supported the Reformation. He surely felt he could not lose either their support nor—in many ways—their protection. Whether reasoned or merely an emotional reaction, his encounter with both the revolt and the rise of the Anabaptists surely tempered his continuing to promote the common priesthood. His primary concern was to ensure that the gospel be given free course.

The Anabaptist movement could also, for Luther, be understood as originating out of his promotion of the common priesthood. The Anabaptists took seriously Luther's insistence that every Christian was a priest and concluded they had no need for clergy. They also saw in government a primary source of evil and oppression. Since baptism was one's entry into civil citizenship (as maintained in medieval practices and continued by the Protestants), they refused to allow their children to be baptized as infants. For Luther, both the Peasants' Revolt and the Anabaptist movement were grounded in blatant heresy that needed to be eradicated.

While bringing down torrents of judgment upon this "radical" side of the Reformation, he turned his attention to accenting the need for an educated clergy. He also began emphasizing the authority of government and called for obedience to all in authority. He preached obedience to the mayor and officials of the state, and spoke strongly of obedience to fathers and pastors as a significant expression of Christian faith. In his Large Catechism, discussing the Fourth Commandment, he included obedience to spiritual leaders in the same manner as obedience to one's father. In the early Reformation he was seen a hero because he questioned the most sacred authority of his day, the Holy Father, the Pope in Rome. He now insisted on obedience to authority in proximity to everyday relations, though he never lightened his critical judgments of the pope. Some would argue that in this turbulent period Luther planted the seeds that would grow into a passive German national character whose citizens were often seen through the lens of modern history as blindly obedient to their rulers. It may also have provided the cultural seeds that later assisted in the realization of a style of pastoral leadership characterized as *Der Herr Pastor,* a strong authoritarian figure, and this style of leadership was transported to the American pastoral scene. (A similar leadership style, however, may also be recognized in North American churches whose origins are related to other European cultures.)

The key issue here is simply this: Are there biblical grounds for maintaining a special divine call of those ordained to the church's public ministry, one that is different from the biblical basis for God's call through Christ for the ministry of the laity? I will argue in these pages that the biblical passages used to support the unique calling of the pastor are just as clearly and just as frequently seen as referring to the whole body of believers. One verse often quoted is the first half of Hebrews 13:7, while the rest of the verse is neglected. An early English translation reads: "Remember them which have the rule over you" (KJV). A modern translation is more faithful to the original: "Remember your leaders, those who spoke the word of God to you; consider the outcome of their way of life, and imitate their faith" (NRSV). Here is a clear affirmation of both the importance of the pastor's proclamation of the gospel and the important character of the pastor, shaped by the gospel that provides a model for the faithful to emulate.

The Episcopal (Anglican) Church is generally recognized, especially by Lutherans, to be the "high church" among Protestant churches, with great attention being given to the role of bishop and priest, and with the sacraments held in high regard. Interestingly, within the *Book of Common Prayer* is "An Outline of the Faith," commonly called the Catechism. In the section on ministry, the first question is: "Who are the ministers of the church?" The answer given is: "The Ministers of the Church are lay persons, bishops, priests, and deacons." Notice that "lay persons" are listed first. Then follows the second question: "What is the ministry of the laity?" The answer: "The ministry of the laity is to represent Christ and his Church; to bear witness to him wherever they may be; and, according to the gifts given them, to carry on their place in the life, worship, and governance of the Church." [10] The instruction regarding the ministry of the ordained follows the instruction regarding the

10. *Book of Common Prayer,* 855.

Baptism

laity. Lutherans like to think they have, from Luther, the great insight to the common priesthood of believers. Why is it that the Anglican community has clearer statements on the subject, as represented in their official orders of service, than Lutherans have? The efficaciousness of preaching and the sacraments resides not in the person of the pastor nor in the power of the people. Luther's centerpiece of all his reforming efforts is his insistence on the authority of the Word: nothing less, nothing more. There is no other authority than the Word except that of the Holy Spirit, which (Luther insisted) breathes life in people by igniting and sustaining faith through the word, indeed, spoken by persons.

Much counsel has been given to pastors and congregations about the church needing to be consciously aware that the pastor has a *divine* call for ministry, and that such should sustain pastors against any and all opposition to their ministry. To the laity, the divine call of the pastor may suggest that in various ways the pastor must be obeyed, or has some strange power or authority greater than that given to all in the word of our baptism. In many ways, Protestants fall back easily into the medieval myth that ordination conveys a special charisma, a unique gift of the Spirit, which makes the word effective, and gives the word its power. Not so! Is not the charge for obedience, as in the Small Catechism, a call for obedience to the faith, as in total trust in the word in Christ![11] To be sure, respect for all in authority is expected of all Christians; however, it is not an absolute trust as is the nature of faith's trust of the Word. It should also be said that emphasizing the common call to ministry of both pastor and people is in no way a lessening of the important assertion that the pastor has a divine call. What has been said is an effort to insist that both celebrate the call of the gospel in their respective lives, and that each lives out that call in various callings—in offices and vocations. And in each of these callings, both pastor and people are able daily to recognize both God's strong role in leading each of us to our respective callings, and the Spirit's daily support in our difficulties to maintain faithfulness in our respective callings.

---

11. For a review of this issue, especially an alternate approach, see Wengert, *Priesthood, Pastors, Bishops*. A critical review of Wengert's book by Luther scholar Dorothea Wendebourg supports the position I have taken. It should be noted that the Lutheran Church of Australia, in arguing against the ordination of women, insists that Christ instituted the office (and therefore for males only). See Wittwer, "Authority of Scripture."

When speaking of a pastor's "divine call," it is meant that the call is from God, though admittedly through the prayerful deliberations of the congregation and the larger church. Why cannot such be said of the vocations of any Christian? Their call to faith—and from faith to life's vocations—is a call from God, though indeed through various human, earthly entities, and—where Christians are involved in the process—prayers are assumed. Does the claim of a special call to the pastor give any greater authority to the office of public ministry? In what way, if at all, does this assertion provide any added reason for the people to give greater obedience to the pastor?

The Power of the Word in Baptism and Formation of Christian Community

Infant baptism, while not mentioned in the Scriptures, was early understood as an appropriate practice of the church for the simple reason that the initiation of faith is a miraculous gift of God, not something humans do or achieve, nor a reward for having reasoned the truth. The evidence of faith is confession, reflecting genuine trust in God's promise, assurance of grace, undeserved love, total repentance, and full acceptance of forgiveness. In addition, baptism has always been understood in the Scriptures as God's initiation of the believer into the community of Christ-connected people: the wider church. Thus faith not only trusts God's gift of forgiveness, but faith also maintains an awareness of God's acceptance of us into a unique community—a community openly accepting of others regardless of their circumstances and conditions. What Luther clearly saw in Scripture and taught—the common priesthood of all the baptized—needs to be seen and understood when being baptized into the community, the church. The insistence that all believers are priests is not an excuse for individualism: that one does not need others; nor that one can stay at home, read one's Bible and pray without regard for Christian community. Baptism is predicated on the assumption that acceptance into the church means Christians surround each other not only with love and prayers but also with the word's instruction in the faith. And without that continued growing in the knowledge of the word and faithful service in Christ's name, our baptism remains "valid" (God's promises still remain), but we lose its benefits.

Parental Ministry

Parents should recognize their unique calling as God's primary agents in nurturing their little ones. They need both pastoral counsel in this calling and genuine support from their church in their ministry of Christian teaching within the home. The Christian home ought to be a greenhouse for growth in ministry as holy priests. Where siblings are present in the home, they too are the continued objects of parental faith active in Christ's love, as the parent encourages the same with even the smallest child. In their earliest play groups, parents are surely saying, "Share those toys," and "No, you should not take that toy from your brother." While not every exhortation is followed by faith words, in the larger context of the home the confession that as Christians we are active in Christ's love needs to be pervasive and needs to be shared creatively with the children. Parents and grandparents—that is, the immediate family—are the primary witnesses to God's presence both in words and actions—that is, the love known and shared in Christ. In such a context, the little ones begin a lifelong practice of Christian faith and Christian ministry.

One of the families at the parish of St. Peter's, referred to earlier, is representative of some in our congregations today—maintaining homeschooling for their children. My earlier contacts with this phenomenon were religious fundamentalists who were convinced that public education was of the devil, and the only escape was to keep the children home and teach them the truth of science and of God as only they could. However, as the years passed, especially as I served in seven interim ministries, I began to discover a very different, though small, breed of parents who felt they had the time, the gifts, and the skills, to homeschool their children. They simply felt they could educate their children better than could the traditional school. Studies of this phenomenon indicate many are succeeding well; test scores generally show advances. However, it is also clear that only a minute percentage of parents are able to homeschool. For many, homeschooling is not possible; simply to survive, both mother and father must work, and/or they lack the training and education that would enable them to do the job demanded by home-teaching. And yet this phenomenon of homeschooling ought to bring us back to what was obvious in the homes of early Christians, and was called for by Luther and pastors following the Reformation—home-teaching of the Christian faith with the support of the pastor and congregation. If you wish to see a sign of an inverted congregation, look for active home instruction of the Christian faith, certainly in concert with the classes offered by the local congregation. In a sermon delivered in 1528, Luther addresses the fathers and mothers by saying: "Every father of a family is a bishop in his house and the wife a bishopess [an "over-see-er" of the faith]. Therefore remember that you in your homes are to help us carry on the ministry as we do in the church."[12]

For an indication of how serious Luther considered this aspect of Christian education to be, look at his classic text, the Small Catechism. A preface in various early publications had these words: "The head of the house should teach these biblical truths to the household." Around the kitchen table and in bedrooms before sleep, the catechetical instruction was coupled with Scripture reading, prayers, and hymns. In the year following the collapse of Soviet rule in Central Europe, my wife and I had the pleasure of teaching for a short time at the historic Lutheran Lyceum in Bratislava, Slovakia. It is a classical high school begun at the time of the Reformation, closed by the Nazis and kept closed by the Communists; it opened again only months after the fall of the Berlin Wall in 1990. As I began teaching a senior class on Christian religion, I was frustrated at how little knowledge the class had of Christianity. Then one day it dawned on me: these sixteen-year-old students and their parents had been born under the oppressions of both the Nazis and the Communists. Churches were often closed or abandoned during both oppressions; the Lyceum was closed for fifty years. This very much limited parents and children from any instruction in the Christian faith. In my attempt at teaching, and as the students and I became closer, I discovered there were a few who had a well-worn Bible; that their parents had dared to maintain in their homes biblical instruction and Christian worship, refusing to let their oppressors win their minds and those of their children. They baptized their children; they did so aware of the high risk of persecution by the state for administering Holy Baptism. Many others in my class appeared to have a strange, blank look when I spoke of God, let alone Christ. These were subjects foreign to anything they had ever heard or learned either in the community or in their home.

Back in the US my recent experience while substituting as a confirmation instructor brings me to wonder if in so many places we are coming close to the conditions in Bratislava in 1991. In these confirmation classes I found a considerable lack of knowledge of the basic truths of

12. *LW* 51, 137.

the Christian faith. Few were able to verbalize that they have been made right with God through Christ and his forgiveness. Christian instruction of children is crucial for the future of the church, and church leaders obviously recognize this. Attention to the development of new instructional material indicates that the leading church educators are struggling in this regard. But do we pastors of congregations and Christians in the pew recognize the importance of this task? In only four of the seven congregational interims I served had the previous pastor maintained a personal, active presence in teaching confirmation. I certainly affirm the delegation of tasks and shared ministry in the life of the congregation, but confirmation instruction demands that the pastor make this a public and personal priority. The pastor ought to be up front, modeling for parents what they can be doing in their homes with their children. Remember, the pastor occupies the office of the public ministry, and central to the office is teaching the faith. Where is that teaching more crucial than during confirmation connected with home-teaching the faith? However, in accenting the necessity of pastor and parent conscientiously being involved during confirmation, it is important that we remind ourselves and others that instruction in the faith (called "catechesis") is a lifelong process and should involve not only the youth but all of the baptized.

Central to baptism is the necessity of a lifelong confession of the Christian faith. Luther (in my judgment) provides an excellent example of such a witness. Here he makes a strong personal confession of his faith, responding to Jesus's account in John 15:5ff (the vine and the branches), and significantly he ties confession with the joys and struggles in daily life: "I know and profess before all the world by the grace of God I believe in that Man [Christ], and I am resolved to remain with Him and to surrender life, limb, and everything rather than deny Him. In this faith I stand and live. Then I go forth, eat and drink, sleep and wake, rule, serve, labor, act and suffer all in the faith in which I am baptized."[13]

---

13. *LW* 24, 230.

4

Our Common Calling and Our Callings

Called by the Gospel

To regain a biblical awareness of the totality of life enveloped in God's design for us earthly creatures, we need to ground our effort in a mysterious yet powerful call by God. To each human God directs a very personal call that brings us together in Christ's church. Christians know the call to be the gospel, the good word God speaks to us in and through his Son. God's redeeming act in the life, death, and resurrection of Christ relates to our daily work and to all of our activities. Without a connection we will merely be busy about religious talk, failing to grasp the wonder and depth of what God wishes to do with us and among us in the entirety of our lives. The gospel, with its gift of faith, illuminates our search for meaning and direction in our daily work, service, and worship.

As Christians who have been taught the faith from the Scriptures, one might expect I would begin with the Bible, with references to specific texts. Rather, I suggest we recall how Luther's Small Catechism has taught some of us. In his explanation to the Third Article of the creed, he insists: "The Holy Spirit has called me by the gospel, enlightened me with his gifts."[1] Nothing could be more personal and contemporary for each of us, in our lives, in our time, and in our peculiar conditions: God has called me, you, each of us, by name, and addresses us very personally and in the context of our personal joys and sorrows. The biblical account

---

1. Luther, "Small Catechism," 1162; see also Luther, *Large Catechism*, 59–64.

of God's initiating and sustaining the call refutes our human quest for discovering God. It is God, the good Shepherd, who is seeking me amid my turmoil and who reaches me, touching me with mercy and grace. The gospel personally calls me to be God's own, to live with God in a trusting, loving relationship.

The call for each of us was personally spoken and heard in our baptism and was clearly restated again and again in our church's varied proclamations of the gospel. A grand and diverse network of God's people relate Christ to me, especially parents, grandparents, Sunday school teachers, pastors, spouse and children, Christian friends—even, at times, strangers.

Above all, the call is personally confessed, often internally and at times publicly, as around the kitchen table or in the Christian assembly at worship. We declare, "Yes, God, I hear you; I believe! While I don't always see and hear you clearly, I do respond in faith, though weak." And so we pray, "Give me faith, pour out your Holy Spirit, give me strength to trust you and your Word and enlighten me." Some would say the call came "once and for all time" at one's conversion or one's baptism. They claim to be able to mark the time and place when they were "born again." While God marked us in our baptism with a lifelong mark, we need to recognize that God continues to call us in myriad ways and never stops calling, even as we are running in the opposite direction. God calls in good times and difficult times, but it often appears that our ears are especially open in moments of sorrow, doubt, suffering, and despair. In this call is the word of grace and mercy, a power for faith and life even to the infant, to those in a coma, and to those suffering dementia. This call is not only a summons to follow, but also a declaration that "I am with you now and always." To be sure, there is an ultimate call for each of us—God's call to pass through death into eternal life—yet even that final call is the central message given in our respective baptisms. The call of Christ conveys dying and rising, life and hope, both now and for eternity. The call of Christ is simply always a call for repentance, turning again to the Caller—God—and receiving God's gift in Christ: forgiveness, mercy, hope, and a fresh approach to the new life now.

Our awareness of God's personal call may have entered our consciousness from varied sources, but its historic grounding is in the Holy Scriptures, beginning with God's initial call to Abraham and Sarah. CNN would have a problem capturing for the evening news the drama of God's initiating a nation from which today three billion people identify their origin: Jews, Christians, and Muslims, all calling themselves "children of Abraham." When God called Abraham to begin a unique journey, no trumpets were sounded; the earth did not shake with a quake; no smoke or fire was reported. God called Abraham and Sarah through strangers at their Bedouin tent in a desolate part of the world. In an almost casual conversation, God singled out these two elderly people and spoke to them to "get up and go" to a distant land. With the call came a promise from God that God would make them father and mother of a new and a great nation, a nation that would be a blessing to the nations of the world. As St. Paul reminds Christians in his Letter to the Galatians, Abraham and Sarah went by faith. The chapters of Genesis detail their and their family's faith-journey, filled with conflict, intrigue, struggles, and hardships, yet always amid the promises of God and the continued signs of God's faithfulness. One early sign that God's promises were to be fulfilled was the culmination of the promise that Sarah in her old age would bear a son who would continue the line of God's unfolding plan of creating a new and truly unusual nation. Indeed, Sarah gave birth. The rest is biblical history, our history, and a model of God's continued calling of varied peoples into a strange and wonderful nation, which in these end of days is called the Holy Christian Church.

Biblical Signs of God's Calling

In this earliest narrative of God's calling and in the subsequent pages of Scripture, many themes reverberate within this subject. Here I will only list a few. God is the caller, and God calls with great power, expressed repeatedly and in various ways. The Psalmist simply declares: "The voice of the Lord is a powerful voice" (Psalm 29). Isaiah records God declaring: "I am the Lord; I have called you in righteousness, I have taken you by the hand and kept you" (Isa 42:6). Calling becomes synonymous with the Word, which encapsulates the very power of God. There are other expressions of God's word power: "Then God said, 'Let there be light'; and there was light" (Gen 1:3; and John 8:12 calls Christ the Light). Or: "The Word [Jesus the Christ] became flesh and lived among us" (John 1:14). And: "The Word was God" (John 1:1). The same God with similar power called Abraham and Sarah to be the initiators of God's own people. And the very same God with all the power of the Spirit still calls people to a similar path. In the Old Testament texts, the caller is known as Yahweh, the Hebrew personal name for the God who called Abraham. God's ultimate voice is heard and seen in the person of Yahweh's Son, Jesus, the Anointed One. At the Anglican Cathedral in Cairo, Egypt, a large stone stands in the center of the church's courtyard. Chiseled into the stone are the words "Out of Egypt I Have Called My Son," a reminder that Abraham's people's journey toward nationhood took them into Egypt. From there Yahweh called them. Seventeen hundred years later Mary and Joseph found protection in Egypt as refugees. Matthew's Gospel quotes Hosea 11:1: "out of Egypt I have called my son" (Matt 2:15). Many of us generally associate Jesus beginning his public ministry with his baptism by John at thirty years of age. However, early in Christ's life the Scriptures affirm God's peculiar activity in Jesus for a journey through time that culminates in his crucifixion and resurrection. As I will discuss later, it often becomes obvious toward the end of one's life how God's call began early to shape a strand of events, which was not always evident in one's earlier days.

The call from God is most personal and intimate; it is direct. Abraham and Sarah's names were changed by their calling, as was St. Paul's. So also are our names changed in our baptism: Christ names us. We become Christ's as we receive our name, both our personal names and the name *Christian!*

Since it is a call from God, it is at times threatening. Following Adam and Eve's turn from God, Yahweh called to Adam, "Where are you?" Adam was hiding from God. God's call was indeed a summons of judgment. Hearing the voice of God in the calling is a summons to stand before God in righteousness. Knowing they had broken not only God's trust but also their relationship with God, Adam and Eve experienced judgment and guilt. As such they could not look God in the eye. Likewise, God looks directly at us. We too are filled with guilt, unless the judgment is heard in the context of Christ's word of mercy—that is, God's declaring, "Your sin is forgiven." Then only can Adam and Eve and any one of us lift up our faces, standing upright before God. Having surrendered our sin in confession, God exchanges our sin with Christ's righteousness. The gift is an alien righteousness, coming from God and from beyond ourselves. ("Alien" means literally "from outside.") In no way is our righteousness self-produced.

Faith is central, and Christian faith is always connected with God's promises. For Abraham and Sarah it was the promise of beginning something wonderful and other such wonderfully new promises as the birth of a son, Isaac, a land for the people, and that as a people they will be a blessing and a witness to others of God's power and mercy. Ultimately, the promise inherent in Christian faith is God's offer of acceptance, decisively spoken in the words, "Your sins are forgiven." Faith receives the greatest of all gifts: God's full acceptance of us with divine love. Thus not with human might nor with human wisdom but through faith do we know that God delivers on the promises of Christ to lead, to heal, and to rescue from despair and death.

The call of God is ordinary, yet within the ordinary God works miraculously. The promise to Abraham and Sarah that they would conceive and bear a son is in many ways very ordinary, yet beyond reasonable belief! The message may appear quite ordinary, "You will bear a child." But what is miraculous, whether young or old, is to experience in faith the awe of birth itself with all its accompanying wonders. Yet these are minuscule compared with the birth of faith, which enables a deep and profound trust in God.

While personal and addressed to each of us as individuals, the call of God is always communal. Abraham and Sarah were called to be and become a special community of God. We are called by God always into the family of God's people, a unique community: the Body of Christ, the church. For Sarah and Abraham the community was a nation called Israel. For us in these days the new community is a holy nation, a peculiar people: God's own people, the Christian church (1 Pet 2:9). The New Testament Greek word *ekklesia,* generally translated "church," has a root meaning of being "called out" or "called together." In the New Testament the word is used to describe the people of God called out and called together.

There is movement in the call. Abraham and Sarah are told, "Get up and go!" The journey, begun with our baptism, is best expressed by the prayer in the liturgies of Morning and Evening Prayer: "O God, you have called your servants to ventures of which we cannot see the ending, by paths as yet untrodden, through perils unknown. Give us faith to go out with good courage, not knowing where we go, but only that your hand is leading us and your love supporting us; through Jesus Christ our Lord."[2] In faith we too make our respective journeys in the Spirit, discovering repentance, renewal, tasks to do, mountains to

2. *Evangelical Lutheran Worship,* 304, 317.

climb, valleys of suffering to traverse, and continued communion with God and the whole people of God, along with the angels and archangels and the whole company of heaven.

The call to "get up and go" may be filled with ambiguities and a lack of clarity, like seeing through a dark glass, yet we hear. Crucial for the Christian is the fact that a calling means that I hear the Caller. For clarity in our *vocations*, we must begin with *invocation*—calling on God in prayer and listening, not telling God what we want to do. We need to learn to listen to God's Spirit giving us insight, letting us know again and again who we are—God's own—and to what we are being called: a life for others. To hear the Caller necessitates stillness and times of quietness on the part of the listener, not easily practiced by many of us in the rush of our days. Bonhoeffer noted: "Silence is the simple stillness of the individual under the Word of God . . . Silence is nothing else but waiting for God's Word."[3]

Our calling is always a call from God to "be in Christ." Our initial call in baptism has clarity of direction: We are called by God for the other, for authentic relationships with people, always in and through Christ. Being in Christ means we are always related to others through him. Luther writes: "A Christian lives not in himself, but in Christ and in his neighbor. Otherwise he is not a Christian. He lives in Christ *through faith*, in his neighbor *through love*. By faith he is caught up beyond himself into God. By love he descends beneath himself into his neighbor. Yet he always remains in God and in his love."[4] In our callings, faith and love are two sides of our one calling. As we go forward in the company of others, we seek the Spirit's enlightenment and guidance in the twists and turns of our lives, with the directional signal pointed towards others and not ourselves. Notice Luther's accent: "[A Christian] descends beneath himself into his neighbor," pointing certainly to the posture of genuine humility.

For each of us, our calling holds eventual insight for our special and unique purposes in our lives as we are pointed outward from ourselves. Such may not be clear as we begin. For some of us, even in old age, the search continues for that "now you see it, now you don't." Yet for many of us, as we do grow older and look back on our careers, we may see how the path took various turns which were unclear at the time. Yet

---

3. Bonhoeffer, *Life Together*, 59–60.
4. Quoted in Lull, *Martin Luther's Basic Theological Writings*, 408 (emphasis added).

now more clearly seen are signs of God's guiding presence leading us, even into our end days. I have already spoken of Abraham and Sarah, but there are some other biblical examples. There is Moses, called by God to lead the people from captivity to the Promised Land. Mary is there to give birth to God's son. Her magnificent response to the call and its announcement (the Magnificat!) is particularly revealing: Mary identifies herself to be the "handmaiden" of God, a servant of God for the nations (Luke 1:38). The apostle Paul is chosen to bring the gospel to the Gentiles around the Mediterranean Sea and on to Rome. So all have their unique calling and their own life's purpose or purposes, though perhaps these are only fully recognized at or near the end of life.

Accepting a call means making a commitment to get up and just do it. Having listened and continuing to listen to the voice of the Spirit in prayer, there is in the call a need for resolution and decision. Let's just do it; let's do the ministry one is called to do. Accepting a calling gives no assurance of easy street; most calls entail sacrifices and faith-testing, and are filled with distractions. Having committed ourselves, we need to keep focused. Thus our callings necessitate accountability and faithfulness to the caller—that is, to God and through others to God. It demands life-ordering disciplines to ensure responsiveness and commitment. It also requires quiet times in order to hear the Spirit of Christ refreshing, sharpening, or perhaps reshaping our callings. One must also be open to new opportunities for service in the midst of current commitments. Indeed, we must always be open to the possibility that we might have taken a wrong turn in life's course, perhaps making a tragically bad decision and seriously hurting others and ourselves. Or in other situations, having been shaken by unexpected events, accidents, and disappointments, one is compelled to reassess one's current course and to explore new options. With such awareness we need prayerful conversation with God, confession, and forgiveness, and a willingness to listen and discern the new.

While sharing a common humanity, each person who is called has special gifts from God, not always quickly or easily recognized. The purpose and primary service of our life may need lifelong review, with openness to new, fresh approaches to the changing conditions of human need. The unique purpose we discern should be thought of as something beyond aptitude, skill, or talent; these are often gifts that advance the unique calling. For example, one may discover that one's lifelong calling is to attract youth to the rich values to be found in classical music. One's skill and talent are gifts to support that calling; they may not necessarily entail personal musical skill. Ultimately we discern our life's unique purpose through the Holy Spirit's enlightenment to both see and hear God's call—a vision of the future—in the mix of who we are in the peculiar circumstances we find ourselves.

The human context in which we hear Christ's call can be overwhelming. From the crying call of an infant at 3:00 a.m., repeated night after night; to the frightened call of a son to a father from the police station; to the knock on the door of a military officer with news of the death of a son or daughter at war; to the home-alone sick friend across town; to the countless calls that enter our lives from those further away, those suffering in war-torn countries, those trapped in poverty, those who hunger, those with little or no medical care—they call out to us for help! Although sensitive and alert to human suffering, we easily become overwhelmed and easily debilitated, and even seriously broken in spirit. As we will discuss later, these overwhelming calls need to be critically reviewed with an awareness of our Christian freedom, which is central to the Gospel.

The Cross and Its Cost

Here I need to focus on a major point, so far not accented: a subject that must envelop all we say and pursue in our Christian calling. Among Christians it may be known simply as "the sign of the cross"—everything that surrounds the cross in Christian faith. I would like to focus on a specific text directly related to our topic, the specific call of Christ to his followers, to take up your cross and follow me. Jesus insists: "If any want to become my followers, let them deny themselves and take up *their* cross *daily* and follow me. For those who want to save their life will lose it, and those who lose their life for my sake will save it" (Luke 9:23–24; emphasis added). Bonhoeffer elaborates wonderfully on this text in his book *The Cost of Discipleship*. We too easily speak of Christians as being *disciples* of Jesus and forget the cost, leading us to a sense of comfort as a follower of "sweet Jesus." If we are going to use the word *discipleship* for the Christian life (as we must), we need to keep Bonhoeffer's word "costly" attached to discipleship. The cost involves both our association with Jesus's suffering and death on the cross, and our own suffering for and with Christ in our Christian life and witness. Bonhoeffer insists:

"To endure the cross is not a tragedy; it is the suffering which is the fruit of an exclusive allegiance to Jesus Christ."[5] Christians have long experienced suffering because they are witnesses both to Christ and to specific struggles at overcoming sin and injustices with movement toward wholeness and peace. Such witness leads to the realization of personal pain and at times death. The New Testament Greek word for "witness" has a double meaning: the activity is *martyeria*, the person is *martys*. The latter may be translated either as "witness" or "martyr." Thus the witness is not to be spoken from within a secure fortress or at a comfortable distance. Rather, the call to take up our cross and follow Christ means testifying to our faith in the risen Christ and daring to struggle, each in our own way, for causes supporting justice. While standing against evil, one surely must be open to the consequences. It means speaking up and acting for one's convictions, which may lead to physical and social suffering, and even to the possibility of martyrdom. It means seeing in one's marriage and in one's professional responsibilities and civic duties the call to confess Christ as Lord. With faith in Christ active in and through us, we are both transparent and at an appropriate time confessional; when the time is right, the Christian names The Name. As we struggle, Christ's love shapes our vocations and services; indeed, the same divine love shapes our struggle for justice and mercy in the midst of conflict and corruption.

Thus our respective Christian callings are connected directly, as declared in our baptism, to Christ's cross of suffering, death, and resurrection. In our baptism we are "marked with the cross of Christ forever." Interestingly, the original German title of Bonhoeffer's *Cost of Discipleship* is *Nachfolge*. The word translates as "follow after" and is the same word used in the German biblical text, "take up your cross and follow after me." This points to the calling of the Christian to be, as a follower, a witness to Christ's death and resurrection; and in so following the Christian is to be a martyr, a witness whose testimony may—for some at least—lead to martyrdom (death). Bonhoeffer's indictment of the Christian churches in the 1930s was their commitment to "cheap grace:" grace without repentance, failing to live the new life in Christ, avoiding witness to Christ, and skirting opportunities to expose and resist evil. His much-quoted words need repeating: "Cheap grace is the preaching of forgiveness without requiring repentance . . . communion

---

5. Bonhoeffer, *Cost of Discipleship*, 77–78.

without confession, absolution without confession . . . Cheap grace is grace without discipleship . . . grace without Jesus Christ, living and incarnate . . . and it is grace because it calls us to follow Jesus Christ. It is costly because it costs a man his life, and it is grace because it gives a man the only true life."[6]

The temptation of the preacher and the Bible reader is to use this text—"take up your cross"—in ways that solely encourage Christians to "bear their cross" in the sense of enduring prolonged sickness or extended personal difficulties. But it means that and more. "Cross bearing" includes being willing to engage in unwelcomed areas where injustices are being inflicted on a person or a people. It does include taking up unspeakable difficulties placed upon us as a given, difficulties given us and our family that we cannot walk away from. As disciples of Christ we bear both our despair and pain, when related to the cross of Christ; and in faith leading to peace of mind we discharge bitterness, ultimately knowing that God is our strength and our hope. Rather than cursing God in sickness and sorrow, we look at God's mercy, taste God's goodness, and still sing with joy even as the tears of sorrow flow. The reason: God's Spirit is among us and within us; that's God's mighty merciful power. In every conceivable difficulty, when taking up our own cross we are lifted high, and there is the witness to God's presence and mercy. M. Shawn Copeland, religion professor at Boston College, in her February 26, 2007, article in the journal *America* titled "To Follow Jesus," articulates the biblical meaning of following Jesus: "We never know precisely when or how the cross comes to us: deep darkness of mind or heart, aching and persistent loneliness, foreclosure of a future, immeasurable loss, diminishment, breakdowns in society, the burden of speaking truth. But when the cross presents itself, we must pick it up and follow Jesus. As we walk, the wide road yields to a narrow way; ruts and obstacles jolt us on the journey. Jesus is just ahead of us, but we see him as if through a glass darkly. Not much is clear. Faith and love, hope and prayer are the meat and bread, sweet and drink that sustain us along with the example of enslaved women and men, who have walked this 'way' before us; indeed, they walk with us now."[7]

The Christian calling, whether shaping our career or our struggle with a particular difficulty, gives us a degree of hope and pleasure,

---

6. Bonhoeffer, *Cost of Discipleship*, 36–37.
7. Quoted in *Context*.

challenge and enjoyment; at least such are important elements of a calling in Christ. There should always be a high degree of joy in service and ministry. If it is seen as a constant pain, a prolonged drudgery, than one is not likely to do the ministry well. Yet the complexities of human life for some are seemingly constant burdens: chronic pain, difficulties, and injustices that are upon one daily and for years. There too one takes hold of faith and the of assurances that God stands beside us and supports us. Without faith we live in desperation, and our callings become either merely meaningless tasks—depressing, regardless how much "spirit" is poured into the effort—or a drive for success without grounding in God's judgment and grace. Even the most pleasant occupation, even the most wonderful marriage and the truly delightful family, will have moments of challenge, at times prolonged challenges. Regardless of what the condition may be, these are the times to call up spiritual courage where one must witness against horrendous opposition and carry on with enormous burdens. At other times, even when apparently free to walk away from a difficulty, one hears the call of God, "Stay in there, fight the injustice, dare to call for justice, and endure the unpleasant reactions of others—including condemnation by some and, at times, even from people near and dear to one."

At the same time, caution is in order, especially in our days of increased religiosity. With so many talking up Jesus everywhere, we need to be as wise as owls in witnessing to Christ. With patience we need to await the "season and the moment" appropriate for the right, ripe time to speak or for knowing when to keep quiet. We need to learn astuteness in finding the optimum occasion for speaking truth in love. We need not jump on every call for social or political protest, nor feel compelled to join every movement for justice and peace. Discernment is appropriate; it is a means of electing among options. However, the fear of being misunderstood or speaking at the wrong time ought not to stifle or excuse one from an appropriate witness.

Nor ought we to suggest that bearing the cross will lead to glory, success, and the elimination of any difficulty or burden. Today, not only among Africa's impoverished Christians (something I personally witnessed in Ghana) but also among middle-class Christians in the US, a theology of glory may be frequently found.[8] This is an assumption that

---

8. Rosin, "Did Christianity Cause the Crash?" 39, claims that "America's mainstream religious denominations used to teach the faithful that they would be rewarded

Jesus will bring you earthly success and personal wealth. The claim is often heard, "If we only would become again a 'Christian' nation, we Christians would experience great prosperity, a new power of world influence, and a nation safe from evil." This is not known in the faith that genuinely identifies with Christ and his cross.

Finally, the Christian calling is a humbling experience. It not only places us lowly and humbled before the mighty presence of God, but it also opens us to the pains of others, always reaching for words that others will understand in sharing our faith and providing help. Using Luther's metaphor, we realize that with all others we are "beggars" before God, all together reaching for the undeserved Bread of Life—the gospel—freely shared in communion with Christ. This lowering of our lives in Christ enables us to be joined with all other people: the learned, the unlearned, the important, and the commoner. But we are never to be caught ranking one higher than the other. Indeed, with Luther we ought to learn to speak various languages and dialects. One scholar saw this in Luther's efforts: "Skilled in the use of language and possessed of a good ear for dialect, Luther was poised to make the ancient gospels and epistles sound like the conversation of villagers in narratives cast in the equivalent of newspaper prose. To translate, write, and speak in the vernacular was one of the most radical and revolutionary choices he made. In fact, the vulgar, gross, and even grotesque barnyard and bathhouse expressions so regular in his work appear to be part of a strategy designed to give voice to and attract the common people who were so often excluded by elites in society and church."[9]

Defining Our Terms

Up to this point we have sought an overview of the Christian calling, anchored in the gospel. Before we proceed with our next chapter, it is important that we sharpen the use of the word calling. I need to identify two specific uses of the same word.

First there is the call of the gospel, our common call to be in Christ—that is, the summons from Christ to be Christian. On this I have

---

in the afterlife. But over the past generation, a different strain of Christian faith has proliferated—one that promises to make believers rich in the here and now. Known as the prosperity gospel, and claiming tens of millions of adherents, it fosters risk taking and intense material optimism."

9. Marty, *Martin Luther*, 72–73.

spoken at length. It is, as has been said, the subject of both the Second and the Third Articles of the creed. Second—to which I have indirectly referred and which I will unwrap in greater detail in the next chapter—is God's *calls* from the various circumstances which we experience in our worldly, everyday life. Examples of this second understanding are many, even heard among non-Christians, such as, "When I interviewed for the position, and they explained what needs were to be met in the position, I really felt the job called me; they and I recognized I had the gifts to meet the demands"; or, "When the accident occurred, and I was the only person around with a car and there was no telephone available, I realized I had to take the injured to the hospital"; or a parent, "When my baby cries in the middle of the night, there's no questioning; it is my call to get to the crib." For our purposes, these examples represent another phenomenon of a "calling" in which God is mysteriously present. The situations are calls for help, and I must ask whether this is "my call" or not? Non-Christians might simply recognize such situations as indisputable necessities, and to walk away from the situations creates guilt or a need for some kind of excuse or rationalization. For Christians, faith recognizes that such situations are a call from God to meet a human need. It may also be a time to exercise the freedom we have in Christ (more on this later). Again, for the Christian, there is the awareness that God cares for an injured person through me or God cares for the world through my career. When we examine long-term commitments—as in a career—and struggle with faith in relation to this, we generally speak of a *vocation* or a *calling*. In effect, the two words become often synonyms for Christians.

To be sure, Christians speak (as I did in the points above) of our Christian calling enveloping both the common call to be Christ's, and our individual and personal involvement in God's calling from within the givens of creation—the unique place where God has placed me. As we proceed I will be extracting the one from the other in order to make sure, first, that we are clear about the gospel's call and its necessity of faith, and second, that we recognize that the callings from within creation are engaged with reason and our senses, yet never engaged apart from faith.

When Luther speaks of those "callings" from within creation, he often identifies them as "stations in life." In his Small Catechism, he illustrates these to be special people, individuals—parents, teachers, employer, employee, spouse, children—to whom we are related by choice, birth, or circumstance. The English word "station" has been viewed by many as too rigid and static. Bonhoeffer, following Luther's insights, uses the phrase "situations of responsibility," thus accenting their relationship while staying with Luther's meaning of "station" as better understood in German.

For the Christian, a movement occurs from the *calling*—namely our call to trust Christ's word, our call to faith—to the *callings* in relationships within God's creation. It is the process of discernment, crucial in the Christian's commitment to faithfulness in daily life. It requires conscious, diligent, and continuous attention. When we speak of a Christian's faith-calling (common to all who follow Christ) and our unique, personal "worldly" callings (tailor-made to our biographies), we need to keep the two connected and yet distinguished. Clarifying again the importance of this task, I emphasize two points. First, the call to faith is specific; it is the "good work and good word" in and from Christ, not to be confused with our own good works. For St. Paul and for Luther, our ethical behavior follows faith in God's reconciling work. We are not reconciled—that is, made right with God—by our ethical behavior. Second, God calls us within the context of our daily activities lived out in this worldly condition. That's where we must discern, must discover under the fog of a fallen world what God wills us to do, which is not always very clear. That God speaks to us in the human complexities is a given for the Christian. Where and how we know which voice is authentic, however, is not always so clear. Luther's understanding on this subject is worth repeating: "We have a double vocation, a spiritual and an external. The spiritual vocation is that we [Christians] have all been called through the gospel to baptism and the Christian faith . . . That calling is common and similar for all . . . The other contains a differentiation: It is earthly, though also divine."[10]

It cannot be known with absolute certainty exactly what God wills for us in our various callings. Yet empowered with the faith of God's clear and good work in Christ, and listening for the Spirit's nudge, we struggle and work at *discernment*. Before a final, crucial decision, we need to take apart the situations in which we live, listening to the various callings for help and the many opportunities among us and beyond us, at times far distant. Then we say yes to some and no to others. And

---

10. *WA* 34 II, 300, 306.

when saying yes, we proceed with the assurance of God's presence. Our response to a call, having discerned what we conclude to be God's will for us in a specific circumstance, is to do it with conviction, with faith and courage, knowing the promise, "I am with you." Indeed, we may say, "This is my Christian calling." And if you conclude you took the wrong course, that the situation is not right for you, then celebrate confession and forgiveness, and be open for the new and be rid of the guilt.

5

The Creation

The Context of Our Callings

I WAS WALKING IN MIDTOWN MANHATTAN, CROSSING 42ND Street into Times Square. An evangelist was standing on a milk crate, megaphone in hand. He called out to passersby, "Believe in the Lord Jesus Christ. Repent! And you will be saved from the fires of hell." A few snickered. Most walked by hurriedly, appearing not even to notice his presence, let alone hear his message.

I found myself listening intently, ashamed that the gospel of Christ was represented so poorly in the center of this great metropolis; but as I also passed by, I began to realize how similar this evangelist's message was to what many of us Christians consider the gospel. Of course, our preaching and teaching are not as crude. If we have grown beyond believing we are saved by our good deeds, then we too may translate the gospel message into God's saving us from the perils of this world. We easily retreat into our comfortable church, as into a fortress, protecting us from an evil world while we enjoy the comforts of this life and wait for our place at the heavenly banquet.

The Times Square evangelist, apparently totally dedicated to his ministry, does say something crucial to our understanding of the gospel: God does save from judgment. But missing is this: we are saved for service, here and now, in a world fraught with evil, yet a world which the Scriptures insist is God's world. God not only created but continues to create, and God remains in control, in spite of evidence to the contrary (think only of the Holocaust in Europe, the tsunamis in Southeast Asia and in Japan, and the earthquake in Haiti). The Word, however, affirms that God is present everywhere, yet hidden within creation. Until our death—which for us Christians is the end of time—the call of the gospel is a call to all the people of God for ministry and service in this broken, pain-stricken, wretched world—God's world! Indeed, God calls all the people to join together with all others who seek justice and who work to maintain a civil society and to secure the common good. To be sure, seeking those objectives is not the ultimate objective which God has for the creation, but it is the penultimate concern, a temporal concern that maintains a world capable of hearing and receiving the gift of God's grace—that is, the gospel (1 Tim 2:1–6).

The message of the Times Square evangelist with his megaphone is but one example of questionable declarations of God's word. There are indeed others. Evangelical Christian fundamentalists may be the flipside, gathered in their megachurches by the thousands, supported by their literalistic reading of Scripture, claiming to know God's specific will as they affirm political agendas and openly support political candidates in the name of Christ. Then too, in the view of still others, the mainline churches may also be as guilty. Struggling for what they consider a faithful and a responsible public church, they are often seen by many to have lost their biblical grounding. An article by Walter Mead in the prestigious journal *Foreign Affairs*, lists the ELCA along with other historic mainline churches as "Liberal Christians [who] are skeptical about the complex doctrines concerning the nature of Jesus and the Trinity that were developed in the early centuries of the church's history . . . And their skepticism often also extends to the physical resurrection of Jesus."[1]

Mead's article makes a broad generalization and gives no indication of the bases for his assertion. We may, however, assume that he along with many others with similar views relies primarily on public statements and press releases issued by the church's official spokespeople. If that is so, is it a legitimate question for us to ask, "What is today the primary image given by the historic Christian church in their current effort to be the 'public church?'" To use a behavioral science question, what is the current "brand," the "logo," the image of the Christian community projected by its public pronouncements? We may take issue with Mead on two counts. First, though the Christian Church, including the Lutheran church, has never been monolithic in its theology, the faith

1. Mead, "God's Country?" *Foreign Affairs*, 30.

of the early church as confessed in the historic creeds remains central. Many find it difficult to articulate this confession of Christian faith in the public arena for fear of being identified with the fundamentalist, evangelical crowd. By its very nature the church is public. Indeed, when we speak of the office of the *public* ministry, the ordained are called to speak very much in public. At the same time, we ought not to give the impression that the ministry and confession of the laity—the people—is a private matter. When faithful to its calling, the Christian church in various public venues addresses issues that give testimony to Christ as Lord and Savior and to the relationship of that confession to a life of love and a striving for justice. This is surely our struggle today, and a subject we want to pursue throughout this effort.

Second, I find Mead's conclusions unscholarly and irresponsible when he assumes that a Christian community and many of its members cannot be both deeply committed to the faith of the historic church and at the same time be socially and politically concerned. In much of the long tradition of the church, those faithful to the Word have recognized worldly justice is not the same as Christ's righteousness. The gospel does not equate Christ's righteousness with worldly justice, nor Christ's peace with earthly peace. However, let there be no question: the people of the Word are called by that Word to engage critically and vigorously with worldly issues and never to retreat, collectively as church and personally as Christians. How the faithful project this conviction and practice is important for our work through these pages.

Whatever our identity—parent, citizen, pastor, bishop, employer, employee, student, teacher, soldier, politician—for each and every one of us the connection and distinction between the word of God's grace and our Christian callings in daily life is both challenging and necessary, and dare never to be taken lightly. This is true also of the corporate church. How we settle on the connection and distinction have significant implications for the shape of all our ministries, vocations, callings, ethical responses—indeed, for Christian witness and for all our worship. What knowledge and what insight for ethical behavior has God disclosed and by what means? Similarly, what unique authority does the Christian claim from God when addressing a particular social, political issue or in shedding light on our vocations? What does the church share in common with non-Christians that enables us to work together toward a more civil society, toward a higher level of justice and worldly peace and the common good? And what has God conveyed to me, as a Christian, that enlightens my choices of a career and of allegiance to a political party or candidate? What guidance does God give me in the midst of my daily tasks? Using Luther's recommended lenses, let us examine the two distinctly different self-disclosures of God, which I trust will both inform and energize us, as well as assist us to recognize what limits us in each disclosure.

God's "Back Side" and "Front Side"

The source of our unique knowledge of God is crucial. In order to grasp the manner in which God is known and involved in today's world, we need to distinguish two entirely different self-disclosures by God. We dare not mix or confuse the two—God's *act of creation* and God's *act of redemption*. These two concepts are known by various phrases: "God's left- and right-hand reigns," "the Kingdom on the left and on the right," and "God's law and gospel." While these phrases may themselves provide different insights and may be distinguishable, they have fundamentally similar meanings.

God's "Back Side"

"God's Back Side" is an expression used by Luther, lifted from Moses's encounter with God (Exod 33:23). When you experience God from behind, you cannot fully recognize who the person is, though you may be able to know a little something about the phenomenon in whose presence you stand. One senses the presence of a god, a feeling of might and awesome power. In addition there is a sense that this all-powerful one lays demands and expectations upon you. Recognizing such, one is not always comfortable. The discomfort expresses something of the weal and woe of the human experience in its confused awareness of God, a God who may appear at times as all-powerful but so often appears impotent to rescue the world in its moments of self-destruction, leading to so much suffering, pain and despair.

Looking at God's back-side from the perspective of Christian faith, God's will is seen being expressed within a sin-inflicted humanity. In spite of what may humanly appear to be God's weakness and —as in the Holocaust, as in a massive tsunami—*through the eyes of faith*—the Almighty is known to be present within the fallen world, certainly hidden, not fully known. Sin has blinded us from seeing God in the fullest sense. In the analogy of the Genesis account, God's eternal will is clearly known, illustrated with Adam and Eve's intimate relations with their creator. In breaking that trust, man and woman became distrustful. No longer in a trusting relationship with God, they felt judged and guilty, and they lied and hid. Those who focus solely on God's creation find their knowledge of God very limited. Our corrupted human nature and our spiritual blindness make us incapable of seeing God clearly, when God's back-side is all we see. God's presence is blurred, distorted, and often confusing and disturbing.

What we may know from this phenomenon is never absolute, yet there remains one conclusive reality in this worldly context. Though seemingly hidden, God's final verdict on my life is a constant awareness: Death is a certainty. Yet what is known about God's will in any situation (including the meaning of my death) or in any moment of history is never an absolute. Social and political ambiguities are always present. Efforts by the best minds often lead to contradictory insights and explanations. Luther is most insightful in his explanation to the First Article of the creed, which article is regarding God's creation and creating. There Luther lists God's gifts to humans in our worldly experiences. Among the many gifts, he lists three that are central to our concern here. Luther says: "God has given me and still preserves my body and soul: eyes, ears, and all limbs and senses; reason and all mental faculties."[2] Thus Christians share with all humanity the common gift of our senses and the ability to think and to reason together. As we struggle for civility, it is reason and our various senses that are God's gifts, the primary tools for achieving social change and justice within our human communities. It is important to connect, as Luther does, human reasoning with our senses. Before rationally analyzing a condition, we may have a sense that something is corrupt: the situation has a feeling of something evil; it may even "smell bad." Civility among humans is not achieved simply or solely by reason nor by the mere discipline of cognitive, rational thinking. Our emotions, our imaginations, our dreams, all our senses, all the arts surely must be honored and respected along with the discipline of reason as we both listen with all our senses and work with all our intellect for a more civil society.

---

2. Luther, "Small Catechism," 1162.

And for these gifts, reason and all my senses, along with all other gifts to be found in the creation, says Luther: "I *owe* it to God to thank and praise, serve and obey him."[3]

As humans experience this corrupted world they feel a need to "do the right thing." Humanity senses a common understanding that we *ought to do the good and avoid the bad*. If you read Luther's explanations of the three articles of the Apostles Creed, you will notice that only in this explanation of the article on creation does he conclude with the word "owe"; a better word is "ought," used in earlier translation. It is conspicuously missing in the second and third explanations (redemption and sanctification). The word here in Luther's original German edition is *Schuldig*, a word closely associated with law—that is, what one *must* do or what obligations one has in view of what one has received. Its connotation is that you have a *duty* to do something in view of what you have received. But the "ought"—the "debt"— is neverending: you are unable to be dutiful enough of pay back what is expected, thus you feel guilty, never able to achieve a full measure of service to match those good gifts you have received. Here there is constant duty and no freedom. Such is the ultimate nature of life when limited to the back-side of God's rule, a life of "ought" and guilt. Such is also experienced by Christians when they live under the law and not under Christ's grace. More about this "ought" later, especially regarding our Christian freedom in Christ.

Along with a sense of duty to do good, there is another shared experience among Christians and non-Christians. Expressive of God's will embedded in humanity is the reach for "the good life" amid conditions that are at times less than good, indeed even bad. The world and its people, religious and nonreligious, may—on many occasions and in various circumstances—agree, "Yes, we crave peace," especially when exhausted by strife and war. This yearning may lead to common, reasonable agreements. It is in the best interest of all to work for justice, put down an injustice, seek integrity, be decent, enjoy the beautiful and avoid the ugly. and somehow achieve a common good. The goals of such desires are often elusive. Intense public debate ensues in every community as various proposals are advocated. Consensus is difficult to achieve. Yet, standing before God's back-side, one may realize an awareness of God's presence and God's concern for the creation and its creatures. Missing are specific directives from God on how and in what way we should resolve

3. Ibid. (emphasis added).

our differences or achieve our objectives. Obviously God leaves us to struggle using primarily the gift of "reason and our senses." Though the pursuit of what is good is mixed with conflict and bitter differences, one cannot give up. The alternatives are often too horrendous! Humanity generally appears to know this but often lacks courage and leadership to respond creatively toward effecting just and fair social change. Indeed, often missing is the willingness to compromise—that is, the mutual will to give up personal treasures in order that the community might achieve civility. And yet one hopes all will pursue sensible solutions that would not compel either a compromise with evil nor an abandonment of decency and truth.

Christian faith recognizes that this push and pull within and among humans, to do good and put down evil, is a manifestation of God's law embedded in creation. However, not everyone who experiences the law in creation will attribute such to God's lively presence, nor should Christians insist on such recognition when working with non-Christians in pursuit of a social problem. In short, God's will to preserve creation, while not understood by the world, is still mightily at work in the stuff of creation. It is God's willpower that preserves the world from self-destructing, thus enabling some degree of civility to persist. God's willpower works its way through individuals and communities; it presses them toward a vision of a better life, a more fair and decent life than they are perhaps now experiencing. Individuals, families, neighborhoods, states, and unions of states can experience a disease-infested, war-torn condition and simply conclude that this is not the way it ought to be. A collective conscience can insist that we can do better. And collective efforts at reform can be made. God wills a good world; God wills fair and decent communities. God wills peace, attainable through men and women who persistently work for justice. Diverse communities—including nonreligious people, Christians, and people of other faiths—can work together toward establishing higher levels of civilization.

With sadness, many of us have at times recognized a consistent—and persistent—human inclination to foster and condone evil: human atrocities, holocausts, seemingly endless calamities, unreasonable destruction of human life with bitter hate, even divisive strife between husbands and wives and between parents and children. History is a witness to the rise and fall of civilizations, to a succession of histories, to the success and failure of achieving the good while obliterating the gains that had been achieved. With Luther we may say, "the devil, the world, and our old sinful flesh" obliterate the paths to peace and civility. And more often than not, evil appears to succeed—often as much *in us* as "in them," as represented in any and every community. Faith, however, recognizes the wonderful human reach for noble ends and its failure as signs both of God's will for a better world and of our fallen human nature. At the same time, we may also feel a spiritual and mental void in efforts to explain human disasters and human atrocities inflicted especially on the poor and the oppressed, from which the privileged and powerful are seemingly so often spared. Yet Christian faith calls on us to persist, never abandoning the fight for right, never denying God's mysterious presence, power, and will for a better world.

Ironically, our human nature often resists God's efforts at provoking us to work for a better world. We humans so easily and so often engage in a human game of claiming to do good and then faking it while doing evil; of wanting to see good done yet not doing it; of feeling guilty and doing some good to get rid of the guilt. Yet in and through such actions God does accomplish a divine intention of setting some things right in a very fallen world. Faith recognizes this. The good that humans achieve in society is both desired by God and to be praised by Christians, even when accomplished with less than honorable motives. Theologians have named this good behavior "civil righteousness." This is a righteousness that God wills, though it is distinctly different from what the theologians name "alien righteousness" (that is, foreign to anything human), which is given by God through faith in Christ. Again, keep in mind God's two Kingdoms: one in the realm of God's created, fallen world, in which civil righteousness is sought, with reason making the judgments about "good and evil"; and the other, in which God gives mercy through Christ, imparting alien righteousness that is grasped by faith, not by reason. The latter is the realm of God's right-hand rule. Unless we distinguish these two realms of God's rule, our Christian understanding and the practice of our daily callings will be distorted, conflicted, and the gospel becomes merely another source among many for a noble solution to a human condition.

In spite of evil, God's will is known among all humanity (though seldom acknowledged) as the voice that insists on fairness and decency; it is a call for avoidance of evil; it presses us to pursue the good. When the proper expectation is not achieved, there is guilt. At times the guilt is subtle or suppressed. Other times, restless on our pillows in the dark of night, we agonize and struggle with an awareness that what was done was wrong! Then, as St. Paul says of our natural condition, we either excuse or accuse (Romans 1 and 2, especially 2:15–16). A mental exercise begins: we rationalize; we account for what we did that was good, weighing it against what we did that was wrong; or we consider what we will do tomorrow to rid ourselves of the "bad," the guilt. Or we get rid of our guilt by blaming all on another, as Adam did with Eve.

So we practice what theologians call "self-justification," working toward "self-righteousness." This can lead to self-destruction and to serious harm to others and to self. Or it can also lead to great works of kindness, enriching the lives of others while giving one a feeling of redemption, an apparent loss of guilt—but this is an illusion. While this might not be God's design for achieving great things for the world, it does further God's interests, that good be done! While feeling free of guilt and enjoying the good feeling, many are empowered to do even more good. Doing what is good is humanly satisfying, and the good feeling motivates us fallen humans to do even more good, subtly providing us with self-justification, if we sense God's judgment.

This leads us to a biblical understanding of sin in our own lives and within societies, which Luther characterized as "the return curve" of sin. It is the thought and activity of us humans that go out to another with some form of goodness and kindness, in the hope that it will return, ultimately giving us praise, glory and personal satisfaction and ridding us of guilt. Luther's phrase for this in Latin is *incurvatus in se*, "the curve back into self." This profound and persistent reality of sin's curve—that is, self-interest—is the driving force of the arts, governments, and careers, including sex and the family. We even feature this self-interest in public signs: "Drive carefully; the life you save may be your own." Adam Smith, in his *Wealth of Nations* (1776)) wrote: "It is not from the benevolence of the butcher, the brewer, or the baker, that we expect our dinner, but from their regard for their own interest," and economists today will seem to agree.[4] An analysis of this obvious feature of sin, the egocentric nature

---

4. A recent book by Steven D. Levitt and Stephen J. Dubner, *Super Freakonomics* (2009), reports the extensive research by economists in questioning the reality of authentic altruism. The important chapter related to our theological concern is chapter three, an excerpt of which was reprinted in a *New York Times* article titled "Unbelievable Stories about Apathy and Altruism" (October 16, 2009). This quote (taken from newspaper article) supports what Luther understood of the "curve of sin": "Most giving is, as

of our human condition (self-interest) may provide genuine short-term advantages for change. It may also ignore long-term disadvantages of specific decisions related to one's own self-interest, often leading to earthly disasters. This is easily illustrated today in matters both of human ecology and of international politics. The American farmer in the 1920s thought, in his own self-interest and short-sightedness, that he could till the soil for all it was worth without consideration of long-term effect—only to discover, as the drought arrived and the winds blew, that the rich topsoil was blown away and the land became unproductive for years. Internationally, following the First World War and the disintegration of the Ottoman Empire, Winston Churchill (representing England's great power at the time) drew the boundaries that now identify modern Middle East nations. They were drawn in the interest of England's political and economic advantage with disregard to long-term political consequences, leading to extended regional conflict which engulfs much of the world today. Even closer to home, a parent may find that the way to gain order in the family is to insist on strict adherence to rules set by the father, never allowing for growth nor fostering personal freedom and responsibility as the years progress. Public decisions of government and all other institutions can too easily fix a problem with a short-term solution to the advantage of a few, which in time only leads to long-term devastating consequences for many. It is generally agreed today that the surrender terms severely imposed on the Germans by the victorious Allies following the First World War failed to assess the long-term effect. The "V" in the name of the V-2 Rockets the Nazis dropped on London in the Second World War stood for *Vergeltungswaffen*, meaning "reprisal." Leadership is crucial in leading us humans from a comfortable, self-satisfying solution to a solution that calls for greater personal and national sacrifice. The difference in leadership at the conclusion of the two World Wars was decisive in shifting the self-interest of the victors to a long-term view and commitment. Harry S. Truman, the US president, and George C. Marshall, Truman's Secretary of State, insisted

---

economists call it, impure altruism or warm-glow altruism. You give not only because you want to help but because it makes you look good, or feel good, or perhaps feel less bad." And: "It may appear altruistic when you donate $100 to your local radio station, but in exchange you get a year of guilt-free listening (and if you're lucky, a canvas tote bag). US citizens are easily the world's leaders in per-capita charitable contributions, but the US tax code is among the most generous in allowing deductions for those contributions."

on what came to be known as the "Marshall Plan." Rather than lowering Germany to a subservient role of indentured relations to the victors, the US decided to provide aid that would enable Germany to develop a positive identity with a high and healthy sense of national esteem. Of course, when speaking of the United States' glorious, gracious Marshall Plan, we seldom confess to the fact that our government recognized a frightening "Big Red Bear" (Russia) looking toward Germany and the rest of Europe, ready to subject these nations to Russia's oppression. So in our understandable self-interest, our government called on us to sacrifice with higher taxes and massive gifts of food and material to our very recent European enemies. The US especially enhanced its national self-interest by the generous reconstructive work in Germany. So in our self-interest we quickly made friends with Germany while gaining ground in preventing Russia from taking over Western Europe. Great and good leadership, both Christian and non-Christian, needs to learn from history, asking, "What are the long-term consequences to our immediate solutions?" We need also to recognize that short-term solutions may too often favor the present generation at the expense of the next generation. Might Christians have a "gift," if properly exercised, to lead the nation in calling for sacrifice now, in order that peace and justice might be a greater possibility later, and be willing to personally sacrifice now for the benefit of future generations?

Christians, however, do not have a monopoly on achieving great acts of sacrifice or acts of love, either in public life or family relations. Great reforms are often achieved by calls for advancing one's self-interest leading toward greater common good. Jeremiah 29 illustrates this fascinating dimension of the human motivation for good. The prophet suggests Israel should "seek the welfare of the city where I have sent you into exile, and pray to the Lord on its behalf, for in its welfare you will find your welfare" (Jer 29:7). Do good even to those who are not of your faith; indeed, pray for them—that is, the people of Babylon—pray for them. It is in your own best interest to do so, for in Babylon's peace is your peace. England's Prime Minister Benjamin Disraeli, in his much-quoted dictum on foreign policy, pinpointed what is true of government as it is ultimately true of everyone in a fallen world: England's foreign policy has no interest except England's self-interest. Ultimately that may be said of most of us most of the time. At the center of sin is our self-centeredness.

Indeed, there are biographies of wonderful acts of love and devotion to others, painful struggles to overcome social and political evils, by people who disavow religious belief or who affirm a religion other than Christian. And to be sure, there are great, historic love stories of countless people who were in no way Christian, who grew beyond self-interest as they loved others with great personal sacrifice. It is important to lift up the good that society or individuals are capable of doing and have accomplished, while at the same time being deeply aware of the beastly, seemingly inhuman, behavior to which humans are susceptible and of which they (we) are capable. Great social good has been accomplished against the will of the community and in spite of bitter opposition, which—at times—comes from Christians. Too easily we Christians can assume that only Christians have shaped the good features of world history, failing to recognize what indeed God has accomplished through those outside of the church, in spite of various opposing forces. Sometimes a secular social movement and its successes open the door for somewhat similar changes, years later, within the church. Women's suffrage and the ordaining of women clergy is an illustration. The women's suffrage movement following World War I was often fiercely attacked from many Protestant and Roman Catholic pulpits, and often denounced by church-going husbands, ridiculing their wives and others for insisting on the right to vote. The leadership of the suffrage movement was indeed generally Christian, but given the sharp attacks from mainline churches, leaders often moved their allegiances to the far-left side of the churches, many becoming Unitarians. The enactment of the Nineteenth Amendment (1920) gave women the right to vote, but the first Lutheran woman in our country to be ordained into the church's public ministry took place much later—50 years later (1970). Had not the country agreed to a major change in its position relative to women in public life by adopting the Nineteenth Amendment, it is very doubtful that the church could have succeeded in ordaining women. The Civil Rights movement that led to the passing of major pieces of federal legislation is a different story. In many ways it was a Christian movement, begun by African American southern Christians who dared to protest at great personal risk. They were later joined by northern Christians, Jewish citizens, and many nonreligious people, while also experiencing significant opposition from some Christians in both the North and the South of our country, including Lutherans of all brands.

What we have covered in these past pages applies to God's will—God's law—being effected in human life, earthly events, and human history. It is the worldly mix in which the Christian seeks his or her various callings, never apart from God's fallen world and, never isolated from non-Christians. Here I have lifted up what theologians have called the *civil or political* understanding of God's law, along with brief references to the Christian alternative. In our next section, we will focus on the same will of God, though not distorted by the world's fallen condition. In and through the Word revealed in Christ, the same law and will of God comes into sharper view, now not as civil law, but as God's *accusing law*. In the words of Moses, in the giving of the Law on Mt. Sinai, in the pronouncements of prophets, in the lessons of the Psalms, and especially in Christ's own words of criticism—in all this, the law of God is seen bringing judgment and necessitating redemption.

God's "Front Side"

God's other self-disclosure shows God's "front side" and a power of God different from that known under the law in creation. Here the means of knowing is quite different. In Christ we do see and hear by faith, empowered by the Holy Spirit—not by reason. Even by faith, as St. Paul says, we see through a glass darkly. Yet we do see, and the picture is clear enough. When looking at God's front side, we are confronted by the broken, painfully stricken body of Christ on the cross. God's Son is suffering for us and for all people, clearly revealing through the eyes of faith that God not only exists, but that God is merciful and truly cares. The word from the cross is simple, "This is the Son of God, achieving redemption for all." Here we discover God's reconciliation and redemption. On the cross, faith recognizes God's Son. There God's Chosen One lifts up his countenance and conveys peace. His life and death usher in God's ultimate reconciling work. In him we hear, see, and receive God's forgiveness and acceptance; the old is made new; death is over-come; the resurrection is a reality known in faith. The distrust, self-deception—indeed, the war between heaven and earth—all are ended for those with faith. This is, as the Scripture declares, Christ's peace, a unique peace, unlike the peace that the world gives or the peace that we may achieve through reason and civil righteousness. The same law of God embedded in creation is revealed by Christ for all to discover. It is the cutting character of the law: the accusing law. The biblical account of God's self-disclosure is not solely about a God who works for the world's civility, but also of a God who insists that humans be righteous as they live amid God's holiness. In the presence of God, sin and sinful humanity cannot survive. That is clearly the point made in God's appearance on Mt. Sinai and in the giving of the Law, the Ten Commandments. There Moses stood before God's back side. A similar image is God speaking to Moses from the burning bush, before whose presence Moses shuddered and was frightened and fearful. Thus God's law both promotes civil righteousness and—when fully revealed—demands of all of us righteousness and holiness—saintliness—beyond our ability to achieve. And without God's righteousness bestowed upon us through Christ, we live a spiritual death.

Christ reveals a deeper and different view of the nature of sin, saying to his disciples: "You have heard that it was said, 'You shall not commit adultery.' But I say to you that everyone who looks at a woman with lust has already committed adultery with her in his heart" (Matt 5:28). Jesus here is speaking of the Sixth Commandment. Again, those who have obeyed the law and have not committed adultery may try to claim righteousness before God, but not before God's accusing law. Christ goes to the heart of the matter: "Whoever lusts, commits adultery." So also with the Fifth Commandment: "You should not kill." In the political process, governments pass laws forbidding murder, perhaps sometimes based on the Laws of Moses, but more often on the basis of the law embedded in creation. Reason realizes that killing is simply not good for any one or for the community. But God's law probes deeper, to the level of God's demand for righteousness, to the "heart" of the matter. Jesus in effect insists that whoever has anger in his heart has already committed murder (Matt 5:21). In allowing God's holy law to illuminate the hidden parts of our life, we become convicted and guilt-ridden, and recognize before God "that all have sinned," and that includes me!

An important insight of Luther is this: *God never demands anything of us that God does not also give us.* Thus law and gospel embody both demand and gift. The law of God accuses us of sin and demands righteousness before God. The gospel, the all-powerful Word that God speaks in Christ, conveys to the believer grace and mercy, forgiveness, acceptance, the gift of Christ's righteousness, and the indwelling of the Spirit to grasp the gift. In faith we have received what Scripture calls "Christ's righteousness." This is technically called an "alien righteousness"; it is foreign to anything human, truly God's righteousness, God's divine holiness, God's sacred love. With Christ, who is brought to us in the word and sacraments with the Spirit, we have his holiness and righteousness. This is always in contrast to our human efforts at achieving *righteousness* before God, which is an offense to God. With this in mind, we can understand the biblical declaration: Christians are "saints" of God, members of a "holy nation," and Christ's body, the church. St. Paul expressed his goal this way: "That I may gain Christ and be found in him, not having a righteousness of my own that comes from the law, but one that comes through faith in Christ, the righteousness from God based on faith" (Phil 3:8–9).

Thus Christians live with Christ's righteousness as they live in the body of sin. Luther describes this reality in Latin as *simul iustus et peccator*, meaning "at one and the same time righteous and sinner." As Christians we continue to find ourselves to be self-serving, indeed, very unrighteous, guilty even of hideous crimes. This knowledge summons the Christian once again to the cross. There we may clearly hear God's declaration of grace, of undeserved mercy, and of forgiveness. Faith clings to this gift and to the promises of God, and responds with a resolve to "amend the sinful life" and to struggle with Christ's love for a spiritually healthy self-acceptance, as one also struggles in Christ's name for good among all people, and for a resisting of evil.

Stations or Situations in Life

Observing the law within creation, one may recognize those various "oughts" experienced in our daily existence that shape peculiar circumstances in our lives. These situations Luther called "stations"; Bonhoeffer called them "situations of responsibility." They are commonly experienced—yet truly unique—"givens" in each life. A definitive study of Luther's understanding of vocation by Gustaf Wingren brings clarity. According to Luther: "A vocation is a '*station*' which is by nature helpful to others if it be followed."[5] It is a circumstance amid human relations in which I sense that I must do something; and when I pursue the sense of the situation, regardless of my motive, others will be helped. These situations and circumstances are the opportunities we encounter in daily life: formal, as in an occupation or marriage; and informal, as in the multi-

---

5. Quoted in Wingren, *Luther on Vocation*, 4.

plicity of unintended relational circumstances that we daily encounter. These are situations that "call" us. In responding, we will most likely deliver some benefit to another, assuming at least we have some sense of goodwill and not evil. The classic example is the Good Samaritan. In the course of his travel, happening upon an injured man alone at the roadside, the situation called him (as it did others) to respond, to be responsible. The Samaritan did respond, and the bloodied man was helped. The situations we encounter call out to us in various media and with differing words to offer help. The biblical awareness of God's mysterious presence is seen in calls by God to us from the person or persons in need. While there is much more to be mined in the parable of the Good Samaritan, here we merely recognize an illustration of Luther's "stations" in life, a relational opportunity calling for service.

The situation may be impersonal or inanimate, yet ultimately it is humanly relational. An example: During a storm, you are alone along the river bank, and you observe the dam is about to break. A town is several miles below at the river's edge. The situation calls for you to do something to save those below, to avoid another Johnstown Flood. While some—for various reasons—pass by, you cannot. Without a lot of internal, rational deliberation, you drop what you were intending to do and now focus on warning those who live in the path of potential destruction—and you may not even know anyone living in the town below.

In the section on baptism, Luther's Small Catechism gives us another insight regarding "stations," that is, those particular relationships through which God calls one to be an instrument of care for others. But in this section of the Catechism Luther points us to the flip side of this subject: If you want to know what sins to confess, consider your recent situations in life, those relations where you were called on but failed to respond, or responded with something less than God's care. Here are some: how we acted toward father or mother, son or daughter, husband or wife, or toward the people with whom we work, and so forth. Luther suggests that we may ask ourselves whether we have been disobedient or unfaithful, bad-tempered or dishonest, or whether we have hurt anyone by word or deed. So those relational situations in daily life are not only opportunities for service and ministry, they are also specific moments in which we failed and sinned. They provoke confession of our sin to God and evoke faith to enjoy the grace God gives. With the cleansing of heart and mind, the Spirit leads us with greater sensitivity both to listen more carefully to the cries of others and to seek the skill, strength, wisdom, courage and resources to help more effectively. In all of this, the Good Samaritan is most exemplary.

God's Creation and Creativity

Luther speaks first and foremost of God's creation in personal, contemporary expressions as he taught in his Small Catechism, "I believe that God has created me together with all that exists." When confessing the First Article of the creed, he asks: "What does this means?" And answers: "God has given me and still preserves my body and soul: eyes, ears, and all limbs and senses; reason and all mental faculties."[6] Thus, with Luther, I may say that the Holy Spirit has empowered me to confess God's mighty creative activity here and now in my very life and sustains my life in so many ways. With such faith, I can easily celebrate God's handiwork over eons past through the evolving of the universe or universes. When speaking of the biblical account of the creation, some assume God had a pattern for the creation, that God set it in motion, and that through the centuries it remained unchanged. Such a stagnant and frozen view of God's creativity refuses to allow God to be God, to continue the creativity and the evolving of life and matter into changed new forms. Thus we need to keep before us a current ordering of the universe for which God is free to shape as God wills. We may experience God's current creative ordering of everything with both awe and praise to God. In the mix of God's creative processes, there are, however, discernable orderings of the creation, recognized certainly through the eyes of faith, but also with varying degrees of empirical evidence.

The Peculiar Balance within the Creation

The creation and its varied conditions often appear to be in an ecological balance. Overstressing one side of the equilibrium leads to adverse conditions. Extensive cultivation of the soil leads to erosion which leads to a loss of important minerals which in turn leads to low productivity and an inability to support life. In other words, if you stress the creation in any one part beyond its basic constitution, something adverse generally happens, though this can often remain unnoticed for years. Surely one may assume that there are limits to each facet of God's creation.

---

6. Luther, "Small Catechism," 1162.

This is what theologians have often said of an order to creation. Yet this presents us with a dilemma when searching for direction in our calling, when we review what God has given us, and when we ask what God is calling us to be and become. How many of the limitations are truly given by God? And how much of what we might identify as limitations is just culturally dictated? And how might we take a "given" and foolishly compel change that results in an ecological imbalance leading to personal stress and serious social problems.

History is chock-full of moments when the doomsayers insisted that if mankind launched into a radically new enterprise, God would bring damnation upon all parties related to the effort. As the Wright brothers began their effort to develop a means of flying through the air, some preachers were heard to say, "If God intended humans to fly, humankind would have been born with wings." Had the Wright brothers and their kind listened to the culture, we might still be earthbound. Or consider the young person who aspires to become a professional quarterback or is determined to make the Olympics in figure skating—and then tragedy strikes! An auto accident results in a spinal injury and confines the once-aspiring athlete to a wheelchair. Certainly there are those news stories of an unusually driven person who refuses to accept the doctor's dictum, "you will never walk again," or, "never again will you make a figure eight on ice," and in spite of the odds they go on to accomplish feats way beyond the doctor's imagination. What can we learn in all this?

One, there are limits. While given the great potential to grow and work toward becoming something we are not, despite the counsel of others, some goals are unattainable. The truth remains: humans are limited; we are not god-like—a factor each of us needs to accept. A person of small physical stature, with great personal discipline and good coaching, can learn to lift weights far beyond what others of similar stature could ever achieve. Although we know that nearly every human record thought to be unbreakable has, indeed, been broken, we still must accept the fact that there are limits, and the limits may provide some insight into what direction our callings may take.

Two, we need to question both the culture that unfairly limits some from reaching beyond certain goals and any counseling that sets inappropriate barriers to a potential as well as to the overcoming of disabilities toward success. Illustrations are vast in numbers. The biographies of many of the great people of history are replete with accounts of their overcoming obstacles of personal weaknesses that would inhibit most of us. Teddy Roosevelt was sickly as a child and had to be tutored at home while others his age were in high school; yet he became the leader of the Rough Riders and a president of our country who dared to travel the nation, initiating the National Parks. Eleanor Roosevelt, who as a young person had deep feelings of inadequacy, was very self-conscious of her awkwardness and her lack of physical beauty. She possessed no noticeable ability at public speaking, but as an adult became one of the most admired leaders of her time and a forceful speaker before thousands and millions through radio. With profound resolve she overcame personal deficits and succeeded in spite of her apparent lack of gifts. Winston Churchill, a stutterer in his youth, became one of the most stirring and eloquent orators of modern time, inspiring England and the free world to stand strong against overwhelming opposition as his country endured the Blitz. Each of us who has lived out a career may need to look back to moments when we might have frustrated someone's vision of a large and bold new future. And those still in the midst of their life's work may want to be a bit circumspect in considering how they might be unfairly limiting—rather than opening and advancing—the future of someone with whom their calling puts them in contact.

A fifty-plus ordained woman was interviewing for a call within a synod on whose staff I was serving. Studying her resumé, I realized that in her student days she had been in a religious studies program at a fine Christian college with which I was familiar. Since I knew the man who had been the department head during her student days, I asked if she had known my friend who, at that time, was a bright, rising star among young theologians, a recent PhD from a distinguished university, and known to be a really "with it" professor. The candidate quickly smiled and indicated her appreciation for her theological growth under his leadership. But she also commented, "I went to him one day [in the 1950s] and said, 'Dr. Bob, I want to become a pastor.' He told me that as a woman that was not my calling, and that I shouldn't frustrate myself with that goal in life." Then she said with some haste, "Last year I met Dr. Bob at a conference and reminded him of what he had told me forty years earlier. With a near tear in his eye, he said, 'Please forgive me for what I did then.'" If anyone wants to be harsh on the Dr. Bobs of the world, let them first be aware of the forgiveness each of us may need to seek forty years from now. One ought to shudder when one confronts the resistance women have encountered, especially from men, in efforts to break barriers to reach new plateaus of achievement.

In addition, the attitude of the teacher toward a student, the parent toward a child, the supervisor in the workplace—oh yes, the pastor toward the congregation—all can make a great difference in the level a person or a group may achieve. I can remember a session with the principal of the local high school while in the eighth grade, just prior to graduation. He stood before our class, preparing us for the selection of courses and consideration of a career as we were about to enroll in high school. I remember only one thing he said: "If you cannot spell, then do not consider a future in anything related to writing." I knew myself a poor speller, so I took his words at that moment as an absolute: no writing career for me! Little did the principal know that in my lifetime I could learn to spell. Never a great speller, to be sure. Still I have lived long enough to learn to spell with a degree of accuracy—using the spell-checker on my computer.

The potential for our growth is astonishing and advances should be encouraged, but only until there is indisputable evidence that a particular calling is *not* one's calling. There indeed are limits beyond which one is incapable of going. We are created and are not the creator. So in discerning our callings, there is the need to be circumspect, to take careful inventory: not first of our limitations, but of our gifts and our visions, daring to recognize—when necessary—that there are those unbending limitations.

A comment by Truman stays with me: "If you can't stand the heat of the stove, get out of the kitchen." That is generally quoted to suggest that if you are in a circumstance that is riddled with conflict and it is "doing you in," find another vocation, another position. At times another option is unthinkable. A person elects a career and finds a position that gives one all the freedom of self-expression one desires; life seems most comfortable. Then suddenly things can change, as quickly as day changes to night. Unexpected conflict within an organization breaks out; or within a family with a history of tranquility, a major crisis develops. The situation becomes unbearable, and it seems as though there is no escape. We need continued reminders that, for a Christian, a calling is always in the flesh (as well as in the Spirit), where inevitably there will be disagreements that all too often lead to conflict and serious disruption of the status quo. While it is not always mandated, one may need to persist—strengthened by the Spirit and (I hope) assisted by others—and not give up. Then there are times when what had been your calling no longer is, no longer a context for a specific responsibility. There is a time to move on; you have hit your limit and then you listen for that new calling and respond to another vocation. Indeed, those who seek and seemingly find that most serene, blissful, nonthreatening marriage or that glorious, comfortable career may need to hear the story (fictional, I suspect) of a man in the 1930s who sought to retire to the most peaceful place he could find on earth, never to experience conflict and war but always be a place of peace and serenity. He chose the romantic island of Guam—a place where only a short time later one of the most deadly battles and bloodshed occurred in the South Pacific. So again, until God calls us from this land of opportunities and from this "vale of tears," we are called within the context of God's creation, through faith, to maintain a life of love for others. In our next chapter we shall explore more carefully how to discern our callings within God's creation.

6

Discerning Our Callings and Serious Considerations

"A New Calling" was the caption of a brief article in the *New York Times* reporting that former White House press secretary Michael McCurry had become the Sunday school superintendent at his Methodist church in suburban Washington. The news media seldom identify a person as having a "calling," unless (as in this case) it is a position associated with a religious activity, generally Christian. You can be certain that the *Times* did not report his appointment as White House press secretary as a new calling. Does this kind of reporting reflect a practice by many Christians that has entered our common culture, namely, limiting an understanding of Christian callings to religious matters? I think so.

As a young pastor, working with our congregation's adult education program, I worked up a series of questions to stimulate discussion on the Christian calling. Some questions were, "Which of these expresses a 'holy service?' Your career? Your work in and for the church (usher, committee member)? Is teaching Sunday school a more 'holy service' than assisting in the annual spring church clean-up? If you were to serve on a campaign committee for the election of a blossoming politician, a candidate for public office, could you view your work on the candidate's behalf as a 'holy service?' What is holy about your daily work, your occupation, your marriage, or your family?"

As you might guess, participants classified the subjects of these questions as "holy service" the closer the subject came to the "religious" nature of the church. Teaching Sunday school ranked the highest. Serving on a committee to elect a politician did not receive a favorable reply. Service to one's family generally got an identity of "holy service," but with further discussion, such actions as leading prayers at mealtime or getting the kids off to church and Sunday school were identified clearly as "religious services" within the family. Something is wrong here, and I would like to explore this in order to discern our callings, our "holy services," with family, career, and citizenship, as well as within our congregations. As our life situations change, we need time for discernment—that is, a careful decision process that moves from faith to that which apparently lies before us. This process is the subject of this chapter.

Here I need to reiterate that the Christian, following baptism, lives simultaneously in two Kingdoms, the realm of faith and the realm of reason and our senses. Our approach in this and the following chapters could give an unintended illusion that first we stand in the realm of faith and then make a movement, a crossing to the realm of reason. In truth, we Christians are constantly in both of God's realms, left and right. Christian faith is always lived out in God's creation, and thus there is always tension and an all-too-easy confusing of faith with reason or reason with faith; or the confusing of our senses, especially our emotions and intuitions with faith. However, although we are constantly in both realms, for purposes of clarification I chose at this time to divide them and speak of two separate entities, making (as it were) a movement from faith to the ethical decision, while always anchored in faith. In the gospel, God's reign and power is revealed in apparent weakness, with the promises and gifts of the Spirit coming to us so freely in and from Christ. At the same time, we work with these unique gifts of the Spirit, faith and Christ's love, in the movements of our lives in and through God's creation—where the power of God is present, yet hidden—and engage God's presence daily through our various vocations.

A basic assumption, asserted earlier, should be kept in mind as we proceed. There should be no compartmentalization, no identifying some parts of one's life as spiritual or religious—as holy—and other parts as secular, if not evil, and certainly not as holy. Rather, all of the Christian life is expressive of ministry, bundled in compassion and care for others, witnessing to the risen Christ in word and deed. In previous chapters we insisted, as we must again that, for the Christian, all of one's life is made holy by God's grace through faith. In the pages ahead I will expand on this basic assumption.

If this assumption is correct, then another crucial insight must follow: Our Christian calling that flows from our baptism must be coupled with a process of discerning our various callings in daily life. Christians are capable of making bad decisions: at times impulsive, often emotionally driven and disconnected from faith. The crucial question is: how does one decide on selective ministries (career, marriage, ordained ministry, and so forth) that identify one for major portions of one's life? Rather than a rolling of the dice, we need a thoughtful, prayerful discernment. Rather than merely jumping into the best-paying or most prestigious occupation available, we need a critical interchange with our faith. In such defining moments, in an intentional spiritual exercise guided by faith, we may be able to say yes to one or a few choices while saying no to the many. It is only then that we are able to move on with a feeling of clarity and confidence. Merely claiming to be Christian, or in simply asserting that by virtue of my faith, I am thereby assured (in a mechanical way) that I'm on the right track and that God is smiling, is sheer magic. There is nothing magical about a Christian's decision, whether it is reached spontaneously or through a process of discernment. There is a need for genuine spiritual struggle as a major decision is made. St. Paul called for "fear and trembling" in efforts at discernment.

We may speak about all of the Christian life as Christian service and Christian ministry because this unique service or ministry is grounded in and motivated by God's love in Christ. In the first eleven chapters of his letter to the Romans, St. Paul clearly insists that our salvation ("justification" is his word) is given by grace through faith in Christ, that it is not a work of our own. Then he makes a major shift from the first eleven chapters: he delivers a pronounced "therefore" and goes on to identify the depth and breadth of what flows from authentic faith, from the gift of our redemption to the new life in Christ. "I appeal to you, *therefore*, by the mercies of God, to present your bodies as a living sacrifice, holy and acceptable to God, which is your spiritual worship" (Rom 12:1; emphasis added). Note that the word translated as "spiritual" is *logikos,* meaning "in agreement with the *logos*," the gospel!" St. Paul is insisting that, for the Christian, the whole of life—nothing less—worships God and serves others in thanksgiving. So let's go on, engaging further the wonder and depth of our respective Christian callings: the offering of our whole self to God in service. The primary question with respect to a decision about a calling is whether or not this decision is in "agreement with the gospel," that it is according to the will of God known in Christ.

The Process of Discernment

In the long history of the church, the word "discernment" was not central in discussions about one's calling until recently, in part because the options were few. Now in the midst of apparent multiple opportunities, the word "discernment" is very much in use. To discern means to distinguish among various options, to decide in favor of some things while saying no to others, to select that which (according to certain criteria or values) is right and proper. To discern also means to penetrate through the obvious, through the surface to something deeper, often seemingly hidden. Bonhoeffer adds clarity: "The will of God may lie very deeply concealed beneath a great number of available possibilities. The will of God is not a system of rules which is established from the outset; it is something new and different in each different situation in life, and for this reason a man must ever anew examine what the will of God may be. The heart, the understanding, observation and experience must all collaborate in this task."[1] Discernment today is an appropriate exercise for determining our ministry and callings. Indeed, it is an appropriate practice for a congregation or group of Christians wrestling with a complex issue requiring a resolution. In one sense it describes the exercise of moving from our common Christian calling (our baptism) to situations of responsibility, toward appropriate ethical and vocational decisions and choices, always anchored in faith. Discernment of one's calling is as important for the pastor as for the person in the pew. I would hope that the pastor, and the larger church in the clergy call process, would model for the people an appropriate and a genuine faith-filled discernment when engaging vocational opportunities.

Refining Our Motives: Being Cleansed Internally

An African Christian hymn (originally written in Swahili), appealing for the gift of the Spirit, prays: "Guide our thinking and our speaking done in your holy name. Motivate all in their seeking, freeing from guilt and

---

1. Bonhoeffer, *Ethics*, 41.

shame . . . Not mere knowledge, but discernment, not rootless liberty . . ."[2] Today it is considered important, especially in the competitiveness of our age, for one to prepare properly for a prospective career. You must be sure you have covered the right academic program, learned the necessary skills and, most important of all, demonstrated on a resumé that you have all the right experiences. The focus is on knowledge, experience, and skill. For the Christian, this African hymn reminds us that mere knowledge is not what's most important; *discernment under the presence and influence of the Spirit* is. Human wisdom and knowledge is of value for the Christian only if it is coupled with faith—indeed, coupled with the responsible practice of Christian freedom, thus avoiding "*rootless* liberty." Christians dare not be human butterflies who flit from one job to another without direction and commitment. Similar danger is present in marriage, like reaching for a "trophy spouse" during the "seven-year itch," or in personal relationships, like discarding friends as causally as one finds them. What motivates us is all-important. Christian faith calls us from our own self-interest to the "other." Faith anchored in Christ resists "rootless liberty."

Historian Richard Marius writes: "To those satisfied with their conduct in the world (as most of us usually are) Luther's message was one of radical introspection, intended to drive us not to the enumeration of our sinful acts but to the examination of the spirit that motivated them."[3] Christian discernment means having clarity about who I am as a Christian, and "whose" I am—namely, Christ's. In such an exercise, we dare to question whether we are driven by self-interests or by the Spirit, seeking the needs of others. Such faith identity shapes a broad-brush picture of our life-goals, our unique paradigm, and reaches for spiritually informed decisions on specifics.

While I speak of the immense options for ministry today, I must also assert that our common calling to be in ministry is not an option—unless one decides to renounce one's baptism and to opt out of the community of faith. For the Christian, responding to Christ's call to be Christian entails being in ministry—it is a package deal. If we say yes to Christ's call, we are charged through the Word to be in ministry throughout our life, all day, every day. How our respective ministries take shape lies within the peculiar freedom we have in Christ and our present human condition and circumstance. If you were growing up a

2. Niwagila, "Gracious Spirit."
3. Marius, *Martin Luther*, 305.

Christian in East Germany forty years ago under the oppressive Marxist regime, the political conditions considerably limited your options. Yet even there one had choices, though many of the options had to be measured against the severity of the state's critical and hostile response.

Christian discernment necessitates a careful, prayerful, personal inventory of what God has entrusted to one both through the creation and in the gifts of the Holy Spirit. We need to clarify within ourselves what we carry with us from the word of faith to our various situations in daily life, along with what God has given us in birth and through years of growth and development. Both are crucial in Christian discernment. In the discernment process it is most important that we listen for the voice of the Spirit in and through the Word. St. Paul focuses with clarity on this subject in his letter to the Ephesians: "I pray that [God the Father] . . . may grant that you may be strengthened in your inner being with power through his Spirit, and that Christ may dwell in your hearts through faith, as you are being rooted and grounded in love" (Eph 3:16–17).

The voice of the Spirit calls for daily, personal renewal, beginning within one's own heart and mind. The Christian act of discernment begins with the Word's cleansing our thoughts, our minds, and our emotions. St. Paul's counsel in Romans 12:2 is crucial here: "Do not be conformed to this world, but be transformed by the renewing of your minds." The focus ought not to be copying the ways of the world. Rather there must be a "changeover" from the way of the world to the New Way "by the renewing of your minds." In Philippians 2:5–7, St. Paul urges us to "Let the same mind be in you that was in Christ Jesus, who . . . emptied himself" and was committed to his mission to pass through death for the life of others. Through the mind of Christ, the Spirit cleanses us from within, giving us a new mind a fresh, selfless motivation. Before hearing the closing words of Sunday worship, "Go in peace. Serve the Lord," many of us often prayerfully sing this Offertory: "Create in me a clean heart, O God, and renew a right spirit within me." Unless discernment begins with the Spirit's cleansing of our interior, our choices in ethical and vocational deliberations most likely will be hollow and misdirected.

Of course, decisions are often made that are disconnected from spiritual thought or any exercise of discernment. And we may even have thought we were being selflessly motivated and later found out we were not. To be sure, the Spirit works wonders in various ways. Yet such experiences should never eliminate the necessity to stop, pray, and review as we explore options before us and listen for the voice of the Spirit.

Discernment begins and continues with a conscious spiritual activity. It is very spiritual: the lively activity of God's Holy Spirit in, with, and under the word, as in the bread and wine, clarifying our relations with God through confession and forgiveness, fortifying us against temptation, and empowering us for selfless, holy ministry in all our endeavors. Thus the discernment process—our renewal through Christ's word in and through the Spirit—makes the movement to our worldly context exciting, challenging, and enduring in the midst of strife and discouragement.

Serious Considerations in Discerning Our Callings

In the movement from faith to ethical decisions, what do we bring with us? Above all we bring faith empowered by the Spirit! Certainly we bring our Bible with us in any process of discernment, but how do we use the Scriptures? Are we issued a rule book that serves as a guide, a book of instructions indexed for whatever might arise with each new encounter? Certainly not. Will we hear a clear, unambiguous word that will give clarity in our struggles for ethical decisions and vocational choices? Not necessarily. St. Paul expresses it best when he describes the process of movement from faith to ethical activity: "Work out *your own* salvation with fear and trembling; for it is God who is at work in you, enabling you both to will and to work for his good pleasure" (Phil 2:12–13; emphasis added). There is an apparent contradiction. God is within us, working to bring us to do the divine good. Yet surprisingly these words are preceded by the charge to "work out your own salvation." On the one hand we are not alone; God is at work within us. This is not the same as the pantheist's assertion that God is everywhere and in everyone. Nor is it a human fantasy. The God who is present, as St. Paul insists, is the Christ, the one revealed in the Scriptures and known by faith. He is mightily present with no thought or suggestion of abandonment. While God the Almighty is at work within us, we are given a freedom in charting our course, in making our decisions—"work [it] out . . . with fear and trembling." So let this effort of discernment be approached with seriousness, diligence, and with prayer—indeed with the freedom enveloped in the gospel. This working out of our salvation is grounded in faith, not in an assurance that things will go right, but that in Christ we know that God is at work in us to will and to do God's good pleasure through all difficulties. The work of God within us is the Holy Spirit's presence, keeping faith alive, holding out a vision of God's good pleasure, and inspiring us to break through barriers in order to do God's will. God's presence, the power and might of the Holy Spirit, is consciously and unconsciously present with us through our faith as we make our way through the maze of daily life.

In Christian discernment we are often frightened when we confront an injustice that summons engagement. We all too easily and too often allow ourselves to cut the nerve between faith and engagement. In doing so we may be party to an evident weakness within Lutheranism in more recent years. According to Jaroslav Pelikan, much of Lutheranism following the Reformation—especially as it entered the modern culture—expressed political and social conservatism both in Europe and America because it had severed the nerve of Luther's ethic: "The nerve was the hope and courage engendered by faith . . . This hope [here Pelikan quotes Luther] 'arouses the mind to be brave and resolute, so that it dares, endures, and lasts in the midst of evils and looks for better things . . . It battles with joy and courage in opposition to those great evils.' [Pelikan continues] In Luther's ethic—both in his ethical theory and in his actions and decisions—justification by faith did not induce moral paralysis, but the willingness to run risks, to face the possibility of being mistaken, and to let God make the best of the proximate *justia* to which men could attain." [4] Thus it is important that we recognize that faith embodies hope and courage in following through with discernment and a willingness to risk in order to achieve a greater measure of justice within our communities.

In the dark hour of a deep dilemma we may hear ourselves praying, "God, give me the answer; tell me what I should do, which way to go!" What usually follows? No answer, no sign from God. In our weakness we can so easily deceive ourselves or entertain false expectations. Seldom are signs clear and dramatic. The presence of God and God's answers are not always as clear as we would hope, yet faith remains active. Faith does hear God saying clearly, "With my love, go in my peace, with hope and with courage." We pray as we examine our interior, reviewing and clarifying ethical decisions, making sure our ministries are directed toward others and not merely toward ourselves, that our faith supplies the hope

4. Pelikan, *Christian Intellectual*, 100–101.

and courage to act and to be willing to suffer in our ministry. We need to hear Christ in effect saying, "As I have suffered for you, indeed as I now suffer with you, so also suffer with me." St. Paul again: "Do nothing from selfish ambition or conceit, but in humility regard others as better than yourselves. Let each of you look not to your own interests, but to the interests of others" (Phil 2:3–4). Then hear the crucial phrase: "*Let the same mind be in you that was in Christ Jesus.*" (Phil 2:5; emphasis added). Having the mind of Christ, we have hope and fortitude and are enveloped in the Holy Spirit as we discern and act ethically.

Our prayers certainly do not end as we make our way to ethical decisions. We pray unceasingly with an open mind and heart, listening for the voice of the Spirit along the way. To be sure, many of us have jumped into a new position with little spiritual discernment (when only one opportunity became available); and soon after the plunge, in the middle of the new situation, we began to ask, "Lord, what do I do now?" So often in the midst of a new situation, discernment is clearly called for or might even be seen as a continuing process. Discernment calls for serious consideration and deliberation on insights gained from the history of God's people through biblical times and in times since.

The Nature of Christian Freedom

As a group or an assembly deliberates a crucial decision in the midst of conflict or during a situation of indecisiveness, there is a tendency by some to claim to have a gift of the Spirit that dictates a resolution. No one ought to tell another what to do, regardless of how strongly this person claims to have a "spiritual insight" from God. I recall a synod assembly which was recessed for the night without agreement on a conflicted subject. When the assembly reconvened in the morning, one of the first speakers solemnly addressed the assembly by saying he had been up much of the night in prayer, and as the sun was rising, the Holy Spirit had spoken to him, declaring the will of God—that is, how the assembly should vote. He then proceeded to lay his insight on the conscience of the assembly. One may laugh at the folly of this, yet a brand of spiritualism within the church today often subtly insists on a specific direction or solution because "I have heard the Spirit speak." In sending a candidate's name to a congregation to be their pastor, I once observed a senior officer of a synod reporting that the Spirit had shown a particular candidate to be the special gift of God to the congregation. The word of the Spirit as understood by the officer was the basis on which the congregation ought to accept the person as their minister. The implication was that no other consideration was necessary.

The Reformers had to contend with a strongly committed group, the *Schwärmer* ("spiritualists"), who claimed a great deal of spiritual knowledge and exercised considerable authority on the basis of alleged gifts of the Spirit. Against such the Reformers quoted the Scriptures, instructing the people to "test the spirits to see whether they are from God" (1 John 4:1). With the historic creeds, the church has taught that the Spirit's work is to carry the gospel to the human heart, igniting and sustaining faith, comforting us in despair and, yes, guiding us in all truth (John 16:13). The Spirit's guiding always points both back to the cross—the redemption—and forward—toward the other's need. That the Spirit guides us into "all truth" means that the Spirit guides us to Christ (John 1:17). This is God's right-hand rule, the rule of faith. In claiming a divine authority beyond the Word, the spiritualist obliterates the clarity of the gospel and makes the Spirit a "dictator." Luther saw such people as "swallowing the Holy Spirit feathers and all" and called such excessive and inappropriate enthusiastic spiritualism *Schwämerei*.

At the same time, some ethical and vocational decisions may be made—consciously—in bold contradiction to what some (including one's fellow Christians) would assert. One may hear others insisting that a proposed ethical decision is "unreasonable" and "non-sense"—indeed, "un-Christian." In spite of counsel from others and even one's own rational, personal analysis, a Christian's discernment may point toward an "unreasonable" personal plan of action that may entail threatening consequences, both social and physical. Bonhoeffer is an excellent example. A brilliant young German Lutheran theologian inclined to pacifism, he agreed to participate in the attempt to assassinate Hitler. By the nature of his writings, we can be sure that he made this momentous decision knowing very well that if the attempt on Hitler's life failed (indeed, also if it succeeded), he would hear again Christ's forgiveness and freely accept the severest consequence (his own execution), and above all, await the certainty of the resurrection. Clearly Bonhoeffer saw a decision for himself, one he could not lay on the conscience of others. In the face of a Bonhoeffer-like decision, such an apparent "unreasonable" decision by one person may cause me to think, "Is this right for me in my situation?"

My Christian freedom allows both the possibility of following with the attended consequences or, for valid "reasons," saying no.

Within this apparent paradox, God working within us to do the right, and our need to work it out on our own (and where possible in community and in conversation with others, and certainly in prayer), we need to remember again the centrality of our Christian faith: God's gracious act of forgiveness. Thus with choices before us, and with the certainty of God's presence, we struggle to know and to do God's holy will. This assurance enables us to act boldly and with courage! Christians with faith ought not to go through life as though walking on eggshells; we have a unique freedom as we live by faith in Christ. While never absolutely certain of our direction, in the very act of making a decision we need the reminder that there is ultimately only one absolute certainty: that God is merciful and forgiving, always and in all situations. Hence we live with courage. With both this knowledge and faith, Bonhoeffer undertook his calling, and later courageously walked to the gallows by order of Hitler at the hands of the SS.

Is Christ's Love Strong Enough?

Certainly we bring our Bible with us as we make the crossing, the movement, from faith to vocational and ethical decisions. However, are we sure the biblical gospel and the motivation of Christian love are adequate for making God-pleasing decisions in the midst of life's ambiguous ethical complexities? Don't we need the Law, especially the Ten Commandments, to provide at least a degree of support and some specific enlightenment to our ethics? While not in any way weaseling, let's say both a yes and a no and spend a few paragraphs clarifying what appears in some circles to be a very controversial issue. First of all, if you stay with Luther you must recognize what is consistent in his theology: Neither the Ten Commandments nor the Sermon on the Mount is the focus of Christian ethics; that focus is rather the forgiveness of sins. Yet Luther surely never abandoned the Ten Commandments. Any reading of his Small Catechism clarifies his recognition of the importance of these commandments for the life of the Christian. The New Testament implores us to live not by the law, which condemns, but by the gospel, which saves. Biblical history and biblical accounts in the Old as well as in the New Testament do indeed provide insights into God's grace for Israel and for all. Notice how the Ten Commandments themselves are introduced by reference to God's gracious call and rescue of Israel: "I am the Lord your God, who brought you out of the land of Egypt, out of the house of slavery" (Exod 20:2). In various ways the Scriptures shed light on how God's grace has been at work from the beginning, and this encourages us to appropriate by faith that same grace, operative in and through us in our daily lives. Thus the Old Testament texts—indeed, the whole of Scripture—are subjects for careful study. Through them the proclamation of the gospel is made public in our congregational worship, all ultimately focused on our redemption achieved by Christ, summarized in his words, "Your sins are forgiven!"

The Old Testament constantly bears witness to God's law and grace at work in the life of Israel, and yet something unique happened with the revelation of God's mercy in Christ. The "good spell"—the gospel—broke into human history for the world to hear, to see, and to believe. Christ is God's rescue of us from God's own judgment. Indeed, as I wrote earlier, Christ dramatically takes the Commandments and leads one to ever deeper understanding of the all-inclusiveness of the judgment. Remember how he handles, "You shall not commit adultery"? Yes, whoever has lust in his heart has already committed adultery. No escape from this one, unless it is the Word announcing God's work of reconciliation. Reconciliation? That's God in Christ not holding us guilty of our sins of lust and hate, granting us grace and mercy—the Holy Spirit personally breaking the barriers separating us from God and from one another, and replacing them with the peace of God that passes all understanding and all reasoning.

Christians cannot be reminded too often: The law accuses us of our sin. In Christian faith the gospel frees us from God's judgment; God accepts us and calls us for a life of love. God's gift of his son and all that is included in that gift—especially the divine love carried by the Holy Spirit—is all the power necessary for our motivation in all our ministries.

The question persists: Is this love of God enough? Is it sufficient to govern one's life? To struggle further with this haunting question, we need to look more closely again at Luther's insistence on the freedom of the Christian. Remember the paradox: "The Christian is utterly free, master of all, slave to none; a Christian is the willing servant of all." Professor Marius is again helpful: "The freedom of the Christian is that Christ has done all the work to earn salvation and there is nothing left for Christians to do themselves. Christians are freed from the law and freed from the tyranny of perfection, from the fear of never being good enough ... Only then can we truly let God be God, to acknowledge that God rules all. Only when we recognize this essential truth can God give us the grace that saves us."[5] Marius uses a simple human experience that adds clarity to our discussion. Employing an analogy drawn from common experience, he writes: "If I love someone and am assured of that person's love for me, I do not go to a rule book to see what bargain I must strike, what deeds I must perform, what dragons I must kill to provoke a love I already feel ... Under conditions of trade and bargain, one can never be certain of love at all. If I know that someone loves me, I can enter a warm human bond and have real freedom. I do not have to prove my love by constant effort. Yet what sort of freedom is it? It is obviously not a freedom to do anything contrary to the nature of love itself. I am not free [to hurt or harm one who loves me] ... I am bounded by love, but it is a bondage that I do not feel as bondage. For Luther, the cross proved for all time how much God loves us."[6]

The freedom we have is the power to love others with the love Christ has had for us, and it is in God's design of the Christian life that is all that God gives and such is adequate. "My grace is sufficient for you," said the Lord to St. Paul (2 Cor 12:9). Certainly God surrounds us with the whole company of the redeemed: the saints among us in Christ's church and the saints above cheering us on. All the models of the godly life trust the Word and share the love of God with others.

The Perverse Use of the Law and What Is Appropriate

When the law becomes a guide for living, it is often adjusted for the benefit of the powerful at the expense of the powerless. In a male-dominated society, such as that represented in much of the Old Testament, the religious law as taught and understood by those in power—generally males—declared that a women in marriage was the property of her husband; he ruled over her. And the Sixth Commandment was understood to say that a man should not have intercourse with someone else's wife; to do so was to have the wrath of God upon you, and the penalty was death (Deut 22:22). Subtly, quietly, the male-dominant society could insist that this commandment applied only to marriage; thus men were

---

5. Marius, *Martin Luther*, 267.
6. Ibid.

free to enjoy sex with the unwed women while having the protection of the Law, keeping one's own wife safe from other men. An example is David's lust for Bathsheba and the killing of her husband, Uriah, in order for David—with impunity—to obtain Bathsheba as his wife to satisfy his sexual desires (2 Sam 11). People and institutions of power will frequently justify their own behavior, or shape public policy to their own interests and benefit. It is with this insight that an individual or a group who dares to engage an injustice needs to "count the cost"—to anticipate the violent, defensive, deceptive, vicious attacks inflicted on those seeking justice. Political power (in the church and in the state) so easily and so often shapes legislation and its enforcement to satisfy not the common good but the self-interests of the powerful. The temptation and abuse can just as easily be seen in some pastoral preaching and teaching. When church attendance is poor and giving is down, the temptation is to call forth God's damnation, speak the law, assuming that such judgment will bring the people regularly to church on Sunday and to increase their giving. Good Christian preaching and teaching will avoid twisting the law for special interests or as a motivator for Christian giving and service. God's love known and received in Christ is the sole authentic motivation in the life of the Christian and in the community of faith, the church.

Giving of Self in an Abusive Relationship

What if the caregiver becomes the object of hate and harm, especially in the marriage relationship? This is a serious consideration for our time. Insightful women theologians have in recent years pointed to an apparent problem with the subject being addressed here, that the Christian life means giving yourself to the other with a willingness to suffer, as is necessary, for and with the other. This, it has been shown, can result in an apparent licensing of a husband (most often) for abuse, and for a suffering wife to be left without spiritual recourse and support. There is evidence that at times Christian counseling has instructed the abused woman to stay in the relationship with the words, "It is your calling to endure the pain." I have spoken on earlier pages of the integral ingredient of the Christian calling—that is, life "under the cross" and the expectation of a degree of suffering within one's calling. This can be grossly abused and become frightfully invalid, a sinister distortion of the gospel. Such an understanding of life under the cross is certainly an invalid license for unjust treatment by one party and an unacceptable "hang in there" counsel to the victim. Women pastors have led in offering a different counsel. Discernment here surely means determining when one must exercise freedom in Christ to simply say, "No more! I'm leaving." Yet to simply up and leave, even under the most distressing situation, is not always easy. For many there is no safe space. Where does one go to survive? As the church counsels, "be free in Christ" and take the strength in Christ to leave, perhaps in the dark of night, knowing what added abuse could ensue if the planned departure leads to confrontation. Along with the counsel of freedom, there is the need for a safe place. There need to be places of care and protection where a woman and her children may find refuge from an intolerable situation. The reason so many abused women remain in a daily torture is their entrapment; they seemingly have no reasonable plan of escape, unless the community becomes sensitive and opens a door. This too is a situation that calls for reason and the gifts of the Spirit. Good Christian counseling assists in stirring up the faith of the entrapped woman, providing both spiritual courage and creative support for the person who dares to leave an intolerable relationship. When the abused wife leaves, this can even be seen as love for the offending spouse—that is, no longer giving him the illusion that he is master of his world. Leaving also shows care for and protection for one's children and, most importantly, a consideration for one's own health and protection, thus demonstrating a healthy self-love.[7]

This problem is not limited to the abuse of women. Consider the difficulties of a mother and her children when their father, a pastor, insisted the family had to suffer an inequitable salary and frequent verbal abuse in their suffering under their calling in Christ. At a stewardship conference with laity from various congregations, a pastor was eloquently identifying the Christian life being one of suffering and sacrifice as one gives to others' needs; the speaker's emphasis was on giving to the church. One lay participant reacted with considerable anger. He said, in effect, "My father, a pastor, repeatedly instructed my mother and us children in a similar way, claiming our calling as a parsonage family was to suffer on behalf of the gospel." He went on, "Our family was a doormat on which members of the congregation could verbally trample. They made life hell, especially for my mother, who lived in poverty. I've

7. See Dahill, "Jesus for You."

been suspicious of the church advocating suffering for the gospel since childhood."

Appropriate action is the challenge. It may at times be awkward for a pastor to insist on a reasonable and just salary. One looks for the people to come forward. Certainly the extended church needs to stand beside and in front of the pastor, modeling for the community decency, fairness, and adequate remuneration.

Dividing Secular and Religious

As one examines and re-examines the "crossing over" from our common calling to those callings unique to each of us, there needs to be a refusal to divide the Christian life into sectors of the secular and the religious, suggesting that churchly matters are spiritual and worldly matters are secular. The practice of identifying part of life as "secular," and another part "religious" or "spiritual," is an intrusion into the Christian faith by Renaissance and Enlightenment thinking. Luther's allusive Two Kingdoms theology easily falls captive to this division, leading to a gross distortion. It was and still is incorrectly claimed by some that "the religious" envelops the eternal, the holy, the spiritual, the church; in this sphere God may be in command. And this time-bound (temporal) world is the secular; it is free of God's interference, leaving it to humans to take charge, ignoring calls for divine accountability.

The faith of the people of God, attested to in the Scriptures, recognizes God as the Almighty, the Lord of both heaven and earth. Certainly there is a tension within the Old Testament between statements and ideas—to a degree, at least, anchored in apocalyptic thought that recognizes "the prince of this world" (evil) in control. Yet in the midst of such despair, there is the expectation that the reign of God is at hand. There is hope in the midst of ruthless oppression. The faithful today who are overwhelmed in pain and are suffering unjustly may be certain that the reign of God's grace and peace is at hand. Faith refuses to accept that, at one time in history, the world was held captive to Satan, that there was a time when God was not Lord of all. Indeed, Christ's entering time, God's victory over sin, death, and the world, clearly pulls back the curtain that reveals that God is and has always been Lord over all, the *Almighty!* Faith apprehends this. The Psalms celebrate this truth in word and song. Luther, in his instructions regarding the Two Kingdoms, always insists that God is the almighty ruler and judge of both kingdoms;

God's reign over all is clearly evident in the Psalms. An example, Psalm 24, sings this biblical conviction: "The earth is the Lord's and all that is in it, the world, and those who live in it" (Ps 24:1). First Corinthians 10:26 asserts: "The earth and its fullness are the Lord's." The Reformers and their followers sought to witness to this truth by identifying all of their endeavors as expressions of ministry under God's universal rule. Johann Sebastian Bach signed all his music, both great and minor works, with *Soli Deo Gloria* ("All Glory to God") *or JJ* ("Jesus Help Me"), whether the music was written for the civil court or for Christian worship. The six Brandenburg concertos and the St. Matthew Passion are both signed as an offering to God with thanks and praise. In a similar way Bach signed his other thousand musical works.

Again: Holy Service, Holy Ministry

What the Christian does in Christ is ministry, and thus it is a holy ministry. *Yes, again, holy ministry, holy service!* Luther insists that whatever is done for the neighbor in Christ's love—that is, out of faith and love in Jesus Christ—is a holy ministry. His illustrations are taken from his time and culture. Thus he speaks of the parent, the milkmaid, the cobbler, the brewer. He recognizes that all in God's creation are instruments for the neighbor's good. Luther said in a sermon: "Just look at your tools—at your needle or thimble, your beer barrel, your goods, your scales or yardstick or measure . . . All this is crying out to you; 'Friend, use me in your relations with your neighbor just as you want your neighbor to use his property in his relations to you.'"[8] When serving others through their work and trade, one offers to God and to the community a "holy service," a ministry. Realizing this, that in Christ we are lively and personal instruments of God, surely leads to a certainty that our calling is a "holy ministry," resulting in a unique quality of service, whether coming from one labeled a clergyperson or a layperson. Through faith in Christ Jesus, all the baptized people are God's holy people, called for a lifetime of ministry. While Christians and non-Christians are God's instruments of divine service to others, the call to faith in Christ uniquely cleanses the motivation for service, and instills a consciousness of one's instrumentation by God for God's purposes. All need this cleansing, pastors and people. Indeed, the Christian calling entails a commitment to excellence,

---

8. *LW* 21, 237.

to quality of service, and to a willingness to give the needed time and to accept discomforts in reaching out to others; this calling includes, again, pastors and people.

The worker is made *holy* by God's gift of Christ's righteousness through faith, not made holy by virtue of the service or certain moral behavior, nor by virtue of a special vocation. Luther frequently reminds his listener: A good person does good deeds, but good works, good deeds, do not make a person good. A person is made "good" by God's gracious forgiveness and faith's acceptance of Christ's gift of righteousness. Using Luther's illustration, God gives milk to children through the faithful services of the milkmaid. When living her calling in faith as a milkmaid, her milking of the cow is more than a mere job: it is a "holy calling" and a "holy ministry" it is God's means of giving milk to the child. It is not what we do that makes us holy, but what God has done and gives. And so it should be among us in our varied callings: from the demands of highly complicated tasks to the demands of caring for a child (which, come to think of it, is also a highly complicated task). Christians pursue seemingly mundane as well as highly difficult and challenging tasks with an awareness that God is intimately with them in all their daily endeavors, not merely standing beside them but actively serving others with them in my work.

Our challenge today is to translate the biblical word and Luther's insights into our industrial and post-industrial vocational and ethical situations. Obviously, as in Luther's day, so also in our day: the church (that is, the "people of God") needs to inform, instruct, and model the godly life. From our baptism onward through life, we need reminders that our daily work is an instrument of God's gifts to others. The redeemed, the righteous, the people, the saints of God—all (both clergy and laity) need to be conscious of our divine callings—indeed, to celebrate such in our public worship. And by all means and at the same time, we also celebrate God's "hidden" ministry in and through all people who are responsible to human needs in countless ways, even those not necessarily motivated by Christian faith.

When seemingly everything is understood as an opportunity for ministry, the intensity of an ever-increasing number of "calls" for help becomes overwhelming. This easily can lead to excuses to do nothing or to a burden difficult to bear, a juggling act of heavy objects. We may recognize that we can't do it all; and in not doing it all, some are overcome with guilt and at times depressed, and thus end up doing little. The cry of suffering humanity overwhelms. We are easily led to frustration and despair. Thus we need to be up-front and clear regarding the freedom given us in Christ, the freedom that recognizes the need to discern, among the many ministries, those few specific ones to which we are primarily called and which we ought to pursue and do well. Certainly, random acts of kindness and instantaneous efforts to respond to sudden emergencies or opportunities can rarely be avoided. Yet even for some of us in some situations one may rightly say no. By the very nature of our personal, physical, and emotional limitations, we may have valid reasons to pass up a seemingly urgent call and, as we do, remember that in all situations and decisions we live in the forgiveness of sin. There are times when circumstances dictate one just simply cannot do it. We must resist the call, sin boldly, and believe more boldly still that we are forgiven and you can move on.

Finally, there are countless other subjects that we Christians must seriously engage as we discern our callings. Those which I have addressed above are only my examples, explored for clarification of ethical decision-making. You will want to recognize your own list as you struggle with and are confronted by challenging decisions.

7

Four "Stand Outs" in Our Discernment

Luther and others in their time, as they surveyed the major spheres of human relations, recognized these three spheres as "stand outs" from among the others: the family, the government, and the church. In Luther's time these three stood out as they do in our day, though today each has considerably different characteristics. Family and government are experienced daily by nearly everyone throughout one's lifetime. Today not everyone would identify with church in such a personal experience. The family and government are each unique, distinguishable orders of God's creating, universally experienced and seemingly inescapable for human existence. One discovers dire consequences in avoiding one or the other. For a reasonable life of civility, we must daily find our way in and through each of these, and within each we make ethical choices and pursue our "holy ministries," our callings. The religious sphere, I believe, in one way or another is common to all, though not commonly understood by all to be experienced personally.

We must re-examine Luther's three spheres (family, government, and church), however, because the dynamic of history has forged changes in each, and we are led to identify in our day a fourth sphere: career. The emergence of the industrial revolution several centuries after the Reformation made "making a living" into an entity apart from the family. Likewise, significant change has occurred in both the governmental and the political sector. So also, the experiential phenomenon of "church" has changed immensely from sixteenth-century Europe to the present. The great diversity of today's religious institutions is evident in nearly every community, so we will also examine religious institutions, among which the Christian church will hold our primary attention.

The Family and Making "Bread"

In the long line of human history, the "family" enveloped the common enterprise of making "bread," what we would today call our careers—the economic or the financial dimension of life, which is necessary for sustaining the physical side of life. If the family's manner of making a living was farming, every member was a participant in that endeavor (and this was one reason for having many children). If it was making shoes, not just the father but the whole family contributed to this occupation. With few exceptions, such was typical of all families. They were nearly all engaged in cottage industries, producing "bread" for their own needs and bartering their own products for goods produced by neighbors. Thus Luther saw obtaining food and goods for survival as integral to the family, not separate from it.

With the coming of the industrial revolution, "making a living" became an enterprise distinguished from the family and therefore a fourth "stand out." Today father and often mother leave home "for work," and as children grow into teens, they frequently take work beyond the home. Realizing and accepting this obvious change in the ordering of life, we must examine "career," the making of a living, as a separate entity, though for many it is still integral to family life. But if truth be told, one's occupation, career, job is often the dominant dimension of an individual's life-experience, often felt to be more important than, and sharply separated from, the family. In some families, respective careers are in great tension; in others, careers are integrated into the family's daily rhythm and routine, especially homemaking and child care. Decisions to marry and form a family are often delayed until one's profession is more fully established. In still other situations, given the commitment to a career, family is not considered an option, though as we will see one really never escapes "family." Too, the concept of "family" in many places is dramatically changing, increasingly evolving in nontraditional formations. In any case, today we must explore these callings (occupations, careers) as separate from family, yet related. Thus I will first explore our callings in the family and then our work, our careers.

Discerning Our Callings in the Context of the Family

The Census Bureau defines family as "two or more persons related by birth, marriage or adoption who reside in the same household." Family, in what follows, is understood as an intimate community of people (or merely two people) who have known one another over an extended time, or a group drawn together in a close and intense relationship, having been together in difficult situations. Each member of a family feels the other members would, as is often said, "Be there for me if I needed their help." In effect, by the nature of the closeness and the time together, this "family" has come to know something of each other's history, hopes, pains, and disappointments, and so also has this "family" learned to know you. You have lived close enough together to have hurt one another and still remain joined together, though sometimes fragmented and with members in conflict over an extended time. These are relationships which sociologists identify as our primary relations, as contrasted with those identified as secondary, the folks with whom one has passing contacts but not substantive relations. Thus for our purposes we want our callings to include our various extended families as well as our immediate family, shaped in various forms. I will, however, first focus on our immediate family. Learning from our immediate family, we should also learn something of our callings relative to our extended family.

The immediate family includes those to whom we are related by blood, law, and contract (mutual agreement). They are also those with whom one has lived at one time under the same roof, but who now have moved on and still remain part of a family. Families generally try to come together again at certain times, celebrating births and weddings and supporting one another when grieving at family funerals and during other crises. Many have learned of a family member breaking away, only to return to the family at an unexpected time. Then too there are those small groups in which we have found ourselves where deeply personal feelings were generated, especially when as a group we have gone through difficulty. Many such groups have profound meaning as a "family," though now scattered yet keeping frequent contact. Members of a US Marine platoon who trained and fought through life-threatening conditions often define themselves as a family. Indeed, the military trains these men and women to become like a family, trained to protect each other, to risk life for the other. And on returning home, many continue to keep close contact. For others, especially those who may live alone, there is the small group at work or at church or in one's apartment building, a group that has known and supported one another over many years. These groups become molded in one's mind as one's family, a unique, intimate support group.

Luther's use of the word "stations" has clarity of meaning when applied to the family. He identifies the word "station" and its meaning in the Small Catechism's list of people with whom we might carefully review any ill done or any good not rendered as each deserved, like father, mother, siblings, people long known to one, and those with whom one interacts closely, frequently, and regularly. The sense of the stations in life also would tend to offer the images of moving on from one station to another. While that's not the meaning intended with Luther's German word *Stand*, a "station or a unique situation in life," its imagery may be helpful. If, however, we connect Bonhoeffer's words (situations of responsibility and accountability)—which I judge to be similar in meaning to Luther's stations—then those people in our respective families compel special attention. Here there are established situations of responsibility, unlike informal, casual contacts.

Indeed, one might insist that in the immediate family we are brought together in a manner in which the family itself is a situation of mutual responsibility, for survival, comfort, and joy—a unique unit. Each relationship calls for a distinct response, and collectively and corporately the family remains a "station" (a vocation) within the larger community for immense social and political contributions.

Today our distorted sense of independence often assumes a need for distance from our family, especially as a person struggles through adolescence. In biblical times, one's identity with family was maintained long after one left home. You coupled into your name who your father was and from where or from whom your family originated. Thus we have Jesus of Nazareth, son of Joseph, of the House of Jacob. In spite of our best efforts today to leave home, many of us still return home despite family conflicts or personal feelings of alienation. Nearly everyone looks for those opportunities to return, to make that last visit before "Pop" or "Mom" dies. Many families have frequent reunions.

The home is a "greenhouse" wherein we learn to identify the weeds that threaten life, to recognize the various foods needed to sustain life, including and especially the Bread of Life, and to experience the "fruits of the Spirit" for sharing with many beyond the family. It is in the family that we learn early that it hurts to live among people, that we have a need to be protected, that we need to seek confession for what we have done wrong to another, learning to ask for forgiveness. Indeed, it is in the family that we witness the birth and growth of humanity, its pains and joys, its enemies and defenders, especially in the struggle against evil within and outside the home. Faith within the home draws deeply on the gifts of God's presence and the power in Christ. One need only go to any work environment to experience power struggles and snide undercuttings. But we also experience them within our homes, and there—in a somewhat controlled setting—is the place to find spiritual resources for growth in withstanding these problems later at the playground, at work, and in our marriages. Speaking of life together in the home, Luther reminds us that it is in the home that: "God's mighty battles against Satan are being fought. Here it is that unrighteous men are forced by God's law to serve others for their self-mortification. Here it is also that righteous men are empowered by God's love to serve their neighbors freely and gladly."[1] Here, in the intimacy of the family, the parents are the "bishops of Christ," shepherding the household as God's holy people, teaching the faith, modeling the godly life, supporting each other in ministry to one another, and—as a family—ministering collectively and individually to the neighborhood and the world. Here we struggle for a new posture in parental leadership, maintaining a strong parental role while realizing that one must gradually allow children to gain self-confidence and the need to live responsibly beyond the family rules and regulations in order to grow into adulthood. Here indeed we practice as a family the art of Christian discernment, wrestling together and individually with calls for help and needs to be met, and recognizing unfair conditions and engaging them with love and wisdom. The home is an important place for discernment, which is needed for its own sake, and it provides for another generation an appropriate model of faith's engagement with various human conditions and opportunities for ministry. Bonhoeffer adds these practical instructions related to our life together in the family: "In a word, live together in the forgiveness of your sins, for without it no human fellowship, least of all a marriage, can survive. Don't insist on your own rights, don't blame each other, don't judge or condemn each

---

1. *WA A* 8, 23.

other, don't find fault with each other, but accept each other as you are, and forgive each other every day from the bottom of your hearts."[2]

The Family in Christ

Among Christians, relations within our immediate families will always be "in Christ." How inappropriate to say among Christians that some members are "in-laws." One member of our family, my son's wife, who by tradition in our country would generally be called our daughter-in-law, led me to a fresh insight as she joined our family. Shortly after their marriage, she indicated her objection to that title of daughter-in-law. Nor did it appear right for our children's spouses to think we thought of them as "in-laws." My wife, Trudy, and I agreed: something was not right in that expression; it was too cold. Christians live above the Law; we relate to each other in and through Christ's love. Thus those who enter our family should be known not as "in-laws" but as fellow members of a special body, our Christian family. By faith we live together "in Christ." As Christians, we wish to be joined together in the mystery of a human family that is enveloped in Christ's love, rather than being merely related by law (of marriage or adoption, for example). When a member of the family maintains a faith different from the Christian faith or espouses no faith at all, we respect their integrity. They are fully and totally accepted with the same love that all others in the family receive, just as Christ accepts us: totally, warmly, and lovingly, just as we are.

Children early demonstrate a self-centered nature and frequently compete with other members of the household. Siblings, as they move away from their parents' household, may often continue as adults the competitive behaviors they demonstrated as children and keep score as they interact. Living in the law? "Let's see," one family calculates, "we don't need to visit my brother's family; they haven't visited us for years." Or keeping an account, one decides, "My sister Jane gave our daughter an expensive gift for graduation; now I guess we're obligated to reciprocate." Or the parents, in later stages of life, reflect on how much they gave to their children and how little the children give in return. Something is amiss in such family scorekeeping. The family is the one place in which we learn to give and share without expectation of return. This is where we learn God's grace—freely given to all—and where, empowered with

---

2. Bonhoeffer, *Letters and Papers*, 46.

God's gifts, we are called to extend the same grace to others. To be sure, it is also the place to begin to accept situations of responsibility, not allowing the free gift of grace to disable one from being responsible. Here too we learn to be grateful, expressing genuine thanks for gifts received, and we in turn, at an appropriate time, give freely without expectation of return. The home is also the place where we learn to express gratitude for the gifts received, both to God in prayers of thanks and to those who give to us. From a young age we learn to express those personal words of thanks. While parents need to teach their children to say "thanks," we also need to teach them to give without regard for anything in return.

Henry Nouwen writes: "When someone accepts a gift, he admits another into his world and is ready to give him a place in his own being ... When the gift is accepted, it acquires a place in the life of the other ... [However] between people, it is quite often more a question of trading than accepting, and many people are even embarrassed with a present because they know of no way they can reciprocate. 'It makes me feel obligated,' they say. Perhaps the challenge of the gospel lies precisely in the invitation to accept a gift for which we can give nothing in return. For the gift is the life breadth of God himself, the Spirit who is poured out on us through Jesus Christ."[3]

The Energizing of the Hug

In every family, the members live close enough to step on the toes of others, to elbow each other, causing hurt that is more than physical. In some cases we leave long-lasting scars, which at times break open and fester openly. Family reunions, special celebrations, and gatherings can often have tense moments. At such times, memories of ill will cause anger to resurface, related perhaps to interpersonal conflict experienced years ago, even as far back as when they were young children. There then closely follows a resurfacing of unresolved guilt or suppressed anger. Surveys reveal that often many family members feel a certain stress when the gang gathers. Some are fearful: "What from our history will break open as we gather?" Being in Christ, one would hope there would be quiet, informal, deeply personal expressions one to another, that we could practice what we pray in the Lord's Prayer: God "forgive us our sins as we forgive those who sin against us." This gives even greater

---

3. Nouwen, *With Open Hands*, 62.

meaning to those hugs among family members, perhaps with a tear or a smile, enabling an ever greater bonding with love and an ever greater life together as the family gathers with a new and genuine sense of joy and freedom.

Those acts of hugging and genuine acceptance at the appropriate time can be tremendously energizing. My parents and grandparents were of rural Northern European stock; they practiced little or no public displays of emotion or affection, no hugging or kissing of the children. My father on several occasions told us of his experience just prior to the family's buggy ride to the church funeral of their father. Once all were properly dressed, his mother had all five children sit on the living room couch. There she sternly told them. "Let no one, not any one of you, cry during the service." That seemed to be my father's only memory of his father's funeral. Fast forward. While I was in the seventh grade, during the days of the Second World War, my father was working in a Chevrolet defense plant, often seven days a week and long hours each day. I was in a group of bigger boys from our parochial school charged with gathering, sorting, and stacking scrap iron and used rubber tires. Material was piled high on our school's playground until a semitrailer was parked in the yard; then we had the task of loading the scrap iron onto the truck by hand—our contribution to the war effort. Often when the evening's work was completed we were on our own, giving us also time to prowl the neighborhood like something of a street gang. I was becoming "street smart" and "book dumb." Mother of course assumed we were working all those hours. Not so. And my grades clearly suffered. The inevitable had to happen. Time came when I had to hand over to my father a very bad report card. His disgust quickly became evident. I felt the heat of his anger, especially as he took off his belt. But then a change happened! Suddenly he dropped his belt and reached forward, putting his arms around me. With tears running down his cheeks, he hugged me tightly. Spontaneous, not staged; no words were spoken. He was conveying something very profound.[4] I doubt that I suddenly returned to my school work the next day with more seriousness, but I have long looked

---

4. Carey, "Evidence." Summarizing recent behavioral science research relative to touching, he reports the following: "A warm touch seems to set off the release of oxytocin, a hormone that helps create a sensation of trust, and to reduce levels of the stress hormone cortisol. In the brain, prefrontal areas, which help regulate emotion, can then relax, freeing them for another of their primary purposes: problem solving. In effect, the body interprets a supportive touch as 'I'll share the load.'"

back on that moment when I realized not only that my father loved me (I knew that without his hugs), but that his love for me was powerfully focused. I then realized how deeply he was concerned that I would learn to read (actually, I never read a book until my freshman year in high school, and that was a tough go). For reasons I was beginning to understand, he really wanted me to make use of the educational resources available to me, resources which he himself had never known. His hug was a call for me to break somehow with the direction my life was taking; a few older boys whom I knew and admired had already dropped out of high school, joining the Marines. When the invitation presented itself, I was off to our church body's St. Paul's Academy (a boarding school, preparatory for seminary). There I found myself in a much more challenging and highly stimulating environment, far different from the one I had known on the streets of south St. Louis. That one hug from my father, driven by Christ's love, made a major difference in my life and my career.

Each One Us Has a Unique Relationship in the Family

While serving on the staff of the New York office of the Lutheran Church in America (LCA), I came to know and deeply respect the Rev. James R. Crumley Jr., then presiding bishop of that church body. Once, while attending a major Lutheran World Federation meeting in Budapest, he was notified that his brother-in-law had died. The next day he was scheduled to chair an important session of the assembly, considered a very prestigious opportunity, an honor for him and his own church body. However, a tourist agency found one seat open for a hurried flight back to the United States, and he quickly returned to the US. He was highly criticized by some colleagues for having left early. Following the funeral he wrote:

> I believe it to be a genuine spirituality that underscores how only I can fulfill my role in my family. It is the place above all others where God has made me unique. No one else can fill the place for me where I relate to parents, brothers, spouse, and children. Only I am Bob's son, Annette's husband, Frances' father. Here above all other human relationships I have a particular identity. Someone else will be a pastor to the people to whom I was pastor; someone else will be bishop of the church. But no one else will ever fill my place in my family relationship . . . Faith urges me to give whatever is necessary to nurture, strengthen, and build those

relationships. That takes time—time to love, to serve, to enjoy, to celebrate, to mourn—together.[5]

Here in the family, one does ministry as one also learns humility in ministry. Our ministries are shaped in various ways; my father's spontaneous ministry to me is only one illustration. Bishop Crumley's letter is another. And here too in the family, ministry entails an intimate sharing of the hope of the resurrection in a variety of ways. At crucial times it simply means being present, at other times providing specific services—perhaps in goods, but most likely in hugs, laughs, meals shared, stories retold, and past events recalled, in some way or other esteeming the other and avoiding any one-upmanship. Much could be said in this context about the callings of mothers and fathers, and ministry to one's children, modeling for later generations how to carry on the calling under the same Spirit. We cannot overlook the opportunity to be reminded that, in the family, father and mother model Christ's "emptying of oneself" for others, in radical contrast to "lording it over" others, especially one's children. Parents minister to their children in Christ from below, humbly, lowly, not looking down from above. Such is expressive of the inverted church in the home.

Ministry is relational. Experience in the family daily illustrates this. Ministry is always personal and people-related; and nowhere other than in the family does one find so many opportunities to carry on ministry. Our prayers may be said in private, but they must be, first and always, Christ-related and so through Christ, people-related. This is best illustrated by the interchange in the Lord's Prayer: we cry to God, "Forgive us our sins!" Then, still in the presence of the Holy One we turn to family, neighbor, and the peoples of the world. Seeing all through Christ, we again cry out to them as well as to God, "Forgive us our sins!" Indeed, either in the company of fellow saints gathered in public worship or alone in our prayer closet—since we are in Christ, that interchange is a holy relationship. And so as we engage our daily callings, we are aware that the God we know in Christ is not against us but for us, beside us, before us, and always with us in our relations with others. How to make that more complete and genuine in our daily life is our common objective. Nowhere is there a more leveling dimension of the church than the request for the forgiveness of sins both in the church and in the home.

---

5. Crumley, "Dear Partners," 6.

Christ comes lowly to us, empowering our appeal for and assurance of forgiveness as we simultaneously reach out to others for their forgiveness of our sins against them and to meet their special needs. This is the heart of the Christian outreach, an expression of God's grace being given to another without any expectation that it will be returned. Any expectation that what we give will not be returned should never deter our action of continuing to reach, with God's love and grace through Christ, to each within our family and beyond.

As we live together as family, which is often unlike any other relationship, it is very hard to feel any freedom to say, when need is evident, that I have no responsibility, that I'll pass on this cry for help. Some may say that such situations place one in bondage, an enslavement to serve. Not so. Even the word "bondage" as Luther used it in his essay on the freedom of the Christian is actually a "bonding" to another in love. Certainly a child can be abused by parents, unfairly compelled to work or to serve at the pleasure of the parent. Or a child, in turn, devilishly provokes parents to anger and depression. To be sure, the freedom in Christ allows a child, as we discussed earlier of the abused mother, to call for help and to be removed from an unhealthy, hurtful parental relationship. In such abusive situations it sometimes happens that the child, once physically able, picks up and moves out. Such a child may need the support of others and the assurance that one's freedom in Christ may call for breaking an unbearable domination of a parent. Yet one needs some degree of a "reality check" in order to be sure one is not simply using one's freedom as an escape from what is called for, perhaps menial work within the home, which though probably unpleasant, in nonetheless necessary in order to maintain the family's survival.

Witnessing to the Christian faith is not the role of the pastor alone, though the pastor is primary, a public supporter of the families to whom he or she is ministering. Speaking God's judgment upon sin and proclaiming God's gift of forgiveness in Christ is every bit as much the calling of the parent and of all the baptized as it is of the pastor. Early on, children should recognize the strong commitment of their parents to their faith through modeling and speaking what is central to their life. As children grow into adolescence, parents may find themselves in need of a great deal of wisdom to know when to be quiet and listen, and to know when a verbal Christian witness is in order. Yet we parents need to be transparent, allowing even those who may be in rebellion to see the heart of Christ in the forbearance of mom and dad. As parents we need help from others, pastors and fellow Christians, to learn to share faith. To do so when the children are very young enables the gradual development of the skill of listening and responding later at the appropriate times.

And finally, with our strong attention to the family we must offer a word of caution. There is a real temptation to look upon our children or other members of our family in an idolatrous manner—that the sun is rising and setting on each member—so that one's family becomes the whole of one's life. Some may by their practices appear to be praying: "God protect me and my wife, my son and his wife. Us four and no more." The family that lives in Christ and breathes the Spirit does indeed pray for one another, but they are also praying and caring for many beyond their home. The parents' prayers for their children should also encircle prayers for all the children of the world. In summary, as the Christian family learns to "empty itself," it bows low in service to others and to its larger community.

Above I spoke of an extended family, such groups as a military platoon or co-workers, with whom one has served through long and at times difficult conditions. Can we not simply insist that what has been said above about the areas of our callings—our situations of responsibility—are just as applicable in these extended family relationships as well? To be sure, the situation of responsibility is generally most clearly seen and felt in our immediate family, but what is experienced there has much wider applications.

Discerning Our Vocations and Career Callings

There are, as I see it, four contexts that contribute to shaping one's career path. The first is a somewhat unconscious process, which is nevertheless very influential—simply growing up in a family. Many of us, from our very early years onward, looked to either our father or mother or both as the role model for our future lifelong work. This occurs not necessarily by lectures, but more often by quietly catching feelings that mix with other ingredients in shaping our callings, our vocations. Regrettably, with mother and father leaving home each morning for work, the children of the household often have little firsthand awareness of their parent's profession and work. There are creative ways many parents have found that enable their family to relate meaningfully with what goes on beyond the home in the workplace.

The second context leading to the shaping of our career is what happens in one's various educational experiences—school and college—along with a summer job, or through those commercial agencies that offer a program of career-planning. Again, it may be a role model who has the greatest impact, especially teachers or a pastor. The third context is the process of re-evaluating one's career: rethinking things, often in "mid-career," which perhaps leads to a second or third field of work. This rethinking is sometimes accomplished alone but occurs more often in consultation with others.

The fourth context is what happens—or should be happening—in our churches. In efforts like this writing, through the work and the words of others within the church, and especially through the Scriptures, it is hoped that we obtain assistance in enabling our Christian faith to shape a fresh vision of our life's work. Such should be a significant dimension of the role of the church: assisting the family and individuals in the exercise of Christian discernment in one's lifelong pursuit of one's callings, our vocations. Specifically, one ministry of the church is to allow the gospel, the Christian faith, to shape our various occupations throughout our life and especially at those twists and turns when searching for new direction.

The first context, the influence of the home, can be a powerful influence in sharpening one's career, providing the values that give meaning and purpose to one's various callings. This may begin even in early age. If mother and father enjoy their work, children catch the feeling and something is ignited within them. They catch the quality of the family, especially the parent's integrity. They discover what it means to be on time, to do work with diligence, and to be accountable. Certainly adult conversation within the home contributes to directing children toward their vocations and to the development of a sound work ethic. Opportunities for children to follow their parents through a work day can mean a great deal to a child's expanding view of his or her opportunities in the years ahead. As children grow older, significant others within the larger family become additional role models.

In some cases, parental influence can be overbearing. I have known a pastor whose father was a famous clergyman. For many years, within the family, it was taken for granted that John too would become a pastor.

And John, feeling he was not free to choose otherwise and holding his father in very high regard, did not want to do anything to offend him. So he became a pastor. His performance was generally judged to be mediocre, certainly not up to his father's reputation. Within a year after his father's death, John announced his resignation from his parish and began retooling for a new career. Counselors often indicate the high number of adults who spend a good deal of time struggling to get out from under the expectations of one parent or both. Such heavy influence may often apply even to the type of person one is expected to marry and to the level of success parents expect their children to achieve. For a child becoming an adult, it is often most difficult to move beyond a parental entrapment. While holding high and noble goals for our children, we will also do well to make sure they know their freedom, and to let them know that this freedom centers in and needs to be drawn from their faith.

No one should fault parents for wanting the best for their children. But are we overdoing it in our day? Parents today are often being labeled "helicopter" parents—constantly hovering over their children, unable to let go, complaining to the high school counselor or college dean if their child has been given a poor grade—without thought that it might be the child's problem (or even the parents') and not the institution's. Often the highest goal is financial success for their children's future, a comfortable career, great financial rewards—indeed, a life with considerable prestige would also be fine. A source for humor in New York City centers on efforts made by the wealthy on the Upper East Side to register their expected child—shortly after conception—for acceptance in the highly prestigious schools for early childhood development. This is assumed necessary for later acceptance at an Ivy League university. At all the major bookstores, the shelves on early childhood development reflect the great interest of many parents in mastering the task of giving one's child a head start in our highly competitive society. It is not only commendable but also an indicator of the high value that parents place in their children to achieve the ultimate in success in later years.

Many of our caring professions like medicine, long considered a special career of compassion and sacrifice, seem to have become for many a twisted, financial-success-driven enterprise. A 2006 article in *The New York Times* gives specifics to this drive: "Doctors have become so interested in the business side of medicine that more than 40 medical schools have added, over the last twenty years, an optional fifth year of schooling for those who want to earn an M.B.A. degree as well as an M.D. Some go directly to Wall Street or into health care management without ever practicing medicine."[6] The University of California, Los Angeles, has annually conducted a survey of some forty thousand entering freshmen. *The New York Times* recently (2010) reported on this research: "In 1971, 37 percent responded that it was essential or very important to be 'very well-off financially,' while 73 percent said the same about 'developing a meaningful philosophy of life.' In 2009, the values were nearly reversed: 78 percent identified wealth as a goal, while 48 percent were after a meaningful philosophy."[7] Current curriculum in universities and colleges reflects a major shift toward an expectation of financial success following graduation, and is accompanied by a reduction of courses in the humanities.

The second form of "career counseling" comes through institutions that appear too often to be focused on assuring future vocational success for our children. In high school and college the candidates for a profession will have access to tests, counseling, psychological examinations—all attempting to match the individual's abilities, skills, and interests with the current job market, generally centered on achieving success. But we should also add, as Anthony Kronman (dean of Yale Law School) writes, critical of this American pursuit: "there are many parents today who yearn for their children to have an education that goes beyond the merely vocational and equips them for a challenge larger than that of succeeding in a career."[8] What is the church's and the Christian family's approach to this success-driven culture? Kronman's recent (2007) book may be helpful. In my judgment it might have been subtitled: How our educational institutions have given up on challenging students both to search for and to assist them in finding the meaning of life. His thesis maintains that centers of higher learning have discarded the importance of the humanities—literature, poetry, history, religion, and the arts—all long considered subjects that explore with depth the meaning of life. In his judgment they are now replaced by both the research ideal (that is, the only way to truth lies in the hard sciences) and by our cultural phenomenon of insisting everything must be politically correct. The latter restricts open pursuit of

6. Uchitelle, "Gilded Paychecks."
7. Zernike, "Making College 'Relevant.'"
8. Kronman, *Education's End*, 6.

truth and discussion of conflicting positions by assuring that no one's feelings or beliefs are affected or offended by the outcome.

What Kronman argues for in the university might also be said of the church. The university—and here I would add the church—should be, in his words: "not just a place for transmission of knowledge but a forum for the exploration of life's mysteries and meaning through careful but critical reading . . ."[9] In the church this could be addressed through gospel proclamation, faith-centered conversation and discussions, and biblically focused forums engaging our human predicament and career possibilities. The sermon, indeed the whole program of Christian education, should be an interactive process among all the people, openly struggling with the mystery of God's will and word, helping us to catch glimpses of God's holiness shining through and upon us humans, pointing us to the purposes and meaning God conveys in Christ. The whole world of heaven and earth is there for us Christians to explore; to pursue with vigor and courage; to bring heaven's light to earth's mysteries; to aid others in lessening human suffering, injustices, and life's sorrows; and to shape our hopes for the future. Here is the Servant Church, helping the people pursue their vocations, shaped by faith and empowered by Christ's love.

For those in pursuit of life goals and life's occupations, the church should offer something more than merely data gathering, dogma unattached to life or dogma attached to success-focused efforts. The "more" is connecting the gospel and faith (and all the rich biblical insights related to the gospel) with the humanities, or if you prefer, the daily newspaper. The gospel and faith should never be separated from the rich accounts of history's long search and struggle to achieve an answer to the question of the meaning of life. The call of faith surely elevates our vision to noble goals, calling for risk, never assuring one of financial success, daring to travel paths others have never taken, and endeavoring to achieve creative accomplishments that move our society from where it is to where it could be.

Christ's gift of freedom from the oppressors and oppression—be they our parents, teachers, or a commercially driven culture—is a treasure each of us should exercise with diligence, letting it be a strong influence in shaping our children's values. Gradually we may want to set our children free to work out their own careers—indeed, with some fear

9. Ibid.

and caution; yet ultimately as they grow older to also grow free of us as parents. I look back with gratitude to my father. He was not ashamed of his work on the Chevy assembly line. But he also clearly gave evidence that he did not expect me to follow him in his line of work or that he envisioned some glorious, financially successful future for his son. On several occasions he told me, "All I want you to be is someone who does not have to carry a lunch pail to work." While living in Stamford, Connecticut, and working in New York City, I traveled with the "briefcase brigade" on the Metro North commuter train to Grand Central Station. I often chuckled, thinking what my father would say if he saw me and discovered that, along with work-related material, I also carried my lunch concealed in a brown bag in my briefcase. Given his frugality, he would have liked that.

Success is indeed necessary in order to achieve a level of subsistence by which one is not dependent upon handouts. But how much financial success is necessary to sustain life adequately in today's complexities? We may accept what my mentor Professor Pelikan once said in a sermon: there is a rightful role for a Christian to pursue "righteous ambitions" in contrast to "self-righteous ambitions." For some, their very occupation in life, their work or their career, fulfils their life and has meaning. One's career may clearly be seen as God's instrument for serving others' needs without a drive to achieve wealth. For others, especially in today's automated workplace (my father as an example) it is difficult to see God's hand in an eight-hour day, driving the same rivet into four hundred auto frames as the assembly line moves ever faster past your work station. My father found meaning in life with the check he weekly brought home to feed the family, to educate his children, to give to his church and community charities, and to create a savings to sustain him and my mother in their retirement. The meaning in life for my father and my mother was surely enriched by finding satisfying services within their church, as well as by the thrill of over thirty years' participation in the growth and successes of his union, including obtaining decency and respect in his daily work in his time and for others who would follow. He also found meaning in the friendships he gained through his union and in the mutual support during the stresses experienced in his work. I am not aware that his church significantly assisted him or his kind in recognizing the nature of Christ's calling in their mechanized occupations. We must do much better for our children and grandchildren.

Discerning Our Callings as Citizens

The second of Luther's three spheres of human relations was the government or the political sector. From the first century (and even before) through to the time of the Reformers in the sixteenth century, "the powers" were known to be "out there, up-above," centered in kings and emperors, popes and bishops, the military, and people of the court. These powers held great influence in one's daily life. In fact, the power of the state and church often blurred. In many ways the father's rule in the household represented a reach of the government. And in the person of the clergyman, the reach of the church and government extended into the life of the family. Yet symbols and centers of political rule and power remained distant. The Christian calling of the citizen was primarily that of obedience to the powers that be.

In the modern-day Sunday litany one often hears the important petition to pray for all in authority—the president, our governor, the judges, and our mayor—that they might lead with justice and wisdom. These lines echo the appeal in 1 Timothy 2:2 that we indeed ought to pray for all in authority. These petitions are most appropriate. However, with a high degree of thanksgiving, we Christians today ought to recognize that the "powers" are no longer limited to those above. Today they are shared among us "down below," in our constitutional right of protest, our freedom to seek public office, and our being entrusted with a freedom to vote both for and against public policies and elected officials when we deem them worthy or unworthy of our support. The litany's petition reflects the church's long history of living under authorities often known to be beyond the people: they were from "above." Absent was any thought that power could also reside in the people, even among and within the lowly peasant. Consider what dramatic changes have happened with the rise of democratic governance, government by the people—though there is a continual struggle for its full reality. However, students of democratic government have long recognized that such government is highly dependent upon an informed citizenry who exercise their rights and who engage personally in the political process, struggling with others in pursuit of good government through wisdom and moral courage.

A concern for the common good is highly important—that is, a willingness to support and to serve without bondage to special interests, attending to legislation and enforcement of laws in the best interests of the community and especially of the disadvantaged. Such noble commitment can be shared by both Christian and non-Christian in our local and national political organizations. Church leadership, however, needs to model that, for the Christian, the motivation for this commitment is Christ: God's love known in the word and sacraments. This is our source of strength against the common temptation to judge candidates and public policy on how well they support me and my family with disregard for others' needs. An apathetic, uninformed, self-centered, irresponsible electorate opens the door for rule by self-serving elites and even an autocratic rule. A saying is attributed to Plato: If the wise disdain the task of politics, then they must suffer being governed by fools.

Very simply, the prayers of the church for "all in authority" must regularly include all of us. Political power and authority have now become the inheritance of the people—indeed, also of the people of God. It shapes our Christian callings as citizens. Today, sensitive to our "area of responsibility" in our political context, we surely need reminders that we, the public, govern by "divine right." Faith recognizes this to be a gift of God, thus calling each Christian to "be responsible!" The Christian community ought to be in the forefront of calling elected officials and the voting public to the reality that good government costs and taxes are the *sine qua non* to sustain government. An informed citizenry, along with an energized Christian community, will insist that raising funds for the support of all aspects of the government should be an open, debatable dimension of public discourse and not a threat to the official's electability. The challenge for the Christian community within the public sector is to demonstrate its willingness to support and to propose legislation that might be personally costly but will achieve the greater good. With such a constituency, elected officials are more likely to engage difficult and sensitive issues with open accountability to the people. To be sure, greater attention to the cost of government should include a careful monitoring by the people and the exposure of financial abuse and self-aggrandizement.

Today, from one perspective, one might say that the political order has been inverted, or at least considerably flattened. Our political leaders now may genuinely be seen as "servants of the people," not rulers who lord it over their constituents. We are now even free under our constitutions to protest the laws that some of us may consider unjust and to work for change or to offer ourselves as possible political officials. Obedience to government is obviously still available in the person of the police, the IRS, and the military. Those who lead us are to be held in honor, especially by virtue of the office they hold and by virtue of their integrity, dedication, and commitment, especially as they work to meet the needs of the least among us. The political process today even allows for orderly protest through a free press and the right of assembly. In times past such activity was seen as seditious and rebellious. Today, amid many alternatives, Christians may want to seek opportunities, unlike conditions in the past, for our callings as citizens, participating in upholding our constitutional governments, willing to run for public office, and assuring justice for all people. Many more Christians ought to prepare for and seek public office, not merely for the general improvement of their community and especially not for special self-interest groups. Christians should recognize their unique opportunities in local and national politics to promote strategies that genuinely enable the disenfranchised to take their seat beside the wealthy and powerful in the chambers of government and in the corporate world. The common good is our primary goal. Christians need to discover their "holy callings" in the civic arena. The avenue to achieve this is through the powers that be, specifically, through careers in government, participation in one's political party, and the exercising of our right to vote. Lutherans have long been lax in this sector.[10]

To be sure, in government as in all other sectors of the creation, corruption is pervasive at all levels. The nearly constant reports of political and governmental corruption frequently become an excuse for some Christians to opt out. Since corruption is so prevalent and so pervasive, some Christians assume they should avoid involvement in politics, even avoiding the ballot box on an election day. Rather these corrupted conditions should encourage a greater commitment to one's civic calling. Remember our earlier discussion of ministry under the cross in the struggle for justice amid injustices; in such battles there is likely to be much pain and a high degree of deceit, deception, and ruthless power plays. Luther calls for a vigilant awareness of the

---

10. "Lutherans Take Office," para. 3. According to the Pew Forum on Religion and Public Life, "Catholics make up 30 percent of the 111th U.S. Congress [Year 2009] . . . Baptists form the second-largest group with 12 percent, followed by Methodists (11 percent), Presbyterians (8 percent), Episcopalians (7 percent) and Lutherans (4.5 percent)."

inescapable reality of evil that lurks in all the orders of creation, including the church and government, within all organizations. Our callings in any sector of our daily life are never isolated from the corrupted condition of this fallen creation. It is within such conditions that God summons Christians for ministry. It is clearly our common ministry as Christians, in cooperation with others, to work in and through various political processes toward both greater civility and the common good. God's call is to compel the powers to bend in the direction of a civil, decent, and just life for all citizens in God's world. Working toward this goal means engaging the powers, that is, powers twisted by corrupted people for self-serving purposes.

Each of us needs to be circumspect, making certain that we ourselves are not contributors to such twisted practices. Discerning our calling from the Christian perspective includes facing head-on the earthly powers that be, twisted and abused as they are by humans. Social and political power is an instrument inherent in everyone's calling. Though the powers that be are often so twisted and abused, including by Christians, that should not sway any one from engaging them nor from being a participant in the powers, lest we prevent ourselves from becoming a power for good. The twisted are encountered in our everyday activities wherever power is present: in the church, the government, the work place, and the home. Yes, included here are the politics encountered in our vocations, twisted powers even within us. In such areas of accountability and responsibility the Christian knows the daily need for confession and forgiveness in Christ's name, either as a citizen or as a politician and, using the Catechism's words, for resolving to amend the sinful life—that is, to get up and get going with the struggle to do what is right and to resist what is evil. Former Senator Paul Simon of Illinois, a Lutheran, often insisted that the way to rise within the ranks of a political party was to begin at the bottom. To parents he would say that they might dream of their child one day becoming president of our nation or holding a significant position as an elected official, but begin now by preparing him or her for major positions of leadership. Parents might consider modeling for their family by giving service at the lower positions, the less prestigious ones, like service in the local Parent Teachers Association or service on a committee of the local city government—especially those positions not considered desirable and often going unfilled. And what can be done in the local congregation? Adult forums could be scheduled inviting political candidates, such as those running for mayor, to share their goals and objectives if elected and to be questioned by Christians in a civil, nonpartisan manner.

Especially as citizens we need to let Christ's light shine through our vocations, and that light is made especially bright when we dare to give ourselves in costly, often painful, service for the common good. Politics generally calls for costly service and is often made more difficult because of one's refusal to accept contributions from sources expecting special, self-centered, self-serving services in return.

The Christian Community in a Pluralistic Society

In this changed and changing world we need a careful effort at discernment, both regarding our callings within the organization of the church and in how our common Christian calling relates us to our new neighbors—often strange to many of us, quite different from us, and unlike our neighbors in the past.

First it is important to look back at a seemingly more simple society, the time following the Reformation, and contrast it with conditions today. The landscape in Luther's day was punctuated with church steeples reaching heavenward, high above even the civil courts. The Peace of Augsburg in 1555 solidified an agreement among the conflicting parties that the faith of the prince would be the same for the people. So the church in any one area projected a powerful, unified presence; their communities reflected an apparent common religious identity. Neighbors gathered at the same church; their baptism identified them as both a member of the Christian church and a citizen of the state, all subject to the prince. Preaching called for the Christian to give alms for the poor, but gradually the local governments began "community chests" to fund those in need. Stewardship programs and fund drives, so common now, were unknown. The organization of local churches called for little service from the people—at least very little compared with the demands for volunteer services in today's congregations. To be sure, then as now the local minister appealed for the young (men) and for the brightest to hear God's call for the study of theology in order to become a pastor. In fact, the call to the public ministry through ordination often drowned out any call for ministry in daily life. In most Lutheran and Protestant churches, Luther's emphasis on the common priesthood was known and often accepted by some as an excuse for avoiding regular

Sunday worship. One did not need the clergy to go to God with one's prayers. The emphasis on the callings of the parent would generally be heard. Under certain social and political conditions, a citizen's call to the military could be viewed as a special service for God, along with an emphasis on God's call to obedience to those who govern, including the father and the pastor. Then as now, through this less than perfect church, God's kingdom continued to come among the people. Faith was strong; pastors were dedicated; Christian love was real. Public worship was often inspirational and attractive, assisted by great composers, dedicated church musicians, and vibrant hymn singing. Yet as the centuries progressed following the Reformation, especially with the emergence of the Industrial Revolution, little attention was seriously given to the ministry of the people in their daily life.

I have a personal feeling about the reason for this failure. While I was a young pastor in the Philadelphia area, I was enrolled part-time in a graduate theological program concentrating on Luther and his understanding of the Christian calling. My parish ministry was in the very early stages of the development of a new congregation, located in a far north suburb of the metropolitan area. Among our small initial membership was Rudi Guenzel. I cherished his leadership. He was the kind of lay person every pastor would treasure. The congregation was in the phase in which we had to organize. There was no need yet for attention to the construction of a church building or major fundraising. While we had a number of dedicated members, few were comfortable with the intricacies of developing a new congregation. Rudi was different: a longtime Lutheran, highly committed and experienced in church work. He had the gift to identify, encourage, and recruit others to serve in leadership and on committees. Whatever the task, he could organize others to work with him in getting the job done. He was also open to the new, not bound by the traditions of his previous church life. He was what many of us would call a healthy pillar of the congregation.

My sermons, reflecting material from my graduate studies, made much of the Christian calling for all of us in the sectors of family, career, and citizenship. One day Rudi came to me, saying he and his wife, Marion, having listened to my sermons, had discussed their respective calling and concluded this was the time for him to make a run for election to the City Council. To do so he would need to relinquish much of the time that he had been giving to our congregation. My heart sank! I did everything to cover my disappointment. I assured him that he surely had our blessing, though internally I felt a great loss. He assured me that he with his family would continue to be present for worship and all other meetings when able. Truthfully I was not very excited that he chose a special role in government, reducing his services in our church—in spite of what I had been preaching! Years later, continuing my interest in Luther, I began to recognize that Luther had had something of the same experience I had had in confronting the organizational needs of the church. Earlier I reported on the first phase of his reforming career, that is, Luther's battle focused on the hierarchy: the pope and bishops. They were the ones thwarting efforts at reformation. They were the ones claiming to be the sole authorities and the only authentic ministers of the gospel, denying to the laity their rightful role as priests in their daily life. Thus Luther's sermons and his accent during the first half of his career are peppered with illustrations and exhortations relative to the ministry of all the people in their various vocations and denunciation of those who thwart such ministry.

A significant change occurred for Luther in mid-career, a change somewhat similar to what occurs today in many of our congregational experiences. By 1525 he was confronted with major new problems. He found himself in time-consuming efforts that now diverted him from his earlier concerns. It became shockingly clear that many priests had gladly left their Roman allegiance and now claimed allegiance to the evangelical churches but had little knowledge of the biblical and theological insight represented by the reforming movement. Confronting this fact, Luther had to give time-consuming attention to the spiritual and theological education of the clergy, relative to the word and Scripture.

Second, with a sizeable emerging church body and without bishops crossing over from the Roman Catholic Church, Luther and others had to give considerable attention to redeveloping an organization among the churches and creating accountability of pastoral practices. Consequently, following 1525 the context of his reforming mission had dramatically changed: and with it, his accent on the ministry of all the people was not as noticeable. His attention, understandably, for reasons of rightful necessity, focused on the pastors and the organizing of an ever-expanding institutional church in Germany. And so the focus on the ministry of all the people diminished as he gave attention to re-educating the clergy and establishing an organization that would manage the life of the movement.

There may be similarities today with Luther's attention in his day. One might say that the compelling nature of pastoral leadership today in many North American congregations is heavily focused on maintaining the church's physical plant and obtaining the money to support the church's budget. Likewise, so much of the pastoral leadership is centered on the necessity of recruiting and organizing the laity for ministry for the church as an institution. Many pastors seem to be unable to promote the ministry of the people beyond service to the local congregation. They may so promote in sermons, as Luther did, but their congregational programs belie what they teach. Recruitment and training of the laity is centered on service and ministry to and for the church as an institution, not that such is wrong, but it is wrong when it is limited and drowns out the broader calls for the peoples' ministry in daily life. I am convinced many of us want to get beyond the limiting of ministry to the church as an institution.

Through the second half of the past century this problem was frequently discussed and experiments were undertaken. In the 1960s the church increasingly made the transition from the urban areas to the suburban ones. Although many felt euphoria at seeing these new growth centers, some saw such growth as an illusion. During that time one could in some mission circles hear the accusation that the church had become guilty of "property-idolatry," a judgment that the intense and tremendous building efforts at the time were idolatrous and a diversion from the church's authentic mission. Indeed, there were creative efforts at that time to increase multiple use of churches' physical space. In a newly planned, huge city—Columbia, Maryland, outside Washington, D.C.—integrated facilities were developed so that a Jewish congregation and two Christian congregations could share space at different hours. The building had moveable walls, creating a unique interior environment with appropriate appointments for the respective religious groups. The innovative effort was successful for a number of years. Then with a change in leadership came a downturn in membership, compelling the Lutherans to sell to the Roman Catholics. In another experiment, a Congregational Church in Burlington, Vermont, received national attention for their commitment never to own property, but to stay—as a pilgrim church—in rented quarters, free to move as needed. Years later I preached at the dedication of a church's educational facility in Burlington. I mentioned that the church has long recognized the need for sacred space. I recalled the effort in their town where a Christian congregation had committed themselves never to own a building. I mentioned I had never heard if that bold effort really succeeded—and this was the only time someone answered me aloud during a sermon. A man responded, "They bought land and built a church." To my knowledge we have few models surviving from those days of experimentation in the mid-part of the past century.

Today, with the swift movement of people from one community to another and the often sudden changes in the demographics of an area, churches built for one generation suddenly become nearly empty in the second or third generation. Consequently, in following years, a small number of members become saddled with the high cost of maintaining a building that is often far beyond their physical and financial means. Attention to outreach, perhaps to a new and different community surrounding the church, is neglected as primary attention is given to maintaining the large physical plant and obtaining adequate income in order to afford a full-time paid pastor. The issue is not the nonowning of property, nor the congregation's refusal to build a building, but it is the need for a fresh, creative approach to building church facilities—similar to efforts that were made in the '60s—to find greater simplicity and multiple use of church space. An analytical formula may be helpful: Calculate the total cubic feet of your church facilities (not just square feet but cubic: that's space that must be heated and repaired) and divide first by the number of hours these facilities are used in a year, and then divide by the number of people using the facilities. The space efficiency may be seen to be appalling, especially compared with other public buildings. Have we allowed our attention to the institution to muffle the call for Christian ministry in our vocations and circumstances of responsibility beyond the walls of the congregation? Certainly an aspect of our Christian calling is maintaining centers for worship, education, and fellowship; this we cannot abandon.

The local congregation often gives a public witness that the church exists for its own survival. Much time is spent calling the people to help maintain the church's physical program and calling for more willing workers when the numbers shrink. People are recruited to support the physical plant, pay for a pastor's salary, and oh yes, worship and be educated, leaving very little time and energy for exercising their mission beyond their own four walls. In New England, in a phenomenon perhaps similar to many other places in our country, Christian congregations are increasingly shrinking in membership, going from being small congregations to being even smaller. In many of these churches, 90 percent of the annual budget is designated for maintaining a full-time pastor and the upkeep of the property. Signs are clearly evident that a good number of medium-sized congregations may, in a short time move to the small-church category. The report of relatively recent (2008) research of Christian giving across the US in all denominations indicates: "70 percent of all congregational income is spent on local operations—on things like wages, salaries, benefits, supplies, and services needed to maintain current operations. Another 23 percent is spent on acquiring and improving local church buildings."[11] Thus while most of the money that North American Christians give is spent on their local needs, the report documents how little is spent on missions, social and medical development, and poverty relief outside of the local congregations, particularly outside the United States, in ways that benefit people other than the givers themselves.[12] National church offices report with understandable pride the figures given for hunger and social service issues, yet these figures represent a small percentage of the total monies raised by the local congregation, especially when compared with what is kept for congregational, institutional needs.

Historically some seminaries and church-related centers have given creative attention to rethinking ways of restructuring the local congregation for mission, especially the small congregation, although such ought to be applicable to all sizes today. Regrettably, many of the past experimental or demonstration efforts have failed. Church mergers of two congregations often dwindle down rather quickly to the size of one of the two congregations before the merger. Two-point parishes sharing one traveling pastor are no longer acceptable in most places. But the troubling situation cannot be overlooked or ignored. We need new models of congregations that continue to reach out to their changing communities, enabling members to serve and energizing them to recognize ministry in multiple areas beyond merely serving the congregation as an institution. Only with a change in overall congregational

11. Smith et al., "Who Gives?" 26.
12. Ibid., 28.

programming will we be able to fully engage our other major missions beyond the walls of the church and allow time for accomplishing them. The problem is not recruiting more for "church work." There needs to be a greater balancing of the time and energy focused on the maintenance of the local church and the time allowed for shaping a vision, for encouraging and supporting Christians beyond their local congregation, for demonstrating ministry in our four "stand outs": the family, our citizenship, our careers, and—indeed—the church.

The sermons I hear today as part of our stewardship programs generally call for the "sacrifice of our whole lives" to Christ and neighbor. We sing, "All that we have is thine alone, a trust, O Lord, from thee," then almost in the same breath, the congregation's annual check-off sheet is given to each family, requesting them to identify from the list how they are willing to serve the church exclusively as institution. Absent is the challenge to examine all our time, "all that we have," asking what part might be given to the congregation, what part might be given to community services either through the congregation or separately (both can be seen as Christian ministry), and how much time is appropriately given to our careers? Why not include in stewardship efforts, as part of a year-long approach, questions about how Christians might assist each other in their ministries as citizens, in respective occupations, and of course within their families? The same can be said about assisting the families of the church to review their family budget in a "spiritual" way, listing what they give beyond the self-maintenance of the church, how they expect their dollars to go for mission and services beyond their own community, to charitable fund drives, to political campaigns, and as gifts to people with special physical needs that appropriately may be given directly by the family, not necessarily through the local congregation or other agencies. Helping members to analyze these issues—especially with another list showing what they spend on entertainment, travel, vacations—might raise questions regarding proper balance. This may also be a time to talk about Christian freedom, making sure the church does not lay a guilt trip on its membership by claiming that what you *give* in faith to the church as an organization is more important than what you *do* in faith as a citizen, in daily work, or within the household. While tithing may have been an important subject in the life of the Old Testament believer, there are only three references to it in the New Testament, and in each case Christ reprimands the Pharisees regarding the tithe. His comments are very close to expressing a sneer when referring to tithing (Luke 11:42, Matt 23:23, Luke 18:12). St. Paul's summary of the Christian life is the insistence that faith in Christ results in the offering of one's whole life to God (Rom 12:1). A Christian does not divide his or her life, claiming that part is holy—especially that which is given to God (10%?)—and part is secular, not holy, unaffected by faith.

Our Christian Calling within a Highly Pluralistic Society

From the days of the Reformation until lately, Christians—Roman Catholics, Protestants and all other denominations that have generated over these past years—have generally identified themselves by their differences, how we are "not like the other." For nearly five hundred years Christians have enjoyed defining themselves by how they differ from one another's beliefs and practices. A shift in judgment seems to have occurred following 9/11. Suddenly news reports indicated that the perpetrators of the 9/11 attacks were Muslims. Then followed a steady flow of information that awakened many of us to the fact that Christianity in the United States and Europe has been steadily declining in numbers, while the presence of Muslims is significantly growing in our own country and in Europe. The reaction of many was, "Can't believe that; it can't be true." Mosques are suddenly springing up in prominent places in our cities. My own Yankee town (Worcester, Massachusetts, begun prior to the American Revolution) now has a Buddhist temple, a Hindu shrine, and a very large Muslim mosque with an elementary school. In many Christian quarters the conversation has changed. Now we hear Christians from various denominations saying to one another and to other Christians, "We Christians are very different from those Muslims; they are scary people."

A major challenge in these days for us as individuals and as Christian congregations is to learn to practice Christian hospitality with new and apparently very different religious neighbors than we have ever known. As Christians we have a lot of terrible history to overcome, as does Islam, if we are going to become decent, caregiving neighbors here in our own country. James Cahill, writing in *The New York Times*, explains: "Islamic society and Christian society have been generally bad neighbors now for nearly 14 centuries, eager to misunderstand each other, often borrowing culturally and intellectually from each other without ever bestowing proper credit."[13] No Christian can claim to stand apart from those historically tragic events. Recently, when someone mentioned the Christian brutality against the Islam nations in the Crusades, a Lutheran church leader distanced himself by insisting that the Crusades were an act of Roman Catholic Christians of which we Lutherans were never a part. If one accepts any assertion of the historic episcopacy, one cannot separate oneself from those blood-soaked pages of Christian church history, our history. Indeed, today's Protestant churches historically emerged out of the Western medieval church.

Can we agree with Sir Jonathan Sacks, chief rabbi of the British Commonwealth, as quoted in Cahill's article: "Those who are confident of their faith are not threatened but enlarged by the different faiths of others . . . [Cahill again:] To build a future better than our past, we need, as Rabbi Sacks has put it, 'the confidence to recognize the irreducible, glorious dignity of difference.'"[14] Can we Christians do that publicly, and genuinely acknowledge the glorious dignity of Islam or of Judaism without surrendering our faith, our strong conviction that Christ is Lord, our Savior, our God? How does one achieve the ability to authentically recognize the "glorious dignity" of the neighbor's faith and convictions? Not by keeping one's distance. Not by making generalizations about a whole based on the offensive acts of a few, but rather by seeing the whole in light of history. As to Islam's relationship with Christians, we cannot close the book on those dark chapters of our history, the atrocities inflicted upon Muslims, especially in the Crusades. We do not need to wallow in those sad pages of our history, nor do we need to tromp Islam, quick to identify those atrocities which they inflicted upon our Christian forbears. We might want to sing today as we sang in my youth: "Accent the positive, eliminate the negative." What is to be gained by parading those "evils" of others? This only leads to failed attempts at denying or suppressing our own "evil" history.

As happens in so many chapters in history, 9/11 with all its horror provoked good and bad change among Christians and between Christians and Muslims. One unfortunate reaction has been the chilling effect on the part of both sides of those involved. While living in Cairo, Egypt (1999), my wife and I traveled about town each day in the small Cairo taxis. I would crawl into the tight front seat next to the

13. Cahill, "Peaceful Crusader."
14. Ibid.

driver: more leg room and I was able to communicate with our driver in my limited Arabic. This maneuver also allowed my wife to sit in the back—certainly not upfront next to the Muslim man—and thus respect their culture. Once settled in, I quickly could feel the driver's discomfort at having picked up two Westerners, obviously Americans. My first comment would be, "We are from the United States, living in Cairo; we like Egypt!" A smile always came across our driver's face at that remark. By the time we reached our destination, the driver was relaxed and joking with us. Recently I was with a friend who had lived in Cairo for fifteen years and had recently moved back to the US. I asked him, "How have things changed since 9/11?" "Oh," he said, "immediately following 9/11 people were especially friendly, wanting to assure us they did not approve of the attack on the World Trade Center, but," he went on, "after the invasion of Iraq, there began a chill that our family felt ever since." The good side: In Cairo, as in many other places (including the United States), a few windows have opened, allowing some conversations and discussions, reflecting a felt need for mutual understanding. To be sure, a humble approach to our new neighbors does not suggest any surrender of our faith. Nor ought one to accept any conversation to go one way, namely, Muslims instructing us in their faith and we merely sitting quietly.

Every person and every nation, when proud and self-righteous, will have their eyes and ears closed in relation to those whom they fear. They will see what they wish to see, and hear what they want to hear. The people of faith, again emptied of their arrogance through the internal cleansing with the water and word of baptism, repenting, turning from the "old self" to the new life in Christ—with humility and courage—will reach beyond the cultural and religious barriers to people of other religions, their fellow humans in God's grand creation. As Christian, we can do no other.

8

The Struggle for a Prophetic Church

THE PHENOMENON OF THE FASCIST RISE TO POWER AND of the ruthless rule of the Third Reich has set in motion, in the years since World War II, a critical review of historic Lutheran theology and practices. Some scholars and journalists have claimed that the Reformation planted the seeds that eventually grew into not only a Lutheran social passivity but also, as is often noted, a passivity encompassing much of Protestantism.[1] Along with disclosures of the horror of the Holocaust, the American press all too frequently attempted to identify Lutheran theology, especially Luther's Two Kingdoms, as the underlying historic factor leading to Germany's political and social disaster. The absence of major protests by the German citizenry (the majority considered Christian) became a wake-up call for North American Christians, especially theologians and church leaders—a call for critical self-examination. The years following the Second World War provided a testing ground for Christians of all denominations to monitor their own ability or inability to confront injustices on a national and local level, in both congregational preaching, programming, and churchwide proclamations.

---

1. Heschel, *The Aryan Jesus*, is a recent (2008) example of this research, which documents the extensive role played by many prominent theologians who were participants in "The Center for the Study and Eradication of Jewish Influence on German Church Life" during the Nazi's reign.

A Review of the Church's Public Witness in Recent Years

Even though there were church leaders who strongly protested against the increasing rise of the Nazi oppression, especially against Jewish communities, there was little sign of general protest by the majority within the Christian community.[2] While I was teaching for a short time at the historic Lutheran Lyceum in Bratislava, Slovakia—just a year following the fall of the Berlin Wall—I became acquainted with several lay instructors who were from the Bohemian Church. (This is an offshoot of the very early reform movement led by John Hus a hundred years before Luther. Hus was executed by the church for his efforts at reform.) A number of the lay instructors had been jailed for their protests against the occupation by and practices of the Nazis and later the Communists. I listened for comments from any faculty member regarding an account of Lutheran lay or clergy protest; I was unable to hear anything. A brief review of the movements and efforts against commonly recognized injustices in the American churches over the past sixty years may be helpful. While our focus in this review centers on what the public church's witness has been, I do not want to give the impression that local congregations and consortiums of congregations have not been active in a great many struggles against injustice and active in social services. Our review of the churches' role in these areas—especially when addressing social and political issues from a public, official position—will raise the question of effectiveness.

Beginning in the late 1950s, many social and political observers, including clergy and much of the nation, became increasingly sensitive to the injustices that became front-page news and were pictured nightly on television. Public protests began surfacing everywhere, especially at state and national offices, city hall, the mayor's office, corporate offices, businesses, and school boards. The primary attack at first centered on national issues of poverty and—in the South—on racial segregation, and then—in the North—against subtle yet pervasive discrimination against African Americans. Gradually the protest movement shifted to

---

2. Often forgotten and not always reported were the major efforts of protest in the 1930s by large numbers of Christian clergy, a significant portion of whom were Lutheran. In 1933 it was estimated that six thousand of the fourteen thousand ordained German clergy identified with the Confessing Church (called *Bekennende Kirche*), a resistance effort against the Nazi state. Many of the movement's leaders were later sent to concentration camps or imprisoned. Among them were Martin Niemoeller, Dietrich Bonhoeffer, Hanns Lilje, and Heinrich Grueber. See Lazareth, *Christians in Society*, 9.

the Vietnam War. Students and others were marching before federal offices, the military, universities and other centers of power. The protesters and their supporters were insisting that public policy had to change. Clergy, campus chaplains, and prominent church officials were often seen among the principal spokespeople. In rallies, marches, and public protests many priests, pastors, and nuns were very visible. These were the days of the civil rights movement and the peace movement, two momentous chapters in our nation's history.

Social and political scholars carefully studying these periods of protests, particularly those related to issues of race, generally acknowledge that Christian church leadership (especially clergy, both black and white) played a significant role in mobilizing major sectors of their constituencies. Their efforts, in concert with countless other groups, ultimately resulted in Congress' passing the major civil rights laws of the 1960s.[3] This was a significant accomplishment, given the depth and breadth of racial segregation that the nation had knowingly tolerated since Abraham Lincoln's emancipation proclamation. This was also when, under Presidents Kennedy and Johnson, the federal government began confronting poverty, enacting legislation known for years as the Anti-Poverty Program. It was also the period of the free-speech movement and the very public advocates of women's liberation. Here also many church spokespeople were being heard, though not always appreciated.

Mainline church leadership was generally quite public in its support of these movements. However, as the movements advanced, it became evident to many that pastoral leadership often failed to mobilize the people to engage social and political injustices, as church leadership often wanted. Also evident were signs that many clergy were either unmotivated or ineffective in this effort. Some clergy, many for theological reasons, simply did not accept a role for themselves or their parish in a struggle for issues of justice. In many places it was increasingly clear that the laity's response was often passive, if not hostile, to the calls for social change. Many church leaders began searching for fresh approaches.

One major Protestant response was the formation of the Chicago Urban Training Center for Christian Mission (generally called UTC).[4]

---

3. These are the Omnibus Civil Rights Act of 1964, the Voting Rights Act of 1965, and the Civil Rights Act of 1968 prohibiting discrimination in housing.

4. The major report on UTC, including on many other similar urban (action) training programs, is Younger, *From New Creation*.

From across the country and from nearly every major Christian body, urban mission executives gathered and initiated an ecumenical training program for clergy. It was housed in a large, well-worn church facility at Ashland Avenue and Madison Street, in the heart of a blighted, poverty-stricken section of Chicago. All the major Lutheran bodies were key players in the effort of development, support, and recruitment. Dr. Richard Luecke, a Lutheran pastor, was the director of theological studies. The program attracted a great deal of attention among clergy. Parish pastors—suburban, inner-city, and even some from rural areas—were given intensive exposure to the conflicted urban issues of the day.

Several dramatic experiences stood out for most participants. One was the "Plunge," an early event in the three-week program and an emotional encounter with the reality of urban poverty. Participants left all belongings behind at the Center except for $8.00. They were set loose, at their own private and personal discretion, to experience a personal immersion within the city's severely blighted areas—often among the poorest of the poor—finding their own places for three nights' sleep, and obtaining food and shelter for survival for four days on what little they had. "Scales fall from [the participants'] eyes," is how Episcopal Father James P. Morton, the UTC director, described the experience to *Time* magazine in 1965.[5] The second major experience was engaging "community organizing." The exposure venues varied greatly, from attendance at the largest citywide organization, Jesse Jackson's Operation Breadbasket, to visits to many other endeavors, smaller but just as dedicated. Many religious and community leaders were taking a chapter from the labor movement, specifically, the effectiveness of "people power"—a sizeable number of people united in organized protest against a clearly recognized social or political issue. Key factors were learning how to draw the attention of the news media, to involve public officials, and to arouse a constituency to action. Saul Alinsky, the professional community organizer who was both admired by many and despised by many, was for some a mentor in this effort. He may be best remembered by friend and foe for his insistence that to succeed in any protest one had to "rub raw the sores of discontent."[6]

5. Morton, "Clergy."

6. While ridiculed by many, especially conservatives, Alinsky's methodology was later taken up by the political right—indeed, by some church dissidents against assumed "liberals."

Many pastors came to the Chicago Training Center deeply conscious of the increasing injustices inflicted upon the members of their city churches. Bulldozers were busy, running through the inner city, cutting paths for construction of the interstate highway system, uprooting people and neighborhoods, and clearing many blocks of housing in order to stack poor people into high-rise public housing. Whether intentional or not, the proposed interstate routes through the nation's cities frequently demolished the homes of those with the least political clout: the poor. At the same time, there were massive federal housing projects underway in the 1950s and '60s, and cities saw opportunities to clear immense sections of debilitated housing and stack those who were dislocated into high-rise apartments, making space for new construction—especially commercial redevelopments that would, it was hoped, increase the city's taxable sources of income. St. Louis and Chicago are good examples of such cities. Each cleared huge sections of their lower-income neighborhoods, often blighted areas, and erected (respectively) the Pruitt Igoe and Robert Taylor complexes: huge, dense, high-rise apartment buildings, impossible places to raise children as well as a breeding ground for seemingly uncontrollable crime.

Assisted by professional community organizers, events in the Marquette neighborhood of Chicago's south side became a major news story and the center of theological discussion. A community organization, heavily represented by the churches in the area, carried on an adversarial confrontation with both the University of Chicago and the city of Chicago. The *Christian Century* aired this confrontation and offered a great deal of critical discussion on the subject. The university and the city were seen by many at the time to be recklessly taking housing and destroying long-established neighborhoods of the poor. The movement on Chicago's south side is merely one example of activities current at that time throughout the country's urban areas and a focus of UTC's engagements. The Chicago Urban Training Center was highly effective, when measured against the objectives of the program. Many pastors, and I include myself, became energized through the intense training. However, a problem soon became evident. Many pastors returned to their parishes, highly charged emotionally. They were determined to effect change in their communities through the witness of their congregations and by participation in various forms of community organizations. The training was effective in converting somewhat passive pastors to become highly motivated and now seemingly willing to take risks, often assuming that their back-home members would do the same. Upon returning home, however, pastors often quickly discovered that the people were less than enthused with their minister's agenda. Once the pastor encountered the stark reality of strong resistance and sometimes outright hostility, several responses became common. There were pastors who charged in, battled opposition, and then retreated under unbearable conflict, achieving little; or pastors who hung in with a badly divided congregation. In other cases, congregations gave their pastors (unwritten) permission or tolerance to "do your thing"—such as marching in a demonstration, perhaps even going to Washington, D.C., for a massive gathering on the Capital Mall—but requested, "leave us alone." There indeed were other congregations that joined their pastors and together "took up spiritual arms." With neighboring churches and other community groups they organized and protested on the streets as they engaged local or city-wide injustices.

This observation could be made at the time: Inner-city congregations with a strong component of African Americans were out in front, especially on racial issues; while suburban churches, with few exceptions, expressed little or no public involvement. College town-and-gown congregations varied in their response to the war. Campus congregations composed primarily of students were upfront, able to "march" often with a high degree of unity on the issues of poverty, race, and especially the Vietnam war, and at times, women's liberation. There were indeed a few exceptions. It must be remembered that the military draft, then in full force, added a great deal of fuel to the burning issue of protesting the war. As the years unfolded, one question was increasingly asked in many quarters, "How might pastors better help their congregation to become as energized and as committed as they were?" At the height of this period, a few theologians and a number of church leaders began to ask different questions. One line of questioning went something like this: "Why are we marching outside these buildings and institutions, protesting the ethical practices of those serving inside, when many of these same people are gathered in Christian worship on Sunday?" In some circles answers, to that question began to gain consensus, sometimes for differing reasons: "The local congregation is not equipped to engage these issues," and some went on "nor will it ever be." When pastors did attempt to engage their people, it was often seen as an indictment, leading to polarization, conflict, and little change. The discussion continued, "Let's try something else. Let's find ways of gathering Christians who work in various venues of our cities and exercise less confrontation. Let's practice more and better listening, and where possible, enlist, train, and support a greater number of Christians as 'change agents' for social justice in their workplace, in their communities, and in their churches." This in many ways reflected a bottom-up approach. Thus began an exciting movement of new models of Christian ministry, nearly all ecumenical. A good number were small, though a few were well-funded. Each was designed to reach Christians in their work: commercial, industrial, governmental, and academic. Three of the larger efforts were the Detroit Industrial Mission, the Wall Street Mission in Manhattan, and the Metropolitan Associates of Philadelphia.[7] Funding for these efforts was possible because of the relative wealth of the church bodies in the years following World War II. In many respects these efforts reflected the approaches of German Christians following World War II in the development of the Evangelical Academies. In one sense, this approach took the church to where the people worked, which the church had long attempted to do in campus ministries and in the military chaplaincy.

As the Vietnam protests increased and the nation became ever more divided, funding for these experimental ministries dried up, and eventually all were disbanded by the late 1970s. Subsequent years produced no thorough autopsies—that is, critical reviews to benefit later generations.[8] What we learned in that creative period has nearly been lost. As one who served three years on the Philadelphia project, I can share what I learned and what I gather some colleagues felt in similar ways. Very simply it was this: These creative efforts—gathering Christians in critical, reflective groups in their workplaces or around their common work experiences—afforded a strategic approach to enabling both growth and greater sensitization to issues of social injustices, and provided opportunities for developing cell groups committed to social change. What was attempted then ought not to be passed over lightly; there is more we can learn from this rather brief history.

---

7. Younger, *From New Creation*, 125–27. Younger details the nature and history of these programs.

8. Younger's report of these many programs is apparently the sole published study. Since it is primarily a survey about the action training programs (1962–75), it is generally recognized to be weak as a critical review of the identified programs.

Differing Theological and Ecclesiastical Approaches

On the negative side, a serious flaw was evident: the disconnect of these programs from the local congregation. Following the publication of Harvey Cox's popular book, *The Secular City* (1965), a mantra was often spoken by some: "The local congregation needs to be collapsed into the world." How ironic. I look back on that period from the present and chuckle. The local congregation may not be thriving but it is very much alive throughout the country, while nearly all of our great experimental ministries of the '60s and early '70s have vanished.

During the later period of the civil rights movement, the expectations of those in the movement were severely shaken. With Stokely Carmichael calling for Black Power, the integration movement became fractured. Many, following the shout of Carmichael, claimed that *whites* were again controlling minorities with their claim, "We are all one." They argued that the white community, under the cover of equality and generosity, was still in power and in control, frustrating and obstructing the black people's realization of their own destiny. The solution was that the black community had to move out on their own and take control of their own future through the utilization of their own power, Black Power. This dilemma continues to perplex relations between the white community and the black community. When and how ought the dominant group exercise care and concern, politically and socially, for the African American community or any other minority while in no way controlling it? The self-perception of those in a white activist group may be that they are certain they are noncontrolling and entirely freeing in their relations with a black group, while the perception of the black group may be quite different.

Official Church Proclamations and Testimonies at Congregational Hearings

Resolutions of synods and assemblies, proclamations of church officials and testimonies at congressional hearings—how effective are these? Among many of the mainline historic churches there may be heard various public voices and statements expressing the church's position on certain social issues currently confronting the nation or a state. These are efforts to make sure the "the public church" is heard. A few illustrations of ineffective efforts in engaging a social injustice may be helpful.

In the heat of the civil rights protest period, the large Eastern Pennsylvania Synod, the the regional body of the Lutheran Church In America (a predecessar body of the ELCA) offers an example of ineffectiveness, though their intentions were most honorable. With the majority of their large and influential congregations located in the greater Philadelphia area, they gathered in fall 1964 for their annual assembly in the Poconos, 80 miles north. There, strongly committed spokespeople challenged the assembly to join in the public protests against racial injustices then escalating in the South. In response, the assembly passed several sharply worded resolutions. These summoned their membership to become involved, encouraged clergy to join the protests, and included provisions authorizing the synod treasurer to use church funds to bail out clergy arrested in a demonstration. As the delegates were returning home, these resolutions hit the front page of the major news papers in eastern Pennsylvania. Suddenly the president of the synod (not yet called a bishop) came under severe attack from members of his church body. Months later (March 1965) there came the call from Martin Luther King Jr. for committed followers to gather in Selma for a march to Montgomery. Several pastors of the synod responded and went to their synod president, requesting his public blessing on their leave for Selma. His reply was, in effect, "nothing doing!" The president, though inwardly torn on the issue, felt he could not publicly support their participation in the Selma march, given the adverse reaction to the earlier resolutions by the synod's membership. Meeting in a resort off in the Poconos, the synod assembly had failed to anticipate the reaction back home. As the assembly debated the issues, they had no assurance that the synod's leadership would or could take the heat of a known opposition to such resolutions, or that pastors would return to their congregations and gain their members' support. The voting delegates were either unaware of how their back-home members would respond or, if informed, they did not prepare themselves for the backlash. When the "rubber hit the road," the witness of the Eastern Pennsylvania Synod went nowhere.

My own church body (at that time the LCMS), meeting in New York City for their churchwide convention, passed a strongly worded resolution advocating a practice of "open housing, " calling for a federal law to eliminate discrimination in housing. The resolution was the result of an effort by a highly dedicated, unofficial organization within the church body, the Lutheran Human Relations Association of America

(LHRAA). Once everyone returned home, silence on the issue by the church's leadership was the only response. Efforts by the leadership of LHRAA to compel the church body to publicize the position adopted by the church fell on deaf ears. Nothing happened.

Another more recent example is also illustrative. In the late 1980s there was a protracted strike by the coal miners of West Virginia. The mines were owned by a huge conglomerate whose corporate offices were in Greenwich, Connecticut. In a clever move by the union, a large contingent of miners traveled from the hills of West Virginia to the corporate headquarters of their adversary; there they began picketing the company, attracting considerable attention in the news. Presentations by their leaders, passionately appealing for support, were also made to area clergy groups. The ELCA's regional synod gathered for their annual assembly near Greenwich at the height of the confrontation. A resolution was introduced through the assembly's proper synodical channels calling for the assembly's identification with the cause of the striking union and an assurance to the miners of the church's support for their cause. The resolution was adopted without debate and with no registered dissent.

As a son of a union worker, I was flabbergasted at the ease with which the resolution moved through to the floor and was adopted without objection or question. Because I was also living in the Greenwich area and knew many of the pastors and lay delegates, I made my own informal study of what had preceded the introduction of the resolution. Apparently, the pastor who had promoted the resolution was the only clergyperson at the assembly who had been associated with earlier discussions of the worker's plight. He alone wrote the resolution that advanced to the floor for a vote. He was also the son of a coal miner. As I talked with lay delegates from his church and from other churches of the area, inquiring if there had been any prior discussion within their congregation of the mining company's injustice against the miners, I generally received a blank stare, suggesting, "What are you talking about?" One congregational council person responded sharply, "Our pastor wouldn't think of raising such a resolution at any meeting of our congregation; he'd be laughed at." Following the assembly, the news media made no mention of the synod's resolution. One might conjecture that the press might have reported the resolution had it received strong opposition or if it had failed. Even though many most likely felt negative to the resolution, they did not want to embarrass their church if a negative position was made public; or the delegates concluded that such expressions of social concern were allowable when spoken from this ethereal level. So they quickly passed it and got on with other matters.

We are not lifting up these public declarations by a synod assembly or a churchwide convention to question the appropriateness of a church's public support or to protest on issues of injustice, nor even whether this union deserved such a resolution. These may be extreme examples, but ingredients of the process are similar to much of what happens at churchwide and regional assemblies of our church bodies. The question I raise is simply this: Is the passing of resolutions that have questionable support back home an effective witness of the church? Are such resolutions offered and often approved because of the personal need of those proposing such resolutions, or are they presented and passed to meet strategically the needs of folks suffering an injustice (that is, to correct a wrong)? It is often said that the church in assembly must speak prophetically, and that is, to boldly address issues of injustices both to its constituency and to the general public. If this is so, then one must insist that such resolutions include specifics on how such declarations will be carried back to the delegates' councils and congregations. What might the assembly attach to such resolutions to show that it is prepared to suffer and shed its own blood for the cause of those for whom it claims to share a social and economic pain? Or, if an assembly is certain that the church must address the issue, then the synod's congregations should know and practice specifically that which they have so far failed to do. Specifics ought to be attached to the resolution, pledging each delegate to proceed with a defined plan of advocacy in the context of their own congregation: that is, one should not agree to the resolution unless one is willing to proceed accordingly. Even these suggestions signal a top-down approach, an approach which I am convinced achieves fewer and fewer intended results in today's culture.

Who Stands behind the Church's Public Pronouncements?

A story is told about how Josef Stalin replied to a member of his staff who told him that the Vatican would oppose a plan the Russians were about to pursue. Stalin asked, "How many divisions [of troops] does the pope have?" As church executives testify before committees of Congress, advocating a policy related to a church's statement adopted by the delegates at its assemblies, the senators will certainly listen carefully, but they will be less attentive if there is suspicion that the mass of the executive's church body are not in line with their church body's public statement. Quietly the legislators are thinking: "How many of your members support your church's position?" One reason the religious right has been intensely courted in some political circles in recent years is the fact that they have delivered the votes relative to specific convictions on public policy.

A vital and effective Christian organization, Bread for the World, has been most successful in enabling public officials to be both aware of and supportive of specific legislation related to issues of hunger on local, national, and international levels. Bread for the World has an identified and committed ecumenical membership from congregations across the country that funds a well-trained staff dedicated to alerting its members to advocate for specific pieces of legislation and to assist its membership in contacting their public officials via phone calls and letter-writing campaigns to advance legislation that meet the needs of the poor and the hungry. And because they represent a known, dedicated, and significantly large membership, their official spokespeople and the advocacy by their members attract the attention of both the media and elected officials. Indeed, because their spokespeople are well informed relative to the moral issues of poverty, they are listened to.

When a church official addresses an issue on public policy, one assumes that the spokesperson is able to make a moral argument for a particular issue, and that such may and should have an effect on an official of government, even if the church's spokesperson is not representative of the membership. We have no intentions here of calling a halt to the church speaking on crucial issues of justice. There surely are times and issues warranting a bishop's public statement or a church assembly's declaration by resolution. Our concern is to discover a means by which the local congregation can itself be alert and sensitive to public, moral issues of injustices and can learn to grow with courage in engaging such issues either as part of a body of faith or as individuals in concert with people who share similar convictions relative to the issue.

Personal Risk: A Crucial Ingredient of Social Protest toward Effecting Change

In terms of risk, there are sharp differences among those who protested racial injustices in the South. Ecclesiastical officials generally enjoy an expense account for travel. It is one thing for them—all expenses paid—to protest racial injustice in the South, taking a hotel room and the next morning picking up a placard and leading a protest march. Compare this to the strong witness of an African American in rural Mississippi who dropped his plough, put on his best bib-overall, and with family and at their own expense boarded a bus for an all-night ride to Selma to join with others in the march to Montgomery. Or compare those of us in the North, protected by our civil rights and the police, making our marches and returning home without a threat to our lives with the powerful witness of the students who drove through the night from Chicago to assist African Americans in Alabama with voter registration, knowing their lives were on the line (indeed, three were savagely murdered). There is a direct relationship between the risk a spokesperson is willing to take and the impact of that individual's witness regarding a particular issue. To be sure, the African American farmer from Mississippi never might have been moved to join the march had he and others like him not heard the call from recognized religious and civic leaders whom they trusted. At strategic moments the voices of the bishops for social action is crucial, as is the willingness to accept the high risk of speaking publicly.

The past century cannot be claimed to be a period of great advancement by the Christian churches in their ministries relative to issues of social justice. The failure of the local congregation to energize even a minority of its members to engage serious injustices should be openly discussed and studied. Or perhaps even more disconcerting is the fact that the masses within the Christian community show seemingly little ability to engage major social issues seriously, unless the issue threatens the people personally. In other words, we Christians may not want to be too hard on those German Lutherans and other Christians in their failure to stand up against Fascism as it was rising in power. Our own record on issues far less threatening than those that confronted Germany in the 1930s might suggest that, should such a challenge confront us, we might be as impotent or as asleep as many of them appeared to have been.

The Struggle for a Prophetic Church

Again, how can leadership facilitate sensitization of a congregation—at least a significant segment of its members—toward greater concern and willingness to act with a degree of courage on an issue of injustice? There are no simple answers, but here are several illustrations that I think point to what is crucial. The illustrations focus on examples both of effective actions and of missed opportunities.

Is a Gradual Approach Acceptable?

Rome was not built in a day, nor will one likely find a response in a congregation simply because the pastor preached a powerful sermon calling for change in social behavior. Determination, patience, persistence, creativity, wisdom, and courage are necessary. While serving on the staff of an ecumenical ministry in Philadelphia during the height of the civil rights movement, I was sensitive to my colleagues' critical comments about the apparent lack of Lutheran involvement in the movement. So I was eager, perhaps at times too eager, to lift up reports of Lutheran churches and especially Lutheran clergy's heroic stances when reported in the public press. On the Monday following the killing of the African American Sunday school children in the Sixteenth Street Baptist Church in Birmingham, Alabama, Lutheran pastors in Birmingham gathered to consider what had happened. They were all ministers of white congregations in the city except for one, who was a white pastor of the only African American Lutheran congregation in Birmingham. The latter pastor took the group to task about their passivity and their failure to confront the racial bigotry in their congregations. He challenged them to confess from their pulpits their and their congregation's complicity in that racial slaughter of children, and call their congregations to repentance.

The challenger was Joseph Ellwanger. He and his congregation were actively involved in the civil rights movement.[9] One white pastor responded to Joe's challenge. The following Sunday he poured his heart out in his sermon, acknowledging guilt and calling all—including himself—to confession and repentance. Within several days following the Sunday sermon, the congregation forced the pastor from the pastoral office. It was a national news story. At that time I commented to a small

---

9. At the completion of the Selma march to Montgomery, Pastor Ellwanger was the only white to join with other civil rights leaders in walking up the steps of the Alabama Capital to confront George Wallace, the segregationist governor of Alabama.

ecumenical group of Philadelphia clergy about my pride in the white pastor's bold witness and willingness to suffer for the cause, enduring the consequence of his witness. A black pastor in the group with extensive experience among the white churches of the deep South reacted with anger, showing no sympathy for the pastor nor for my comments. An exchange followed. A white colleague picked up the discussion by asking: "What else should the pastor have done?" "A lot," answered the black pastor. "What were he and other clergy doing for the past ten years in their respective parishes? Those pastors had spent years, as had so many of their colleagues in the white churches of the South, doing absolutely nothing!" He went on, showing a great deal of understanding of the deep-seated racial bigotry and hostility toward anyone publicly advocating racial change within their white southern churches at that time. Then he startled us in using a forbidden word in our northern liberal vocabulary: "gradualism."

He maintained that the southern white pastors never even raised a question about their churches' racial attitudes until guilt struck them because of the death of the Birmingham children. "Why," he asked, "did they not at least work ever so *gradually*, gaining perhaps at least a few like-minded supporters?" He continued, even willing to suggest that pastors might have had to work in an almost undercover manner, knowing that to push too hard on an issue would end any effort to bring about further change, but that to do nothing was the greatest evil.

Could gradualism be an acceptable approach? The civil rights movement was a period of confrontation in the North and in the South. In many situations you could not duck the issue. It was "in your face." At that moment in history you could not go back and begin all over. It was nearly impossible to avoid the issue, though indeed many did succeed in doing so. Regardless of your own (if you were white) or your white church's history, good people could only be confronted, confess, and suffer the consequences, but not wear merit badges, especially when nothing had been done earlier.

A People Convicted against Their Will Are of That Opinion Still

When the first 707 airplane landed at O'Hare Field, I was cutting my teeth as the initial pastor of a suburban Lutheran congregation northwest of Chicago. A congregation in that area need do little to grow.

Christians were flocking out of Chicago, moving along suburban Northwest Highway, looking for a new home and a new church. Sixty members were released en masse from a large, old, well-established neighboring Lutheran congregation. With many of my younger pastoral friends, I shared a concern for developing a congregational stewardship within our parish that avoided commercial fundraising for church support. I soon discovered that the mother churches in the area were very active and successful in raising money through such commercial activities as feeding the Lions Club and holding bake sales, Christmas bazaars, and rummage sales. It also did not take long to discover there was a strong, similar commitment among some of our newly formed congregation to do the same. While planning the design for a building with the architect, a controversy arose among women and men leaders on the size of the designated space for the kitchen and on the budget for appliances.

Soon after my arrival in the area, the editor of the regional newspaper briefed me on the living conditions of migrant workers on the farms near our church: during harvest time they were housed in indecent quarters. Most farms in the area were owned by Lutherans, members of our mother churches. It took little to confirm the deplorable conditions.

The concrete had hardly dried in our new church building when the congregation held a rummage sale and passed out flyers to the migrant workers living on these nearby farms. When I arrived for the opening night of the sale of clothing and household items in the undercroft, I discovered the stairs to the sanctuary were roped off with a sign, "Do not enter." I bristled! Most of the congregation appeared neutral on the issue, though the church council and I we were clearly of two different minds. I maintained my position on discouraging commercial activity as a source of congregational income; they continued committed to such. In other areas everyone seemed happy. The church was growing. Then one Sunday, following the service, I received a call from the circuit counselor (an area dean) reporting that a delegation of two from our church council had come to see him, protesting my pastoral leadership with special reference to my discouraging dinners for profit, bazaars, and rummage sales. I quickly consulted with several wise and seasoned pastors, assessed the situation, and chose (wisely, I thought at the time) not to make it a public issue within the congregation. If I had, we could easily have had a bitter church conflict and few minds would have changed. I simply insisted that a council meeting be held and that a senior official of the District be present for a review of the charges.

A meeting was convened. After an hour-long session, the district's official declared there was nothing that the pastor had done that brought into question my fidelity to the office of public ministry. The official said little more. He could not, since his congregation was riddled with similar activities. Soon after, I was able to accept a call to begin another new parish in the East. The Illinois congregation gave us a delightful farewell. But as the years passed, and as I looked back, I realized that a great deal of the problem lay at my own doorstep. While I did not intentionally despise those who disagreed with me, I gave them little or no time to freely express their position. I began a critical review; I began to question my actions. Should I have hung in there, quietly but persistently showing a better way—a biblical way—of giving funds to the church and thereby gradually reducing the church's commercial activities? Might we over time have enabled at least a small group of us to pursue ministry with the migrant workers and their Lutheran employers, especially finding better housing on the farms where they were working? That would not have been an easy task. Only over the years did I realize that here was an issue that could allow for a definite but gradual plan of slowly but surely helping the leadership, including me and the membership, to grow and change together. I did not have to achieve success within a year. What I surely needed to do, but did not, was to show genuine concern for the opposition as people. They needed genuinely to feel that I cared for them as people in spite of the differences between us or as we together engaged the issue. This is not easy, but it is crucial!

There is a need in every situation to assess the issue that troubles us as pastors and as congregational leaders. Is it an issue of injustices, an issue that is so evil you are certain God calls for condemnation without reservation and without delay? Is it like the days of the civil rights movement, a crucial time for the nation, when you could not take time to do what for years had not been done? Certainly, a nonnegotiable issue was and is the acceptance of an African American person or any other confessing Christian into the life of a congregation. Is it an issue that you cannot duck, but one that needs an ongoing commitment, a strategy, and tactics permeated with genuine love and concern for all, especially for those who appear to differ? But how do you keep from letting this commitment to a gradual approach become the means by which a crucial issue slips from your priorities and drifts into oblivion? Sometimes you need to ask (no, demand) a trusted colleague to check on you regularly, holding your feet to the fire on the issue. You need to report to the colleague regularly what you are doing and what progress you are making as you engage the issue. Such a trusted colleague needs to be a sounding board for a critical review of your thinking and your efforts. What is called for is a loving engagement of the people or individuals as you together make a difference.

Once, when I was beginning a new position, I asked two friends (independently of each other) what advice they would give me as I began my new assignment. They both knew me well and also knew the position I was about to enter. Said the one, "Don't screw up!" Said the other, "Love the people." Neither advice was easy to follow, but I can assure you that the latter charge was the one that would make all the difference in the quality of my ministry — as it would be in anyone's work. What is being said here about a lonely pastor in the midst of a socially insensitive congregation may in another congregation be said of the laity (singular or plural) who are sensitive when their pastor and/or the general membership of the congregation are insensitive.

Should a Church Body Engage in Political Compromise?

What is the role of the people when officials of the church take on a public issue? With the turn of the twenty-first century, we who were living in eastern Massachusetts found ourselves in the epicenter of a major scandal—the disclosure of an ever-increasing number of Roman Catholic priests found guilty of sexually abusing young boys. Among many shocking disclosures were the detailed reports of years of cover-up of this offensive behavior: cover-ups by government officials, prosecuting attorneys, law enforcement officials, and by bishops and cardinals of the Catholic Church in Boston and throughout the state of Massachusetts. For years, faithful, devout, loyal, Irish Catholics enjoyed a clear majority in both city and state governments. They were in near-total control of all aspects of government. So also did the Catholic Church dominate the state with powerful and highly influential bishops and cardinals, and had since the days of Cardinals O'Connell (1907–44) and Cushing (1944–70). During those years, when people made accusations and charges of clergy sexual behavior—whether to the police, the courts, or church officials—they were dismissed and silenced by intimidation or, if forced into the courts or the church's chancery, the settlements that were made were sealed from the public, as were all records of the proceedings and agreements.

Our purpose here is not to replay the tragic and sad chapter in the history of the Christian church either in eastern Massachusetts or as it reverberated across the country. During this period other Christians could only counsel themselves against having joy at other people's sorrow. They also needed to support their neighboring Roman Catholic priests who were often feeling societal judgment on all priests, as though all had been guilty of such behavior.

If cover-up had been the acceptable practice by both state and church for many years, a dramatic change occurred when several deeply devoted Roman Catholic laypeople, prosecuting attorneys in the Boston area, recognized with absolute horror and astonishment what was happening. Conscience-stricken and awakened by their faith, they realized they had to act publicly and against their own church. While daring to engage the issue publicly, they knew that they would encounter hostility from many officials of the church, including Cardinal Law. They knew a sizeable section of the electorate would not appreciate their hanging the scandal before the public. The leading prosecuting attorney had as his high school teacher a priest whom he admired as a student but whom he now recognized as guilty of a most grievous crime. He was compelled to act. After many predecessors had closed their eyes to the hideous conduct of some clergy, an increasing number of elected officials began to support a thorough airing of the conditions and the charges. They could no longer keep silent. According to the *Boston Globe*: "The extent of the sexual abuse . . . , especially the church's efforts to buy the silence of the victims, shook to the core even the most devout Catholics in law enforcement and politics. A culture of deference that had taken more than a century to evolve seemed to erode in a matter of weeks."[10] The investigations and public reporting persuaded a vast number of victims to come forward, and a large number of lawsuits were filed against the diocese, resulting in the convictions of priests in criminal trials and the resignation of Cardinal Law. Court settlements also mandated the Boston Diocese to pay out huge sums of money to the victims.

As the Boston Diocese was making one settlement after another, amounting to millions in payments, the diocese began to insist before

10. Boston Globe, *Betrayal*, 120.

judges and through the press that its treasury was being depleted, that it had no more money to pay out as the demands for continued financial settlements increased. Concurrently it announced the decision to close a number of parishes—all this made necessary, according to church officials, as a direct result of the financial settlements that were draining the church's finances. Many whose churches were being closed and others maintained that the closing of parishes was a cover-up for the fact that there still was money within the treasury of the diocese. No one really knew the true situation. The church's books were closed to the public.

Now we will pick up a sequel to this tragic story, asking the question: If the church, especially the Protestant Church, sees a calling to be involved in governmental legislative processes and discovers a bill with which it does not agree, is the only appropriate response one of mobilizing the Christian community to work politically to kill the proposed bill? Is compromise a responsible posture of the church in the political arena? And does the church find itself too often most strongly present in the governmental process when it personally feels threatened, and less present when bills are pending that would support programs for the poor? And what is the role and engagement of the people—the laity—as officials of the church take up the issue?

Marian Walsh, once a Roman Catholic nun and now a lawyer elected to the Massachusetts State Senate, became the key figure in a controversy related to the state's struggle with the Roman Catholic Diocese of Boston. She proposed legislation that would ultimately be strongly attacked by the religious community and strongly defeated. The State of Massachusetts over many years required all charitable, not-for-profit organizations (including the churches) to file an annual audit with the state's office of the attorney general. In 1942 the Catholic Church, employing its considerable political clout, obtained a change in the law, exempting churches. Since then churches had not been required to file an annual audit of their finances. In 2005 Walsh proposed Senate Bill 1047, "An Act Relative to Charities in Massachusetts." It called for all churches and church bodies in the state to be fully transparent by filing an annual disclosure of their finances (including property holdings) just as the already-existing law demanded of charities. Following open debate, the Senate Bill passed 33–4, a near-unanimous vote.

The bill never got to the House, even for a debate. Suddenly the word went out to all the religious groups, claiming that the bill was a dangerous crossing of the line between church and state. Religious bodies mobilized with great force. In addition to both the Catholic bishops and the Massachusetts Council of Churches, the Black Ministerial Alliance, the Islamic Council of New England, various Jewish organizations, and conservative groups including the Massachusetts Family Institute, rallied their constituents. Bolts of lightning and thunder began to roll across the state. Bishops and religious leaders sent letters to their congregations providing talking points, identifying (in their judgment) the damaging nature of the bill and requesting congregational councils and their members to call on their state representatives to insist that the bill be defeated. The material distributed by the religious organizations claimed the bill would intrude into the rights and privacy of the religious bodies, leading to state control. The elected officials argued that such was not the case, insisting that there would not be and could not be any interference (assuming nothing was being done dishonestly or criminally). The religious groups claimed that the cost of the reporting and auditing would be financially prohibitive. Spokespeople for the bill claimed that this also was not true, indicating that the fees for filing were on a sliding scale: small religious bodies would pay very little; the largest would pay much more. This they illustrated by showing that presently even a Little League baseball team must file a financial report that cost very little, as would be true of small congregations.

Many of these religious bodies claim a role today in being present and active in the public square. They claim to have a right to engage legislation that is just and appropriate for the welfare of the common good, and that they provide a unique service to the community, for all of which they are free of taxation. My question is this: If the religious bodies claim such a position, should they not willingly—as one among many responsible parties to the political process—engage in negotiation and ultimately compromise in order to see a bill passed, one that would have social value though perhaps not to everyone's satisfaction? And when they have the slightest sense that the bill might be a financial burden on them or a time-demanding effort, why are they so quick to go for broke, willing to kill the bill? And why were there no religious leaders who dared to stand against the crowd, courageously asking the legislature to give the religious bodies time, not only for a more careful review that would enable a reduction of the emotions in order that reasonable people—religious leaders and elected officials—might work through specific concerns and problems, but also time for open and free consultation with their membership? In the absence of such voices, in the midst of the emotional moment, the religious community became totally negative towards the bill. This was clearly a top-down approach. The highly organized effort was successful, but the people were not challenged to examine on their own their understanding of and objections to the bill. The people of these religious bodies were simply called to respond negatively, much of the call colored with fear and apprehension. As is frequently seen in a religious conflict, the appearance is given that it is a matter of the "good guys" versus the "bad guys." The emotion of the moment promoted "Group Think," a compelling drive that everyone needs to stick together, muzzle all opposition (even within the ranks), and make sure no one wavers. In a gathering of both elected officials and clergy during the heat of the protest, a senior elected official was heard to say as the meeting was ending, "Too bad the religious community isn't as energized when we have a bill before the legislature that calls for support on a poverty issue."

Working with congregations over many years I have found church conflict often to be most distasteful; and for this simple reason: that church conflict too often centers on absolutes. Each side often views the other as completely wrong, and too often each sees itself morally right. Generally, in the political area, elected officials soon realize they will get nowhere with such absolutes. Lutheran theology, when engaging ethical decisions in the realm of reason and our senses, would have to agree: when engaging ethical decisions, compromise is acceptable and generally necessary. Elected officials have an insight that we in the church should share with them, namely, that in the public arena, compromise is the art of politics. What might have been different if the religious bodies of Massachusetts protesting the disclosure legislation had asked for a time-out? What if the churches had insisted on opportunities to discuss the proposed bill with the elected officials and to involve their membership in open study and free discussion? Might they have been able together to achieve a mutual understanding of the problem and a willingness to give and take, while still protecting constitutional rights and being respective of faith convictions? The church leadership surely should grant the elected officials the possibility that they too were focused on the common good.

Some Injustices May Best Be Engaged Apart from the Formal Structure of the Church

Given the nature of efforts to affect change, we might want to consider the need to facilitate and support committed Christians in organizing and doing their ministry as Christians but doing so not necessarily in the name of the church or under the church's public auspices. Let me illustrate from a personal experience. This is the account of a Minnesota farm boy who became a housing entrepreneur in a poverty neighborhood and who, because of his ministry, became the enemy both of his city and of a highly respected cultural institution. This is really an example of a bottom-up effort at engaging injustices. While I was teaching a seminary course in St. Louis in the early 1970s that focused on urban issues, a student, Jim Roos, approached me as class was ending. He made the admission, "I have just come back from my year of internship, and I learned preaching is not my calling." But that was not his purpose in approaching me. He went on, "I would like to explore a housing ministry in a poverty neighborhood here in St. Louis." He had already done his homework. He had been looking at an abandoned house in a neighborhood very familiar to me.

At that time, the Federal Housing Administration (FHA) was generously mortgaging homes in blighted neighborhoods. In order to secure financing, the seller (usually a speculator) was required by the FHA to bring the house up to code—that is, making sure the heating, plumbing, and electrical systems were all working properly. It was rumored and later documented that corruption was rampant. Speculators, who did not perform the required repairs, could easily pay off the FHA inspector and obtain FHA financing for the sale of the home at a considerable profit to an unsuspecting family, generally a first-time home buyer and generally an African American family. This practice was a forerunner of our present subprime mortgage crisis. The difference in this case was that the new home would need major, costly repairs within a few years (if not months), which was certain to push the new homeowner well beyond any financial ability to hold on to the home. Unable to meet mounting costs, the buyer had only one recourse: abandon the property. As one drove though such neighborhoods, abandoned houses were popping up everywhere.

Jim had a definite ministry plan in mind. The city was willing to sell these abandoned houses at a very low price: they were bringing further blight to already blighted neighborhoods. He would buy an abandoned home, initially do the repairs himself, and rent it at a fair price. With the assistance of several lay leaders associated with Lutheran Social Services of greater St. Louis, he was able to obtain initial financial support from a foundation and was assisted by sound legal counsel. The lawyers, wisely as I later realized, counseled that Jim's program be incorporated as a for profit—not a not-for-profit—program. The lawyers, knowing how controversial this ministry could become, realized a church-related non-profit approach could muddy the waters, leading to even greater difficulties. Later experiences of the organization proved them correct.

While one may question labeling such a program a success, it did indeed catch on. As the years progressed, Jim enlisted a good number of socially sensitive individuals willing to purchase an abandoned home. He trained neighborhood men to do the repairs, find tenants, and help collect rent or enable those who could to buy. Investors were conscious of the high risk in ever profiting from or recouping their investment. Jim and his wife Judy bought a home in the neighborhood and raised their children there. Judy, who had an advanced degree in nursing, served on the faculty of St. Louis University. The greater the number of homes Jim controlled, the greater the conflict with the city, and in later years, with the Missouri Botanical Garden. The latter—a private, heavily funded, historic institution enjoying an international reputation—was also making considerable expansion into neighborhoods where Jim's program had grown. In more recent years, major sections of the city's urban renewal plan covered housing rehabilitated by Jim's organization. As years passed, many of his houses and the houses of those who had purchased their homes were on city blocks that were increasingly earmarked for demolition through the city's right of eminent domain. The city was clearing and destroying neighborhoods and in their place building desirable, new homes close to downtown in an effort to attract middle-income families back to the city and, in the process, eliminating housing for the poor and lower-income people. Thus Jim's program became engaged in one lawsuit after another, sometimes assisted by community lawyers pro bono. City officials saw and still see his program as standing in the way of the city's redevelopment. In addition to right of eminent domain, the city had another instrument for obstructing Jim's work. Frequently his houses required inspection by the city, sometimes for questionable reasons. Just as the FHA inspectors had closed their eyes for a kickback, the city inspectors—with instructions from above to "get Roos"— could find all sorts of fault during an inspection, forcing costs on top of costs.

As the Missouri Botanical Garden began expanding, especially with efforts to bring in middle-income families and upgrading their neighborhood, they too were free by state law to use the right of eminent domain to clear streets of the homes of low-income African Americans. Again major legal battles ensued. Over a number of years, the *St. Louis Post-Dispatch*, the city's leading newspaper, made editorial attacks on Jim's work, claiming he was obstructing the progress of the city's redevelopment. Among city officials and among the many citizens who have long admired the Botanical Garden, there were harsh words for Jim. But he never wavered: he held his position. Some said he was simply stubborn, occasionally winning a court case, frequently losing cases and, at times, sums of money. Those of us who have known him through these years have always recognized him to be a man on a mission with a calling. While he was never ordained, he maintained a strong sense of a Christian calling in his unique ministry, always also present and active with his family in his church.

If you lived in St. Louis, you could also easily join the many who denounced Jim's work. If you hoped for the city's turnaround of its continued loss of citizens (1950, Pop: 856,796; 2000, Pop: 348, 189), you could easily question Jim's work and positions. If you loved flowers and the work of the Botanical Garden, as many in St. Louis do, you too might not have appreciated Jim's work or his court fights. I find myself conflicted here. Personally I have a great love for St. Louis and the Botanical Garden. And yet, with others, I recognize his is a mission of justice for the poor and low-income people on St. Louis' inner-city southwest side. Few others in the area have been known to support these people as Jim's program has and to take financial risks in doing so.

Thus in the pursuit of justice in the public arena, especially when political and economic powers are involved, the effort can become nasty, painful, and costly. And the issues are seldom one-sided. Could a church-related organization have withstood the conflicts, hung in there for the interest of the poor against public attacks, especially by the city's leading newspaper? I doubt it. Indeed, the Lutheran social service agency was a truly creative, innovative, daring organization as I knew it in times past. If Jim's program was structurally related to theirs (as some earlier thought it should be), his public fights could not have been tolerated. A lesson learned: We simply need to encourage and support visionary Christians in the pursuit of justice to work outside the official structure of the institutional church and yet with the support not only of the community of faith but also with non-Christians, as has been the case in Jim's work and service.

This is also an example of the harsh realities you will most likely encounter if you tamper with the powers that be, when economic, political, and cultural values are threatened by your witness. What the Germans call *Realpolitik*, the harsh nature of political engagement, ought not to deter Christians from entering the fray, as long as they count the cost before foolishly engaging an issue. Wisdom and our senses, and at times patience and especially courage, are valid instruments and ingredients of Christian discernment. Yet again comes the reminder that too much analysis may lead to paralysis.

9

Working toward an Inverted Church

I SEE TWO MAJOR WAYS THROUGH WHICH WE CAN WORK TOward an inverted church. First of all, the leadership at the church's highest level needs a fresh paradigm. Rather than focus solely on the mission and ministry of the ordained as the primary, if not the sole, avenue of ministry, we need to turn this around. Recall the words in chapter 1: *The people in the pew, pouring out of the church into their various vocations following public worship, should be seen as the front line of the church's ministry and mission. Below them, uplifting and supporting them, there are the bishops and the pastors and leaders of the congregation.* A paradigmatic change means both a whole new way of commitment—a different way of thinking and acting—and in this case, a commitment to significant change in church programming.

In 1988 the newly organized ELCA's national body included an Office of Ministry in Daily Life, similar to an office in the LCA (a predecessor body to the ELCA). However, after fifteen years, the church's national leadership closed this office for various reasons, transferring it to an office within the Episcopal Church and sliding aspects of its work into another existing division where it appears to be lost to the general public. The issue is even now more out of sight and out of mind in the public expressions of the church. Just at a time when a burst of theological energy is being unleashed through a great number of books on the subject, the ELCA closes its sole office advocating the ministry of the laity.

However, the mere presence of an official office within a church body does not assure that the needs we are discussing will be met. Beginning at the highest levels and moving to all levels, the church's leadership must model for the local congregation and clusters of churches ways to engage the people toward an increased knowledge of and a greater sensitivity to their ministry in daily life. The paradigm proposed does not necessarily require a specific office in order to succeed. Rather there needs to be a commitment to the paradigm throughout the various units of the church, with the presiding bishop's office overseeing its development in all units of the church.

The proposed paradigm also necessitates a critical review of major current efforts within the church that specifically promote programs which train the laity for ministry. When many of these are examined, one discovers they are often primarily training a select group in and for the local congregation's pastoral ministry. An example: a recent report of a synod's lay school of theology focused on a large group of laity in a training session on "How to Prepare a Sermon." The substance of the training for lay ministry was identified with the vocation of public ministry. Clearly absent in the curriculum was any emphasis on a Lutheran understanding of ministry in daily life, ministry in and through various vocations. (To be sure, the schools of lay theology are to be commended for their providing opportunities for a more in-depth study of the Christian faith than is usually available to the laity.)

One of the last major efforts of the Office of Ministry in Daily Life during its ELCA tenure was a demonstration project, a conference on the ministry of lawyers and judges. Gathering in a Chicago hotel, people in the legal profession participated in discussions relative to their work in light of biblical and Lutheran theology, especially the Christian calling and the nature of Christian ethics related to a specific vocation. Its purpose was to test an approach, get the "bugs" out, and make it moveable for adoption to other clusters throughout the country. With the closing of the office, no further programs have been pursued. All should not be lost. Variations of this effort could be made for a wide range of vocations: teachers, people in the health sciences, union leaders, and business executives. There's no end to the possibilities; for instance, a presentation by theological specialists in the field of Christian ethics, setting faith parameters within which the laity would be encouraged to share their experiences. An integral part of this is sharing case studies, seeking critical review and clarification of ethical insight relative to Christian faith and witness in their particular vocation. An aspect of such events ought to be the inclusion of pastors from participating congregations. Their task would be primarily to listen, and then in separate sessions be asked to explore insights gained on how they might be supportive to those of their members whose vocation and profession is law. This is not a put-down. Simply listening as a pastor to the ethical cases confronting the lawyer sharpens an awareness that each vocation is limited in what specifically one can counsel from one's own vocation. This includes clergy. While there is clearly a substantive entity in the message and role of the ordained that needs to be heard (as the same needs to be heard from the laity in each respective vocation), there is also a clearly understood limitation to what can be said. This becomes especially evident at times with quiet listening. Such weekend gatherings could be an outgrowth of the experimental ministries of the 1960s and '70s as described earlier. They would be similar to gatherings at the Evangelical Academies in Germany following the Second World War.

Second, pastors—in preaching, teaching, and model building—need to help those of us in the pew to discover and to clarify our respective Christian callings. We need continued help in recognizing how an active faith moves from a conviction of Christ's redeeming of our lives toward ethical decisions and public witness, as each of us as travels along the Christian way, never isolated but together as members of a body of support, the faith community. We need weekly reminders how our faith, active with Christ's love, inevitably shapes our various callings, including attention to issues of justice. The interactive nature of the Internet offers a model, suggesting opportunity for all kinds of feedback and intergroup discussion on a wide variety of subjects. Many are no longer comfortable to be "talked to" in a sermon; no longer can preaching be experienced as monologue. Clearly we now need, more than ever, sermons that are open for dialogue, including various manners of interactive engagement of the word.

In mobilizing the people for active social ministry, the commitment and the skill of the pastor is most important, as is recognizing the freedom of the Christian when some feel otherwise. While living in St. Louis in the early '70s, I got a call from a friend in New Jersey, Pastor Vernon Schreiber. Many members of his parish worked in Manhattan. He asked if I could help a family from his congregation that was relocating to St.

Louis. He said they were hoping to find a home in an integrated neighborhood. I was immediately struck by this nontypical request. Then a greater shock: Ken Bitter, the father of the family, was becoming a senior financial officer of one of the largest corporations headquartered in our city. They did indeed find housing in the kind of neighborhood they desired. After they settled into their new home, I began to learn more. On an occasion when we were reflecting on our respective work, Ken said that in his position within this Fortune 500 company he had seen a clear calling to demilitarize the program. Once, in a relaxed moment, I asked, "Ken, how did you become committed to such bold social change, such as promoting integrated housing and being committed to a reduction of your company's military production? These are controversial commitments." "Oh," he said, "we were conservatives, religiously, socially, and politically, and suspicious of the civil rights movement when we moved to New Jersey from Southern California. At our new church we came under the ministry of Pastor Vern." He went on, "Just days following the riots in Harlem [after the assassination of Dr. Martin Luther King Jr.], our pastor invited members to join a group going with him on the following Saturday to Harlem. There we would join other concerned groups in helping to clean up neighborhoods that were badly damaged by the riots. Pat and I accepted his invitation, not so much because we wanted to be involved in a social or racial issue, but because our pastor had a most unusual care for people. Though quite fearful, we somehow mustered courage and went to Harlem that Saturday. We swept up broken glass beside others who, we realized, were of a different color. We were sweating together with people very different from ourselves. Together—the first time in our lives—Pat and I sat down with blacks and had lunch together in a riot-trashed neighborhood. There I began to feel their pain, especially when a black man began to explain to us the anger within his people, anger that had exploded into this tragic blunder. Having lost nearly everything, the black store owner was not complaining; with others he was busy picking up the pieces."

I knew Ken's pastor well. Low-keyed, he was not one to give a congregation a guilt trip. He knew the gospel, and from the gospel he shared the love of Christ with the people of his parish and with any person whose need he had come to know. He led his congregation in efforts toward integrated housing in their relatively upscale New Jersey community; he did so openly yet without flair. The local Jewish community gave Pastor Vern and his congregation a B'nai Brith award for courage in pursuing their social ministry, especially for their work toward open housing. Pastoral leadership is all-important in modeling the godly life, which surely envelops personal action, because of a commitment to the gospel and a willingness to take risks for others in need. Pastor Vern was neither boastful nor a loner. Always inviting others to join in, he was careful not to pass judgment on those not taking such actions whether because they were too fearful to join in or were skeptical of the reasons offered for joining in. In the midst of good biblical preaching and teaching, one could not escape the truth that their congregation was called to ministry for others under the cross of Christ. Vern was also known as a pastor who was genuinely felt by members to be one among them, very much a pastor.

A key to sensitizing a congregation is both the word and the creation of opportunities for exposure to alternate lifestyles, especially to social conditions and to public attitudes that oppress others. Such was the effectiveness of Pastor Vern's ministry and the Chicago Urban Training program for clergy. Faith provides the courage to remove the blinders from our eyes, to dare to go to unusual places, to read discomforting literature, and to engage people whose culture and history are far different than our own.

Pastors' spouses may also be strong witnesses and models of the godly life, even in things that seemingly so simple. In the early 1950s, Karl Lutze had just been ordained and had become the pastor of an African American Lutheran congregation in a southern industrial town. He and his fiancée, Esther, were to be married a year later, so Karl began his ministry as a single person. Following his wedding and the arrival of his wife, he began to recognize a considerable increase in the Sunday attendance. After a number of months of still- growing attendance, he commented to a church elder: "Has my preaching become so much better since I've married, attracting more people?" After a moment of silence, the elder offered the explanation for the increase. "No, it has not been your preaching, but the fact that your wife is present on communion Sundays and takes the bread and wine along with all of us." Then a startling truth came out: previous pastors' spouses had gone across town on communion Sundays to receive the bread and the wine in the white Lutheran church. Esther did not. [1]

1. Lutze, *Awakening to Equality*, 38–39.

Travel tours are an often-underutilized means of expanding experientially people's exposure to social contexts foreign to their own experiences. It was Mark Twain who reminded us that "travel is fatal to prejudices, bigotry, and narrowness." Many church bodies gather groups for visits to various fields abroad, generally opportunities to discover firsthand the needs of others. A recent gathering of Lutheran youth, assembled in New Orleans after Hurricane Katrina, demonstrated an inspiring witness to one another and to others. These youth worshiped, socialized, and spent significant time in the midst of this still-devastated city. With decency and care and a significant amount of time, they publicly engaged with the many obvious needs of the people of New Orleans. It was also a powerful learning experience, as evidenced in their reports back to their congregations. But such trips, local and abroad, are costly, leaving behind many who could benefit from such trips but cannot afford them. Many travel tours are often criticized for being superficial. As the locals say in Jerusalem, "Where Jesus walked, the tourists run." It often takes time to live among and deeply identify with another people's culture and difficulties. Yet more attention needs to be given to such educational programs through travel.

While my wife and I were living and studying at Tantur, the ecumenical study center in Jerusalem on the edge of the West Bank, a Roman Catholic priest returning from the Old City told me of a large group of Lutheran tourists being guided through the narrow streets. The following Sunday, attending worship at Christmas Lutheran Church in Bethlehem, we discovered that the tour group was present and occupied nearly half of the seats for worship. After the service, visiting with the group, I learned they had been in the area for two weeks. The first week was as tourists, visiting the biblical sights; the second week, as volunteers, assisting in cleaning up the playgrounds of several Lutheran World Federation grade schools in the Bethlehem area that serve Palestinian children. Palestinians had been their supervisors. This is a good model for other tour groups to follow.

Recently I discovered in my interim ministries that a number of the members were making frequent business trips to and within developing countries. In one congregation, a member spent several months each year in various parts of China. With the encouragement of his pastor and through the assistance of the church's office of missions abroad, he was connected with Christian church leaders in the areas of his visits. There he could, on his hours off, be exposed to a dimension of his host country not generally seen through his business eyes. Volunteers, youth, and retirees are a second opportunity for increased recruitment for short-term services in challenging conditions here and abroad. Lutherans might learn here from their neighbors with whom they were uncomfortable in the Reformation: the Mennonites. Their young adults are often visibly present in various high-risk areas, in difficult and threatening situations abroad. While living in Jerusalem, I became impressed with a program known as "Peace Keepers," which was under the auspices of the Mennonite church. Peace Keepers was a visible group of young Christians, trained to mingle among groups of Israeli and Palestinian youth and to stand between conflicted groups as a street fight began to erupt. That is indeed high-risk. Many of the young people in the program are Mennonites from mid-America. For eight months I served as the interim pastor at St. Andrews, the international congregation in Cairo, Egypt. Our Christian community came from a wide range of nationalities and Christian traditions. Included was an unusual assortment of people, such as a government official from the Myanmar (Burma) embassy who with his wife and small children were in church every Sunday. And present each Sunday was the entire contingent of young Mennonite volunteers, who were housed in a home supported by their church body They actively worshiped with us: following the liturgy using the Lutheran hymnal and that in a congregation staffed by pastors from the Evangelical Lutheran Church in America. The Presbyterians had a program similar to that of the Mennonites, and their volunteers were also present every Sunday. The volunteers worshiping at St. Andrew's were all engaged in down-to-earth services, ministering in the heart of Cairo's settlements of the poorest. I was told by those who knew that there was one, only one, Lutheran volunteer from the US who had been serving in Cairo several years before we arrived. Given the numbers of Lutherans in the US and Europe, compared with the number of members of other church bodies large and small, Lutherans are generally poorly represented in such volunteer services. In very recent years, Lutheran volunteers have been regularly added to the group at St. Andrew's.

Indeed, the ELCA's global mission staff, as is the practice in similar offices in other church bodies, works hard to promote and recruit youth and retirees for service abroad. Yet the number of Lutherans who respond is small compared to the numbers recruited by many of the other church bodies. Is this reflective of a failure to encourage ourselves and others to volunteer for services in contexts foreign to our own life experiences? Does our preaching fail to engage the listener to feel called by the gospel to the challenging needs of people at home and abroad? Are we willing to suggest that service may also call for personal risk? Are we encouraging—especially our youth—to explore opportunities that are available through our church body in challenging ministries abroad? And are we actively encouraging our youth and retirees to consider two years with such groups as the Peace Corps, the AmeriCorps, or Teach For America? In many communities we need to break out of our cultural ghettoes and discover the world beyond us, realizing the exciting opportunities for service in local and distant places.

Needed are those experiences that broaden and deepen Christian awareness both of nearby and distant lifestyles and of people living in conflicted and difficult social conditions. We need opportunities to relate personally to people with social and political lifestyles and experiences considerably different from our own. The pastor and other people in the congregation are models because of their positions, clearly visible before large audiences of people of every age; how they relate to the congregation and others beyond are significant as to the message conveyed. They can be most effective in leading youth especially, as well as people of various ages, to a lifelong concern for service and for a struggle against injustice.

Seminary Education Represents a Challenge

If our pastors are themselves insensitive to other cultures and foreign social conditions, it will be difficult to expect our congregations to experience a broadening of their own perspectives. If the pastor is very important in developing a bottom-up ministry, then seminary training is a place to begin. Seminaries today devote a great deal of academic programming to the area of specialized ministry, generally titled "urban ministries." This is a good development, yet I often wonder if it inappropriately divides our metropolitan areas into rural, suburban, and urban. "Urban" today defines much of the culture of our country. It is difficult to identify today a truly "rural" culture, especially with the prevalence of TV, universal education, the Internet, and access to work from distant locations. Nor ought "urban" be seen as a synonym for "inner city" or "a poverty community." The federal government's housing policy has shifted. No longer is it federal policy to relocate poverty families into historic areas of social disorganization, that is, into the inner city. Now people of poverty are often relocated to housing scattered in suburban areas. Many of our communities today are a broad and deep mix of various subcultures, rich to poor. The well-off and the well-educated are often as emotionally and physically sick as are others in various sectors of our cities. At all times and among all, there are social and cultural factors that generate conflict, suffering, and discouragement, often unique to their place and time.

What is needed is a component of seminary education that immerses students experientially in as many of these subcultures as possible, inspiring empathy and developing skill in critical analysis. In various contexts and cultures, the seminarian (as all within the church) must learn to listen, interrelate, and become skilled at both sharing the gospel and enabling others to share, leading to a deeper exploration of the purpose of life within one's various callings. Through immersion in unfamiliar subcultures, and with proper leadership, the Christian is sensitized and develops a greater commitment to the specific needs of people in their situations of responsibility. This was the concern at Concordia Seminary (St. Louis) in the 1970s that led Bob Bertram and me to the development of a full-time, quarter-long course titled "Theology in Metropolitan Experience" with fourth-year seminarians. It was intensely interdisciplinary and highly interactive with laity in their various work places, representing a variety of social and economic circumstances.

Laypeople Are Just as Capable as Pastors of Initiating and Modeling a Commitment to Social Change, though They Often Work at the Edge of the Official Structure of the Church

I learned the phrase that titles this section as a teenager in the late 1940s through the influence of a woman in our congregation, Anna Beck. She was president of the St. Louis Lutheran Secretaries Association. This was a group of very bright, mostly single women of all ages who were secretaries in downtown corporate offices. Some today would qualify as presidents of their companies. In an effort to find a meaningful service project, she led her group in organizing and staffing a community center on South Third Street, a blighted, "colored," poverty-stricken neighborhood three blocks from the muddy Mississippi. In a rented three-story town house the effort flourished. It was staffed entirely by laypeople: women coming after work at their secretarial jobs downtown, male retirees teaching woodworking, many others recruited from white Lutheran congregations throughout the city. This was a truly inverted, bottom-up, grassroots mission and ministry of St. Louis Christians.

During the summer, white high school students were also recruited. How did Anna recruit? After church on a Sunday in early summer, she approached several of us high school students, stating that we were needed at the Center to help kids play softball. "Which day of the week and at what time will you be there?" she asked, clearly assuming we had no reason to say no. I joined the effort. Arriving at the entrance to the flat, Anna simply handed me a bat and a ball, yelled to the African American boys standing nearby, "Follow Paul and play ball," which we did on a vacant lot down the street. When I returned to the Center with the boys, she handed me some old Sunday school lesson material and said, "Gather your boys in a group and share the Bible lesson." In the course of several years I never once saw a pastor of one of our white Lutheran churches amid the swirling, congested crowd—a gathering of African American children and white lay volunteers—though I am sure some white pastors did occasionally visit. There were several black Lutheran congregations to which many of the children could be directed, but my home congregation was not an option, nor were other Lutheran white congregations in the city. In fact, the Protestant and Catholic churches of the city were ecumenically united as segregated houses of worship.

Anna Beck, a layperson, was obviously a "model of the godly life," a quiet irritant to many segregationists in white Lutheran churches, a gentle but forceful breaker of racial barriers. and an active force in setting children free to become something that the oppression of segregation had thwarted. She led me and other young people, along with countless adult white Christians, to a fresh awareness of the "others" to which Christ's calls us. In her late years she was still serving in the church's missions along the Mississippi, and while I was teaching at Concordia Seminary, Anna was awarded honorary degree.

How Can We Lead People to Engage Issues of Injustice?

The League of Women Voters might be a model, in part, for the local congregation. Supported by their national offices in engaging social and political issues, the League's local chapters are committed to careful, critical review of public policy from various viewpoints. There is careful attention to local issues. They maintain a strong nonpartisan position while modeling for their neighborhoods a personal commitment to local political involvement. Their national office is designed to support the local chapters in their particular studies and concerns. Only on major issues, generally processed from the bottom up, do their national leaders make public, political statements in the name of the League. The League's strength is recognized in its public engagement of social and political issues, its informed membership, and a grassroots witness, not in pronouncements from their national office. Might this, in part, be a significant model for the Christian church?

Experiencing Firsthand a Social Problem and Being Assisted in Following It to Its Root Causes.

Many of us pastors and youth leaders may often be too quick to tell people what the root cause of a social problem is. Rather, with coaching and support, people will grow best when they invest time and energy in discovering the root causes for themselves. For example, a church youth group joins others in cleaning a nearby creek on a Saturday. Even after cleaning the creek, the kids say, "It smells; don't swim in it!" Leadership might want to encourage them to explore why it stinks. They may, as in a case I have known, discover that a meatpacking company upstream is the apparent contaminator. On further investigation, they discover that the company is the sole source of employment in a small town where the plant is located. Encouraged by their youth leader to pursue the problem further, they contact state health officials and realize they have hit a brick wall. On inquiring of officials, it becomes clear that to force the company to meet filtration requirements will surely cause the plant to close, leading many to lose their employment with few or no possibilities for alternative employment. What ought to be done? What began as a local effort follows a line of inquiry that leads one beyond the local, to the state capital and to various governmental departments. The issue is complex and challenging.

Another illustration: In 1973 my wife and I were guests of the Lutheran mission hospital in Amber, India. One evening a hospital doctor took us for a walk through a part of the town where locals tanned cowhide as a cottage industry. They piled their finished products along the roadside to market their business. Russians were bidding for and buying the tanned leather for export. Though it provided a relatively minimal income, it was the major economy of the area. In 1991 we were again guests of the hospital. This time we were driven along the main road leading into town. Tanned hides were no longer piled along the road; instead, there were three large shoe factories. The identity of one company and its relationship to the US was clear by their sign, FlorAm (Florsheim-America). The hospital doctors wanted us to see these factories because processing procedures were now generating serious health problems. Since the factories had begun operating, treatment at the hospital for pulmonary and other diseases had significantly increased, with elevated rates of morbidity. The cause was clear: dye from the massive tanning processes within these factories was entering two of the town's three wells, and it was only a matter of time before the third was also contaminated. The hospital had already confronted local political leaders, but elected officials would not go near the problem. In the judgment of the people and the political leaders, the community was enjoying for once a high degree of employment. They were earning an income far beyond anything they had ever known. The prospect for the future was clear, mortality rates would drastically increase. Obviously the hospital had to protest, to carry their concerns to the officials of the factory, and to put public pressure on the companies to clean up their environmental mess. But it did not take long for the hospital to realize that the solution to their problem rested beyond India. This was one reason for wanting U.S. visitors to share in the awareness of the problem. However, even the hospital officials knew—as did the local elected officials—that if pressure was put on the company, the plant could be moved to another country. This leads one to question the assertion that all politics is local. While an injustice may be local, today the adverse condition can often only be rectified at another place on planet Earth. The local issue becomes very complicated. It may, indeed, relate to international treaties on trade by foreign governments—in this case, our own US. Good people cannot back off, even though correcting or preventing an injustice can become highly political, costly, and complex. As international trade agreements are negotiated, sensitive Christians along with many others need to insist that a U.S. company working abroad cannot inflict environmental damage on the people of the host country. The industry will argue that to impose restrictions of this kind (to stay with the example above) will increase the price of shoes sold in the U.S. Likewise it will lead another company in another part of the world to find another nation that will allow them to make shoes more cheaply and avoid environmental restrictions. So all politics *is* local, but today the solutions reach beyond borders. It is to be hoped that Christians will have the energy, courage, commitment, and wisdom to look at the local conditions and search for solutions—even though those solutions may be complex on both national and international levels.

Planning for Open Forums and Reducing "Church Hopping"

Henry Horn, campus pastor at University Lutheran Church near the Harvard University campus, once told a group of us: "Personally, I have come to question whether a pastor has a right to argue a controversial issue in a sermon." He was not ducking the confronting of hot and conflicted problems, but he was questioning the value and effectiveness of taking a position from the pulpit, where the context limits immediate engagement of the issue by others who might hold considerably different perspectives and convictions. There are issues and occasions in a pastor's career when the judgment of God must be spoken from the pulpit. Surely the pastor must address such an issue in the context of the Christian faith. But it is also wise to arrange for an immediate forum following the service where the subject can be openly aired and discussed.

Most of us want comfort, and especially we want comfort and peace in our local congregation. Few are comfortable when a congregation becomes embroiled in conflict. Many have found a simple solution: church hopping. Church hoppers pick a congregation based on its character. If it's one of those socially sensitive churches, and you are not socially sensitive, then move on. Some will seek one that is Bible-based in a way that never allows the message to give the hearer discomfort. If a new pastor arrives who is not like the previous one (who kept things quiet and peaceable), and the new pastor "stirs the pot" a bit, then move on and look for another church. And conversely, others who find themselves in a congregation that is insensitive to current social or political issues about which they themselves feel strongly will then find a different church. My experience indicates that some pastors feel that this is the solution to conflict within their church. These pastors welcome the development of a culturally homogenous congregation, even at times encouraging some to find another church because they "don't fit in here." I have observed that this modus operandi applies not only to issues of social justice but also to strongly held difference about liturgical practices.

Establishing a homogenous congregation is both theologically offensive and nonsustainable in today's fluid culture. What might have been a unifying social, political, or cultural condition may suddenly—under changing national or local conditions—give rise to considerable differences leading to troublesome disunity and conflict. The only real solution is to establish over time a congregational quality that openly engages differences, seeks common grounds for agreement, and often settles on the fact that we will not agree on certain matters. In such a context it is our faith that keeps us together, continuing to support each other and continuously being bonded together by Christ's love.

Again the effort here is not to expand an analysis of the issues, like the cause of and solution to a stinking river or that the shoes we wear are causing the early deaths of poor people in India. We shall not, and need not, always agree. The real question is, How might we (the people) approach conflict in a more productive manner, with less splintering of the church, while we maintain a united witness to Christ's word? How might we develop greater transparency in our daily life, giving evidence of God's love at work among us—including concerns for justice in the public arena—knowing that any position taken may well be different from that of other faithful Christians? Our congregations need to be truly the body of Christ, the people of God, knowing what unites while open to the changing social and political convictions of their members. Central to the unity of the church is its ability to be the open place where we allow our personal and communal values and convictions to be subjected to the critical light of the word; where both liberals and conservatives find in Christ the courage, to allow faith to shape our callings, our ethical behaviors, and our common witness to our baptism, all the while honoring those whose convictions differ from our own. Can our church develop an atmosphere that permits free and open exchange of conflicting positions? On this, the left and right sides of the church are often guilty of screening out those who differ. Our next chapter may provide specific direction, beginning with church leadership, in improving our engagement of conflict and our ability to retain a greater sense of unity.

10

The Art and the Science of Inverting the Pyramid

The Art of Leadership

LIFE IN A CHRISTIAN CONGREGATION TODAY OUGHT TO BE like a Viennese waltz: so beautiful and glorious that an observer cannot always be sure who is leading and who is following.[1] For the dance to be mutually rewarding and proceed smoothly, the one who leads and the one who follows need time together to develop both the rhythm of the movement and the balance required to master the appropriate steps. In the life of a Christian congregation, the melody that gives substance, unity, and direction to the dance is the gospel. Most important for success is that both leader and follower need to know and hear with heart and ear how the melody shapes and supports the dance. With accomplished dancers as well as with those just learning to dance, there are bound to be toes stepped on and elbows butted. The surface may be more rough and uneven than smooth. Signals will be missed, and directions misunderstood. Yet with the music resonating in the heart and head of each and all, corrections are made, and signs of grace are again recognized in a forward, flowing movement. The important point here is the beauty of life together in Christ. Indeed, leaders and all members are integral to the whole. Any number of metaphors could be used to provide insights into various aspects of what we have been say-

---

1. Portions of this chapter originally appeared in Goetting, "Openness and Trust."

ing throughout the book. The dance metaphor focuses on the congregation as a whole rather than on the "leader." Here the integrated whole is evident. Looking closely one surely does recognize leadership but it is integral to the larger picture.

In times past, several major league baseball teams had coaches who, during the game, were not found on the bench or in the dugout: they were one of the players on the field. They were called "player-coaches." This too might be an appropriate metaphor focusing on the role of the pastor in the life of the congregation and on the pastor's relationship with the people. The player-coach had to do everything that every other player did. He had to be effective and responsible for his position on the team, as each member must. He was as liable to error as anyone on the team. In each inning he had to demonstrate that he was not different from his colleagues, with one exception: he was also the "overseer" of the team. He had to support his teammates, not from a safe place in a dugout, but at the center of activity. One may easily recognizes that the pastor is—at one and the same time—both player and coach. Also the pastor should see him or herself, as never aloof or separated from the people but one like all others, struggling at the center of issues, rejoicing together at successes, and supporting each other and all in difficulties and discouragements.

There is a need to recognize and practice life together in the church as an art form expressing certain skills, evidenced by partners fully committed to a unique relationship and united by the power and depth of the Holy Spirit. As a community of faith we are set free by the gospel to shape the congregation creatively both as a waltz and as a team in a manner that best expresses the Christian life and the church's mission in our time and place. As an art form, pastoral and congregational relations may be greatly assisted by insights from the behavioral sciences. In this chapter I will focus on both the art and the science of leadership within the community of faith. The reader will recognize that much of the terminology used in this chapter is representative of the behavioral sciences. This chapter serves as an additional guideline for practical implementation of efforts to invert the local congregation, and can as well for other units of the church and in our various callings and vocations.

In recent years, a book by Jim Collins titled *Good to Great* (2001) has become a bible of corporate executives; it is the result of major research conducted by a large staff. They carefully compiled and analyzed financial data that identified the major "good" companies and those that are clearly seen, in distinction, as "great" companies, and detailed how some "good" companies became "great" companies. The study, insists Collins, did not initially intend to deal with the CEOs—that is, the character and the leadership styles of those running these organizations. However, once the massive amount of data was assembled and the staff gathered to analyze their material, an unexpected distinction stood out between the CEOs. Collins revealed that those leading the "great" companies were people who "channeled their ego needs away from themselves and into the larger goal of building a great company." It is not that these "leaders have no ego or self-interest. Indeed they are incredibly ambitious—but their ambition is first and foremost for the institution, not themselves."[2] He noted the insistence on the "we" language that is spoken by "great" leaders, "in contrast to the very 'I' centric styles of those in comparison leaders." He also said: "Compared to high-profile leaders with big personalities who make headlines and become celebrities, the great leaders seem to have come from Mars. Self-effacing, quiet, reserved, even shy—these leaders are a paradoxical blend of personal humility and professional will. They are more like Lincoln and Socrates than Patton or Caesar."[3]

I benefitted from the first two chapters of *Good to Great*, which revealed a lot about the need to move beyond being merely a "good leader" toward something greater by virtue of our life lived in Christ. In our churches many of us may simply be too satisfied with mediocrity. The comments are something like this: "Our church is pretty good and our pastor is 'ok.'" Or a pastor may be heard to say, "I don't want to be a great pastor; I just want to be a good pastor." There may be a false humility in settling with simply the good. Because the church is the body of Christ, we cannot settle for being merely mediocre, whether pastor or people. We all have a calling to be the *great* light of Christ, both in our public ministry and in all our endeavors, called to serve with the highest quality in all callings beyond ourselves (the "I") for the life for others in Christ (the "we").

Foundational research by two psychologists, initially reported in *The Harvard Business Review* (1958),[4] demonstrated that specific leader-

---

2. Collins, *Good to Great*, 21.
3. Ibid., 13.
4. Tannenbaum and Schmidt, "How to Choose." The authors were clinical

ship styles may have a measurable effect on follower behavior. Since that article, a great deal of research has followed, much of it very helpful to our interests. *The leadership pattern of a pastor or a bishop may have a discernable effect on a congregation or a primary group within the congregation, or on pastors within a synod.*[5] While I will identify a number of discernable factors, our initial focus will be on openness and trust. These two are really inseparable and are perhaps the most important factors in efforts at initiating and affecting change (viewed from a behavioral science perspective). Key to openness and trust is leadership's movement from being a benevolent authoritarian toward a greater, authentic expression of consultative behavior. The change is one in which the organization progresses from a leader-centered institution toward a people-centered community. A people-centered Christian community is one that is gathered around and centered in the Word, energized by the Spirit for mission and ministry in all aspects of life and work.

There are several reasons pastors ought not allow themselves to sit on the point of the pyramid. The first reason, as I have sought to demonstrate in previous chapters, is this: There is sound, theological ground on which we are able to build, while maintaining strong leadership that is not hierarchical. The proposed model is similar to the pattern of leadership found in the New Testament, a ministry without rank, which can be sharply contrasted with the Old Testament Levitical priesthood. Second, the authoritarian model is generally no longer effective in today's culture. This too I have discussed earlier. Third, congregational conflict is generally directed at the leader in a hierarchical organization. Today that heat often becomes unbearable, leading to considerable discord and to a church that misses its mission. Research has unearthed alternate approaches to leadership that I will examine in what follows.

Leadership Is Crucial

The pastor who is committed to genuine change in leadership from what is commonly recognized as a *benevolent authoritarian* style to a

---

psychologists. Schmidt graduated from Concordia Seminary and earned a PhD from Washington University (both in St. Louis), spent most of his career on the faculty at UCLA in research, as a lecturer, and as a consultant to corporate management. He won an Oscar for his script, "Is It Always Right to Be Right?"

5. Though focused on the church and religious organizations, these insights apply equally to any other organization, including the home and the workplace.

consultative one and at crucial times exercising a *collaborative* style—all things being equal—should over time realize more positive and healthier human relationships within the congregation. Such a movement in leadership initiates a greater openness and raises the trust level both between the pastor and the people and among the people themselves. It should also lead to other salutary changes. The ultimate change desired is a congregational shift from a dependency on the leader to a realization that Christ's mission is carried out through all the people. It is much easier for a leader to change than for the follower community, especially within a hierarchical organization. Appropriate pastoral leadership is crucial to affect this change. This has been demonstrated in behavioral research and in our common experiences. While the change in behavior begins with the leader and as such must be the dominant agent of change, with time change is anticipated and expected within the follower community. Effecting such change is not easy, nor is the effort certain to accomplish all for which one might hope. All too often there are those antagonists, present in so many congregations, who seem to relish complicating any effort, taking advantage of openness, and successfully blocking decent communications. Yet even as progress is slow and often made difficult because of a few contrary persons, one must persist in the effort and be reasonably consistent. The initiation and maintenance of the process very much depends on the strong commitment of the pastoral leadership.

The leaders in mind here are the *"benevolent* authoritarian*"* type, sharply distinguished from leaders identified as "*coercive* authoritarian." Benevolent authoritarian pastors are people of good will, recognized as considerate, with honorable goals and respectable commitments in their ministry. They are most often viewed as good pastors. They have no intention of being harmful; they are highly committed to their faith and their church and may be well liked.

Benevolent authoritarian leaders are often very sure of themselves, very self-confident. At times they are so strongly certain, especially under stress and in conflict, that they give the appearance that they alone have the answers. Many of us have been caught in the cultural myth that problems can only be understood and altered by the professional in charge. We conclude, incorrectly, that only the pastor can "do ministry," since others are not knowledgeable, so slow to catch on, or incapable. To be sure, a benevolent authoritarian pastor might also be an insecure person who takes cover under the cloak of authority and desires to give an impression of both being a nice person and possessing more capabilities than one really has.

There is often a tendency to blindness on the part of many of us who are by culture and training authoritarian leaders. An authoritarian leader tends to be closed-minded, not open to the insights of others. We often fail to see ourselves as others see us. The congregation may see the pastor as a strong person who both enjoys doing the ministry and appears unwilling to share ministry with the people. People are often satisfied to let "ministry" be accomplished in the domain of the pastor, the assumed professional. This may work in some situations. Yet frustration often grows as leaders press for new programs, especially when decisions are made that affect one's values, and one has been kept outside the decision process. Then, lethargy or open conflict often follows. Benevolent authoritarian leaders have long been central to our culture. However, in many situations today, such leaders may be out of touch with member expectation, and this becomes a cause for the increased dissonance within congregations.

In these days we are all capable of altering our leadership styles, leading toward a more authentic Christian realization of a common priesthood. Recall the theological grounding accented in previous chapters. Building on those insights, in this chapter I want to identify specific steps in moving our congregations and various ecclesiastical entities toward what we have been calling an inverted church, in which the leadership is seen and experienced as supportive of the people, and where the people discover that ministry occurs in their daily lives through various vocations and callings. To initiate this growth process, a particular style of leadership is crucial. While we may call it a style, ultimately we would hope it would become the very character of pastoral leadership, one that evokes greater trust and openness among the people.

A System Approach

An organization—like a congregation, a synod, or a family—can be viewed as a holistic unit, a system.[6] It is a multiplicity of human relationships, interrelated, perhaps best illustrated by a circle with identifiable

---

6. The model I am utilizing here has evolved over the past forty years and has been used in various places.

entry points. While many more entry points may be listed, for our purposes we will work with four:

1. Leaders/personnel
2. Structure
3. Feeling Tone
4. Purpose/Reason for Being

The church is here being examined as a system. Viewed as such, when attempting to make major changes one should recognize that, to make a change in one of these entry points, one may be surprised to find unexpected consequences in other parts of the body. For instance, when things are not going well, some within the congregation may work to remove the pastor as a solution to a parish problem. They "succeed," only to discover they have created among a significant number of members a deep and often lasting bitterness (feeling tone) which infects the body for years. This is certainly true also of a synod when it experiences an organized (undercover) effort to unseat a bishop. I do not want to spend a lot of time on this system analysis, but we do need to have it as an important backdrop for what follows. When observing a congregation from these entry points, one should first look at a "hard side," then a "soft side." Using our four entry points for each yields the following.

"Hard side" refers to that which is published or publically stated. *Leaders*: the called or elected personnel; *Structure:* the church's constitution and organizational charts; *Feeling Tone:* as written in promotional pieces: "A friendly church," a "congregation with heart," and so on; and *Purpose:* the church's publicly identified theology and faith confessions, stated goals, approved objectives, and defined programs.

"Soft side," as one might infer, covers those things that are not publically stated, that are subtle yet real. Again, we use the four entry point above. *Leaders:* Are there nonelected, not publicly identified people to whom special groups look for direction in certain circumstances? *Structure*: Are there "underground" networks of people who get on the phone to others when a sensitive subject is before the congregation? *Feeling tone:* What is said (on the parking lot, amid the chatter at coffee hour, to friends and neighbors) that identifies your church or its leadership? "The people are cold." "Lots of conflict." "I don't trust them." Or more positively, "We really are a family at St. John's." *Purpose:* What reasons are expressed to others for "belonging" to the church? Example: "My family has long attended here." Or, "I find here the gospel and a community of Christian faith."

The closer the "hard" and "soft" sides are together and match, the more likely you have a healthy congregation or organization. The more distant and the more disconnected the two sides are from each other, the more likely you experience lethargy or conflict. Where openness and trust are relatively high, generally these two sides are close together. Where they are distant, generally there is distrust and a lack of openness. A lot can be gained by careful examination of each of these entry Points.

Leadership Styles and Their Effect on Follower Behavior[7]

Our entry points for our purposes in this chapter will be primarily *Feeling Tone* (the level of openness and trust), and *Personnel/leaders* (pastors, bishops, and dominant groups) whom I assume are the keys to initiating a change in the level of trust within congregations and synods. The assumption is this: The primary entry point for altering the "feeling tone" (trust) lies with the dominant leadership and/or group. This may or may not be the called or elected or appointed leadership, but one generally hopes it is. In a local congregation the initial focus is generally on the pastor. The dominant group is generally the church council. In their sermons, pastors may call the membership to greater openness and trust among one another. This may be appropriate, but it will have little effect unless the pastor and congregational leadership genuinely practice openness and trust.

A window for observation may at times be the relationship between pastor and the congregation's primary decision-making bodies, the council and those attending congregational meetings. What happens there, especially under stress, is often reflected through the congregation, though these may be two separate worlds—that is, the council

---

7. I credit Dr. Rensis Likert for much of the material in this chapter related to leadership styles and follower behavior. He and his associates at the University of Michigan (Center for Social Research) conducted extensive studies/surveys which support the material, for which I am indebted. He also worked closely with the Center for Parish Development on whose staff I once served. Those interested in pursuing this subject further might read Likert and Likert, *Patterns of Management* and *New Ways of Managing Conflict*. While the research was completed in the late 1970s and others have expanded the research since, I find Likert's work offers clarity and simplicity, continues to be most helpful, and is especially applicable to religious organizations.

and the congregation. In a synod, the window is (in my judgment) the relationship of the bishop and staff to a congregation in the call process, generally the call committee and the council. Here too the feeling tone relative to the bishop and synod may be quite different from that felt by the general membership. It will vary with the situation.

The call process often raises an anxiety among a great many people. Not least is the fear of some that the bishop does not really know the congregation and its unique needs. The people are fearful of receiving a poor match for which they will be saddled for years. There may be a few other times when the congregation is more uptight over what is going to happen, such as when a pastor has been charged with some inappropriate behavior. The style of intervention by bishop and staff in both situations may significantly shape the congregation's trust level and may flavor the quality of the congregation's relations to the synod for years.

Styles of Leadership

A leadership style is a matter of perception by the followers, not one's own self-perception as a leader. People respond to a leader's style based on their perceptions, not on how the leader defines his or her role or leadership. A pastor and council or a bishop and staff may collectively develop a leadership style that becomes clearly perceived by a follower group in a way quite different than any self-perception. As was mentioned above, we can discern four recognizable leadership styles and their resulting effect on followers. They are:

1. Coercive Authoritarian
2. Benevolent Authoritarian
3. Consultative
4. Collaborative

Now I will elaborate on each and on the consequential effect on the follower community, with particular focus on trust. *A style of leadership generally becomes "locked" in the mind of the follower not in times of ease, but in times of stress,* especially through interaction around conflicted opinions.

Coercive Authoritarian

This leadership style uses threatening force, physical or verbal, to maintain control. Seldom is it found to be present within congregations. Examples are: Slandering people with whom the leader has differences; betraying confidences; intimidating, refusing to openly interact with a member of the congregation when there is conflict. Such leaders are known not to speak truthfully under stress. The leader is often so self-serving that he or she is insensitive to the feelings and needs of others. The consequence leads to fear and distrust and congregational discord. I personally believe this behavior is seldom found among pastors, though it indeed may be present in some cases.

Benevolent Authoritarian

Likert's research has demonstrated that followers judge the vast majority of leaders as *benevolent authoritarian*. Those who have worked closely with their pastor and bishop over a period of time, who have struggled with sharply different viewpoints, will tend to identify their leader as controlling, a feeling that may over time permeate the larger body. Certainly some are judged more strongly than others. Indeed, others may jump (unpredictably) into several leadership styles, causing discomfort among followers who are unsure what to expect. This is not helpful in maintaining trust. Culturally we expect leaders to be *strong* people when they are placed in charge of an organization. There is an assumption among those who lead: "Out there are some disagreeing, disagreeable people (generally true). As a leader I need to be on guard. There are individuals and groups who make me uncomfortable. I must be strong and learn to stand my ground." The assumption is also stated that to be a leader is to lead in spite of opposition.

Inherent in this is our cultural proclivity to competitiveness. We too easily see our situation as *"us versus them,"* especially on conflicted issues. We need to take our stand against *them* since *they* are against us. *The benevolent authoritarian cares for people, but is often caught between caring and being threatened by an opposition, especially as differences develop.* It is important that we clearly delineate what is meant here, since it is a judgment on many of us who are pastors, most of whom are healthy, sincere, committed, caring leaders. Very simply, many of us are perceived as being controlling (manipulative?) when caught in a situation of disagreement when both leader and a follower group hold strongly differing positions. Leaders are often seen in such situations as "closed minded," resulting in a lowering or loss of trust.

One reason that "liberal" clergy may often be perceived as controlling is expectation. Conservative people will generally not speak of themselves as being open minded, while (if not actually stated) among more liberal people it is assumed that they are open minded. However, among many (self-assumed) liberal clergy or (self-assured) open-minded clergy, sharp differences often arise between our assumed open-mindedness and a congregation or groups. This might appropriately be called the "imprisonment of our own mind-set."[8] Many pastors carry into their office extensive training in biblical, historical, and pastoral theology. In conflicted situations, one may convey an apparent, absolute authority on matters beyond the Office of the Keys—as perceived by those who may disagree. And frustration rises: How can I argue with my pastor? Look at his or her degrees. Many of us would like to side-step this, but it has become clear that a self-assumed "liberal" clergy person in the interactive relations within a decision-making body will often appear as rigid in his or her positions as a "conservative" clergy person. The "sin" appears to be distributed equally.

Consultative

This is the primary, initial key in raising the trust level in a parish, toward reshaping the congregation's feeling tone, and it works similarly for a synod—indeed any workplace and even the home. Consultative style or consultation may best be understood as a one-on-one relationship. When a pastor or bishop engages as equals others with whom there is disagreement, and when the follower thus genuinely perceives the leader is relating as a peer, a different "feeling tone" will mostly likely be registered.[9] Some among us have learned this skill, and I am certain it reflects

---

8. A phrase similar to this was used by Robert McNamara in his late years, describing himself in his role as secretary of defense during the Vietnam War.

9. The use of the word "consultation" will be understood differently by "professionals," as when a psychiatrist is called to testify in a criminal court case. It is assumed by virtue of the profession he or she is not of equal rank with others when providing testimony as a consultant in the trial. Rather this "professional," it is assumed, has insights which carry authority by virtue of the profession. Recall our earlier discussion in chapter 2 regarding clergy as being different types of professionals who by theological education have not gained insight restricted only to a profession, such as that of

a higher level of trust where they are serving. It is important, however, to sustain this practice with all and not just with a few. Literature that I read early in my career suggested that if you are meeting with a member of your congregation with whom you have a sharp difference, you should be sure to sit behind your desk, or allow the person to be seated while you stand. One instruction suggested that you be sure to have an open Bible, a sign of authority, visible on your desk. Today the literature in pastoral counseling is quite different. The instructions now suggest that when you are counseling or interacting with another person with whom you have conflicting opinions, you ought not sit behind a desk but should have at least two similar chairs in your office facing each other, from which each of you can converse without any obstruction standing between you.

My own inclination through my ministry has been to avoid sitting with the people with whom I know I have strong differences. And when I have sat with such people, my approach has often been to show the other how wrong they are and how right I am. Of course, I have allowed myself to appear to be listening, but not really. As they talk, I am organizing my attack.

I know better. I have been around long enough to know that if I can discipline myself, to hold back and genuinely listen, then better relations result and we can more effectively engage sensitive issues. This does not suggest that one discard one's own position. However, to be effective, leadership will want to be sure meetings are at a time and in a place that is conducive for all, where both parties may talk freely and listen carefully—not standing in the church narthex following the worship service. When a conflicted issue is on the meeting agenda, there may be an opportunity to shape perspectives in a healthier direction. The chairperson who "controls" the meeting (an aptitude we often favor: it gets the meeting done on time) may be the one who tends to put down an opposition: "We don't have time for that here." Can the chair of the council, in the heat of debate, avoid the tendency to put down an opponent and instead honor the right of dissent and insist that we need to take time in order to hear the dissenting voice?

The dissenter must be honored with a *platform* from which to speak freely, assuming he or she is not merely being obstreperous. It

---

medical doctor.

is understood that there is a stated ground rule: no personal attacks allowed.[10] The chair need not support the opposition's position, but should support the opposition's *right to speak and provide the time he or she feels is needed to be heard.* The chair may insist that a vote be postponed until the next meeting. The chair may offer that he or she or someone else will sit with the dissenter to gain an understanding of her position, and that then they together report back at the next meeting. That does not mean one is supporting the dissenter's position, but one does use the power of the chair to be fair, to assure the dissenter an unobstructed opportunity to state a position.

The important question is: Can leaders use their power in reverse order, to turn the power often used to control (limit) discussion into the power to encourage open interchange? To do this, the chair and council must work at getting the meeting's priorities in the right order: spend limited time on what is noncontroversial, and more time on delicate matters (in group or in one-on-one conversation). This is not always easy, but it can be learned. When the opposition is given fairness in deliberations, their position may not sway the majority, but they are less likely to simmer with anger behind the scenes and become the rotten apple in the barrel, negatively affecting others. Very simply, leaders need to feel the negative emotions when a minority perceives *the tyranny of the majority.* While this awareness ought not to discourage decisions by the majority; it does suggest the necessity to give honor to the minority or to the dissenter. The objective should be more than eliminating a "bad apple." The dissenter may well have an original insight, ultimately of significant value to the group, that is perhaps only realized years later.

Collaborative

While a consultative approach is generally understood as one-on-one, collaborative style is a group or a meeting assembled for the purpose of making a decision. In being collaborative, you work toward a consensus. The key word is *toward.* While one may realize consensus is seldom achievable, this ought not to discourage every effort to achieve

---

10. Where the chair recognizes hostile feelings between two individuals in a meeting, he or she would be wise to approach the two apart from the meeting, asking that they meet privately to talk through their personal differences, and that the chair or the pastor offer to be present, if that would help. Such conversation is not appropriate in a public meeting unless an announcement of reconciliation is offered.

consensus in a group's struggle with a crucial matter. In the end, without a sense of defeat, but being realistic, a vote must most likely be called, resulting in some people being on the losing side.

In an authoritarian style, one assumes that the correct knowledge and wisdom resides in the person of the leader who should make major decisions (an assumption by the leader, often at times supported by some or even many of the followers). In the consultative style, there is the assumption that important information and wisdom is to be found in individuals or in the group in addition to the leader. The input of others is necessary before making many important decisions. Competence and insight are genuinely recognized in others as well as in oneself. Collaboration dare not become a technique to achieve acceptance of a leader's or a council's plan. It must be an authentic effort to search the mind of the congregation in order to bring insight and resolution to a problem or to pursue an opportunity. It is time-consuming, and ought to be approached selectively with a well-planned process. When practiced properly it clearly signals that the leadership trusts the people. How do you know what issues or subjects need to be processed through collaboration, or for that matter, when to consult? In a great many of the situations, a leader should be free to proceed unilaterally. One does not need collaboration in determining how many paper clips to order. However, it is an art of leadership to know when to act unilaterally and when to consult, when to collaborate. *When in doubt on how to proceed, consult with people related to the issue. Be sure you are consulting various viewpoints, and be sure you are not seen as merely manipulating matters for your own point of view.*

A few years back, while I served as a congregation's interim pastor, the council felt strongly that the parsonage should be sold. They had carefully studied the matter and had obtained a responsible engineer's review of the building as well as several realtor reports. However, they also knew that a group within the congregation was against the sale. With the annual congregation meeting approaching, it was proposed that the council call for a vote on the sale, and they were prepared to bite the bitter bullet. Then another voice was heard: Why not use the annual meeting to share the fact that the council is seriously thinking about selling the property, that a special meeting be called, after the Sunday service a month later? In the meantime, all the information obtained by the council would be available to the membership. On several Sundays following worship, the parsonage would be open for an inspection by all. The suggestion was followed. The special meeting brought informed discussion from all sides. Then the motion was called, and the sale was approved 64 to 23. Though there were losers, no one seemed to leave the meeting bitter. Had it been pushed through in the annual meeting, it might have passed, but with a narrow margin, and many would have left very unhappy. One may say this is a small matter. But a pattern that is fair and open goes a long way toward raising the trust level within the congregation

A collaborative leadership style is never laissez-faire, as though the leader need not lead but just sit back and let the group decide. It takes courage: courage to allow your position to be openly tested in an arena of a freeflow of countering viewpoints. It places the leader in a vulnerable position. There is risk. You are exposed to the possibility of being shown to be wrong. In fact, the more the follower community recognizes that you, as leader, are willing to listen and to learn from others, and are then willing to change your own position when new insights are obtained, the more ready a group will be to also change. The opposite is just as true. A group is less likely to change if it perceives the leader is obstinate. Here is just one illustration of how openness can engender positive results: In meeting with an individual in a one-on-one session, or in a meeting gathered to discuss a controversial issue, the pastor might say, "I have a position on this subject, but I dare not let my position inhibit a free and open discussion on the subject; indeed, I am certain I can learn from you [*Must be said honestly!*], so let's hear from one another. I want you to speak freely, and I insist that we all listen carefully to each other." In any stressful meeting, the chair (moderator) must exercise extreme fairness in the deliberation. Ground rules for fairness by all parties must be clearly understood. A person who chairs fairly is more likely empowered by the group to rule out of order those who are beyond the rules of agreement.

Before we move on, a word of caution: Too easily the two words—consultation and collaboration—can become merely a management technique (a label) rather than a persistent behavior that flows from the heart and character of the leader. These two words ought to be verbs rather than nouns. Thus, a good leader learns to converse with others in an open, free interchange; never in a one-way "conversation." People experience that it is their pastor's very nature to consult and to collaborate.

She genuinely gives the impression that in much of her conversation with people that she encourages persons to share what they are feeling, including their critical concerns, their discouragements as well as their joys.

Differing Effects from Authoritarian to Collaborative

In what follows I would like to pick up several pertinent subjects, tracing each from authoritarian to collaborative, and see how they will appear differently in each category. A few subjects will be discussed at greater length than others.

Communications

Authoritarian: Opinions, information, and instruction flow from the top down. This is an extreme sign, though it may be more common than one assumes. Preaching may be experienced as a monologue. There is little or no encouragement for response from followers, especially on sensitive issues. In my first parish, I recall stepping before the choir in rehearsal, informing them that I did not wish them to use a choral piece which I felt was inappropriate. After making my statement, I quickly headed for the door. That is how I remember it. I was afraid and did not want to become entangled in their response.

Consultative: Pastor and people communicate freely and openly one-on-one, sharing information and insights that relate to church business and mission. Through the church paper, officers are identified to whom you should speak about a conflicted issue facing the council. People need to be empowered to speak up and to know to whom to direct their concerns, avoiding gossip and griping. Preaching is experienced as a mutual conversation. While perhaps not responding out loud to the preacher's questions, the listener has the sense of being understood as the Word is openly explored. The listener further senses that feelings and doubts and personal concerns are recognized by a mutual encounter with the Word.

Collaborative. Communication moves openly and freely in many directions. Leaders encourage feedback and give evidence of acting responsibly on the feedback given. In fact, there is in collaboration an empowering of people to share their insights and feelings about hot button issues. It is one thing to say, "Let me know what you think." It is another to provide a feedback instrument with which people can easily and clearly express themselves. We need to be sure we recognize appropriate and inappropriate feedback.

Leaders need to brace themselves for frank expressions that are insightful but often leave one uncomfortable. You may learn things you did not expect but are better off knowing. And it is better that the concerns are directed to you as leader than directed to others in conversations on the parking lot about you and your work. Quietly but firmly it should be known throughout the congregation that you want to hear from any member disturbed or concerned over an issue. But unsigned letters regarding your ministry or about conditions within the church are unacceptable.

Once in awhile a member or group within the church proposes a survey, or worse, undertakes a survey of the congregation without formal approval. Generally the survey contains loaded questions about the pastor's leadership; an effort to "gotcha!" Every effort should be made to prevent this from taking place. Surveys proposed with the intent of proving a point should be seen differently from objective surveys designed to ameliorate in the interest of all. When a group or a person is pushing for a preordained outcome, one might want to step back and ask: "Is this a sign of profound frustration that over time an open discussion has not occurred?" As I have mentioned earlier, my experience tells me this will most likely have happened where there is no effectively functioning mutual ministry committee with which concerns about the leadership or other sensitive matters can be discussed openly and civilly. Confidentiality is, of course, essential in meetings of this committee. But assurance can be given to the congregation and concerned individuals that specific requests are being addressed, that frank and open exchange does take place, and it is all in the interest of the church, the pastor and his or her family, the people, and Christ's mission.

Central to any collaborative leader is feedback, a significant form of intragroup or interperson communication. It may be offered in conversation or in print. In a survey of a group or of the whole membership, one ought not expect people to sign their name. It makes for a far more honest response if they aren't required to give their names. However, unless one genuinely requests feedback, and is personally conditioned to receive and internalize what comes back and willing to share the results (in summary) with those who responded, it is of little value. In fact, if a leader has not genuinely indicated receptivity to feedback, one should be very cautious in offering such. It may be seen as a threat to his leadership. Rather than being helpful, it may become a wedge driven between the two of you. It is for this reason, among others, that you as leader need to genuinely convey an open and sincere invitation for feedback, and that you do not see it as a threat to your leadership.

In advocating feedback, I am not suggesting that a pastor or leader develop programs and policy on the basis of the will and whims of others. You as the pastor have your position and you are sure you know your parish well, but you also know you are fallible. You are open to others while not driven or controlled by others and their opinions. Major practices in both congregations and synods need periodical review, and this may often best be initiated through a carefully prepared and objective feedback process.

The call process appears to be the one hot button item among pastors and—at critical times within congregations—that is often dodged by synodical leaders, a subject I have closely observed over fifty years. Few other features within a synod set the trust level more than the call process as played out between bishop and congregation and also between bishop and pastors. It is the primary entry by the bishop and staff into congregations of a synod. Pastors generally recognize that their ministerial career often (humanly speaking) lies in the hands of their bishop. And among the people of the parish during a vacancy (with or without an interim pastor), I have long discovered that there are many rumors that move freely through a congregation, reflecting the high level of anxiety about the process—a process seldom fully understood, especially by the congregation.

While listening, over many years and in varied venues, to bishops and district presidents, I have recognized the following: Too easily a bishop and staff can assume the process is working effectively in their respective synods. On this assumption, they feel no need for feedback or any periodic review of policy and practice by others—but they may be wrong. In other cases, because the synodical leadership realizes there is a high level of unhappiness with the process, they therefore resist opening the subject for review, fearful where such might lead. Others conclude that the unrest over the synodical process is limited to a few, and find in the applause of the many an excuse to avoid critical review. Indeed, I have known over time synods and districts, though few, where the process was periodically reviewed and feedback sought with which to give specific attention to necessary change. Through the years, I have seldom observed a synod or district where one did not hear some degree of grumbling among pastors and considerable dissatisfaction within congregations as they experienced the call process. It would be most helpful if we had some solid data on how well the process is working in each of our synods or conferences and what needs change. Commercial enterprises would never go without a constant review of their practices in a crucial, sensitive interaction that affects so many vital units of their organization. The church has every reason to do the same. Responsible, constructive, critical review is important for developing and maintaining trust within a synod.

The Person of the Pastor

Benevolent/authoritarian leaders speak frequently in the first person, "I," while often referring to the followers as "they." Occasionally one hears a pastor speak of "my" congregation, "my" church council. Some bishops may speak of "my" synod. People speak of the congregation or synod as "they," indicating a sense of distance. Collaborative congregations identify themselves as "we," as "our" church and "our" synod. What is important, however, is that these words are expressive of a larger, personal commitment and not merely window dressing.

Unity

Under authoritarian leadership, unity ultimately and symbolically lies with the leader. The pastor is expected to convey publicly to the congregation the meaning and purpose of the Christian faith. Thus members should stand with their pastor. There is historical grounding here. In the history of the church, the bishop (and also pastors) gradually became the public sign and symbol of the church's unity. In the best Christian understanding of this sign and symbol, the bishop expresses publicly the apostolic tradition in a region of the church. The bishop is the one who proclaims publicly and clearly the gospel in all its purity, and it is the bishop who is a public sign of the unity of Christ's church. The office of the bishop is a teaching office. And surely we ought to insist that the pastor of the congregation be publicly expressive of the same apostolic tradition. And to the bishop and pastor we assert God has given to the church the Office of the Keys, to forgive sins to the penitent and withhold forgiveness of the unrepentant—that is, to preach both law and gospel. Keep that in our churches, yes, but what is the pastor's and bishop's authority beyond this, and how ought that authority be managed?

There are gray lines and often unexamined lines that divide and define the pastor's and bishop's authority in the countless decisions that entangle relationships. Though bishop and pastor rightfully occupy the public teaching office of the church, their theology is never infallible. Here certainly they need to be open to the critical theological concerns of other clergy and of the laity. As we teach and preach the gospel, we need to be open and listening: what are people hearing? Can others help me? Indeed, they can. They can help me hold forth more clearly the gospel of Christ and his cross, which truly and ultimately are the unifying power of the church. The unity of the church may be recognized in the pastoral leadership, but that unity must be represented in the common life and witness of the people.

Initiative

With the authoritarian leader, it is assumed the pastor must be the "mover," the one who must initiate and promote programs. When some members make proposals, it may be seen as a threat to the leadership. With collaborative leaders, the people are encouraged to use their imagination and creativity in initiating and promoting programs for mission and ministry. There are established processes for review and for critical monitoring, along with support for various ministries initiated by people or by groups within the congregation.

Pastors and lay leaders often complain that "they," the congregation, are lethargic. It is a common refrain. "They" are so difficult to arouse to any enthusiasm. Appeals for Bible study as an adjunct to the Sunday service draw only a few; calls for work projects attract the same volunteers year after year; and efforts for an every-member visitation are abandoned, because too few volunteer to be visitors. Most serious of all, while attendance may be good, any careful audit of the biblical and confessional knowledge of the membership reveals considerable ignorance. A great amount of research has demonstrated that the mental perspective of teachers regarding the competence level of their students will significantly determine the level of achievement in a given year.[11] Thus teachers who assume their students' ability level is below an appropriate level will teach accordingly. If the teachers genuinely believe their students are capable of achieving higher levels of competence, the results will be considerably different—even though the students in both classes are of equal abilities.

If pastor and leaders conclude that the membership is lethargic, the people in turn respond accordingly. This is a typical leadership pattern representative of the authoritarian style. Again, if we use a different mind-set—a different paradigm—in which the leadership *genuinely* concludes that all are together in a mission and that we all are both capable and committed to grow in a multiplicity of ways, results may be different. In others words, authoritarian leadership results in a *lack of initiative* (or certainly less initiative) among the people; while a movement over time toward a culture of collaboration will generally result in far greater self-initiative throughout the congregation. The authoritarian leader breeds a dependency relationship of the people upon the leader. Our pastors knows their Bible; we simply go along with whatever the pastors say (until, that is, the pastor takes a position with which we are uncomfortable). The culture in the collaborative congregation assumes that we need to support each other; we all need to engage the gospel, to learn and witness to the faith—and that includes the pastor. We are all capable of learning and serving. A significant key, remember, lies with the attitude of the leadership toward the people. It is crucial in initiating change, even if the congregation has been conditioned over many years to sit back and let others do the work, to let others do the learning and growing. To alter the culture may take a considerable period of time, but it is possible to change.

Conflict

Under authoritarian leadership, conflict focuses on people more than issues: it is generally directed at the leader/pastor and it is person-centered, which is generally very difficult to manage or resolve. One simple reason to move authentically beyond the authoritarian style is

---

11. See Weinstein, *Reaching Higher*. Weinstein carefully reviews the extensive research literature focused on the learning process of children and young adults within schools. Much of the material is transferable to the educational efforts of Christian congregations, including preaching.

this: Pastors (including their family) cannot endure the conflict that is often inflicted upon them. Certainly there are times when one must take a stand and endure the heat, but it is most important that one picks the right issues. In the collaborative style, conflict that focuses on issues more than people can be energizing. As a group matures in its collaborative abilities (increased self-initiative), the group will (one hopes and prays) protect leaders from unfair attacks. The congregation needs to be nurtured in this skill and commitment.

Creativity

With an authoritarian style, creativity and problem solving are assumed to lie with the leader. In collaborative leadership, creativity and problem solving lies within the group, generally more than in a single individual and its proposals are more likely to find greater support.

Stewardship/giving

It is quite obvious that where there is a strong congregational sense of "we," where the awareness that the targets of giving are genuinely understood and owned by all, giving will be much higher than when people feel that the decisions were made "above and beyond" them.

In conclusion, I admit that I have explored leadership in the church by using terminology and concepts that often come from nonecclesiastical contexts, often thought of as secular. I offer no apology. The gifts of God are many among us, and where ideas and information are appropriate and genuinely supportive of God's mission we ought to utilize them. For all and in every way, the calling of faith is paramount. We certainly dare not allow the behavioral sciences to "wag the tail of the Word," but rather to recognize that such gifts may be a vital component among the resources that support the ministry of the Word in the life and service of all Christians.

11

The Challenge of Change in a Conflicted Culture

In this, the final chapter, it is important that I now summarize the vision I have portrayed of a servant ministry, an inverted church. I will briefly lift up several summaries of subjects addressed in earlier chapters. We must also recognize the obstacles that confront us in any effort to achieve a greater practice of our common ministry in the wholeness of our lives, and gain confidence that we are capable of change.

In recent years, the U.S. Army, experiencing a shortage of chaplains, ran a series of full-page advertisements in various religious magazines, including *Lutheran Partners* and the *Christian Century*. Each depicted a military implement, in one case, a well worn army field binocular. Below the symbol was this caption: "Improves the soldier's range of vision, but only a chaplain can help them find the way." Another in the series depicted a battlefield canteen with the caption: "When soldiers are craving more than water, only a chaplain can quench their thirst."[1] Only the chaplain?

These advertisements are in stark contrast to the understanding of pastoral leadership and of the relationship between pastor and people that is advocated in this book. The ads are clearly contrary to Luther's and Protestantism's claim of the common priesthood of all believers. Sadly, they are also expressive of the all-too-common understanding of Christian ministry within both church and society. Christian ministry

---

1. *Christian Century*, September 5, 2006; *Lutheran Partners*, July/August 2007.

is so singularly identified with the ministry of the ordained, and this attitude is deeply imbedded within our common culture. Given this reality it is easily assumed that no significant change is possible. In spite of our circumstances and the cultural resistance to change, we cannot abandon this issue. It is too important for these days and for the days to come. Indeed, our American culture is itself changing. Even the military's culture has significantly changed.[2] And the change offers a model for life within the congregation. The advertisements reported above are contrary to the current practices in the United States Army and Marine Corps. In today's army, soldiers are drilled and disciplined to look after the welfare of one another. In a platoon, each soldier is trained to care for a buddy—that is, to protect and assist each other by every means necessary. The soldier understands the orders to go through the hell of a fire-fight to attend to his or her wounded comrade.

The biblical text "to equip the saints for the work of ministry" (Eph 4:12a) provides an image of a platoon of soldiers preparing for a mission.[3] In preparation for the engagement, the command is, "Get your pack on your back, take up the mission." But the backpack is not something any one person is able to get up on his own back. If one stays with the army's advertised image of the chaplain, each soldier passes before the leader, since only he can put the pack on the each soldier's back. Rather, in the biblical sense of community, the pastor facilitates a process in which each helps one another in putting that pack on the other's back. The exercise does not mean providing people with an exterior, weighty addition to their witness. Nor is the backpack a sign of righteousness or holiness. Those being equipped are already, by their faith, known to be righteous, called by St. Paul *saints!* Christian faith and Christian knowledge include an awareness of the mission and the source of strength, that is, the Word for the engagement. As Jesus said of the yoke, it is light and not a burden. The calling of a Christian pastor and Christian chaplain is to assist Christians to obtain a clear commitment to our common Christian calling and to practice the same in every situation of responsibility. The word of our baptism calls each of us to care spiritually and physically

---

2. Some maintain this is a result of the volunteer army, compelling a different relationship of sergeant to soldiers.

3. There is nothing in the text from Ephesians, "equipping the saints for ministry," that suggests this expanded interpretation of the military. I am admittedly taking liberty with the text. However, the thrust made here is representative of the New Testament's call for common ministry to and for one another by the baptized.

for others with Christ's love and mercy. When lying wounded and possibly dying in battle, soldiers need their comrades to attend both to their physical and their spiritual needs. If this is a pastoral ministry, so be it. Given the ratio of soldiers to chaplains in the throes of battle, a chaplain most likely will not be physically present to attend to those wounded or dying, nor be present for expressions of faith and hope in the bunkhouse or on the landing craft. A soldier's buddy is most likely nearby. Similar illustrations can be made of the multiple situations of the people (all of us) relative to the diverse needs of loved ones and others in need. Within the spirit of the New Testament, pastoral leadership will be assisting the baptized in their common ministries of witness and service where God leads them and wherever they find themselves.

All substantive change in Christian behavior grows out of our self-perception: specifically, that one lives daily within the presence of God. This is a source of strength in renewing an authentic faith, enabling one to confront one's own peculiar sins and weaknesses. As in all Christian ministries, the heart of the leader (as in all) is to be captivated by Christ's presence in a profoundly spiritual manner, reshaping one's personal paradigm and often resulting in a changed public and private posture, especially as one relates to others in an ever-increasing number of changes in the contexts of one's ministry. Henry Nouwen describes a trait that ought to be in the mind and the heart of today's minister, since in his view it is crucial for effective relations of pastor to people in our current culture. What he says of clergy should be said of every Christian who relates to anyone who is in pain, physically, emotionally, and spiritually. He writes: "The minister is called to *recognize the sufferings of his time in his own heart* and make that recognition the starting point of his service."[4] Nouwen echoes St. Paul's deeply felt desire, expressed in his letter to the Christians in Philippi: "I want to know Christ and the power of his resurrection and *the sharing of his suffering* by becoming like him in his death" (Phil 3:10; emphasis added).

Nouwen does not suggest that you as the Christian caregiver must personally have experienced the particular difficulty of the person to whom you are relating in ministry. He is saying that you as a caregiver must identify authentically with "the suffering of one's own time" and that you approach the other on a common human level, displaying an authentic care for the person. In ministry, one's own wounds are not the

---

4. Nouwen, *Wounded Healer*, xvi (emphasis added).

subject to be raised in relating to a suffering person. What is important is the need for the caregiver to convey a genuine compassion. This has surely been generated in the caregiver through his or her having personally experienced God's compassion in their own suffering. Madeline Drexler, a science writer, describes the frequent failure of Harvard medical students to advance beyond merely listening to a patient's heartbeat with their stethoscopes. She wishes them to advance to a level of humane relationship with their patients. She concludes her article with this insight: "As any patient knows, the touchtone of a good doctor is the ability to feel one's heart." [5] We may paraphrase her statement this way: "As every hurting person knows, the touchstone of a Christian caregiver is the ability not merely to listen, but above all to feel the suffering person's heart." Christian ministry must surely envelop an authentic interchange of heart to heart.

My wife has a memory of a day that has long symbolized for both of us the character of Christian ministry, how faith and situations of responsibility not only shape but also compel a specific posture in ministry and may ultimately project a public witness. While on a short assignment in India, my wife and I spent several days in Calcutta (now called Kolkata). While I was busy with other things, she had time to volunteer at several of Mother Teresa's centers serving Calcutta's poor. On one day her volunteering took her to a building that was home to mentally ill women, who had been abandoned on the streets of the city. After warmly welcoming Trudy, the sister in charge led her to a large room, very clean but without furniture or chairs (only straw-woven bed rolls) where some twenty women were sitting or lying on the floor. As the sister brought her to one woman, she suggested that Trudy care for her as she was able. The sister then moved on, giving attention to others who were very ill. For a moment, Trudy was unsure of herself, standing beside and above a troubled human who was sitting beneath her, staring up at her. Trudy's natural response was to get down on the floor, sit beside the women, touching the woman ever so gently. Silent messages were exchanged. The two spoke entirely different languages and they came from different cultures and different faiths. Yet, sitting on the floor, holding hands, stroking an arm, a very unusual ministry was unfolding. Words were spoken in a caring manner, with a warm

---

5. Drexler, "18 Stethoscopes," *New York Times*, February 28, 2011.

smile, even though not fully grasped. The situation and the motive to care dictated a specific posture.

Trudy and I have gone back to that unforgettable relationship on a number of occasions. We have realized those moments provide an illustration, not unlike the account of Jesus washing the feet of the disciples. Both are illustrations of an event that points beyond the event itself toward what ought to represent the whole of our Christian life. In one sense, we cannot replicate either event. I am not sure that today's Maundy Thursday re-enactment of Christ's initial foot washing is that effective in our northern U.S. environment, as its attempts to teach the nature of Christian humility and the appropriate posture for service. To truly learn from a foot washing, you would have to walk all day with sandals in the hot Middle East sun, stumbling over rocks tearing at your feet, and collecting dirt between your toes. With pain and hurting feet, you arrive at your host's home. He is a powerful and most important person, not a slave. Yet he stoops lowly, washing your feet before you gather for the great meal he has prepared for you and others. Such an experience would be most revealing and yet also difficult to replicate authentically on Maundy Thursday or any other day. However, Jesus' words while washing the disciples' feet, "Do as I have done to you," is a powerful text for learning and practicing the Christian life of genuine, humble service in any culture or in whatever situation. The "do as I have done" brings to our mind Christ's coming from heaven above to walk among us, related intimately to our suffering and to that of all others. Christ goes to the depth of suffering, death on the cross, for all humanity. Christian ministry generally calls for a posture by which people are together on the same plane. To be sure, the posture must be representative of the entire life, the ongoing ministry, of the person who stoops to serve.

The quality of our relationship and the place from which we serve is crucial in affecting an excellent ministry. In 1995, while in Guatemala, my wife and I were guests of the Behrhorst Foundation, *Partners for Development*. Dr. Carroll Behrhorst, a visionary medical missionary, very early developed a holistic, community-based approach to economic and social development in poverty areas of Guatemala. Following his death, the creative effort has continued and expanded in various locations with a highly competent and dedicated staff, all working in partnership with local communities. Their efforts center on remote villages in extreme poverty. Several friends long related to the mission were eager to arrange an opportunity for us to witness one of their projects while we were in Guatemala. With a guide and in a jeep we were driven through the Guatemalan highlands deep into a remote area. After traveling rough roads and fording rushing streams, we came to the end of the road. The village mayor and other community leaders were waiting for us with a warm welcome. Once out of the jeep, we realized we were standing on the edge of a precipice, looking down upon the village, which was accessible only by a steep path. Those who had gathered were eager to share with us the important health and agricultural advances their community had experienced through the services of the Foundation. They were also interested in sharing their recent history and presenting their needs as we looked down on the countryside below. There before us were lush fields of various vegetables, row on row of banana trees, and meandering its way through the valley was a river shimmering under the bright summer sun. Nestled between the river and the bluff was their village, El Tesoro. Everything appeared so quiet, quaint, and peaceful; it was difficult for us to connect this sight with the death-squads that had created a killing field there only a decade or so earlier. Within the village, two churches stood out. The mayor was quick to identify his own church, a Pentecostal evangelical congregation (as he described the church), with a building primitive in construction. He then pointed to the other church, which had a large steeple, saying, "That is the Roman Catholic Church, long a center of activity within the village, and the church of my youth." But he was quick to report, "It is no longer the center of community activity, nor is it anymore my church." He appeared proud to make public that he was now a member of the Pentecostal parish; his co-workers were quick to identify with him. He said his congregation needed to build a much bigger church since they had grown far beyond the walls of their original sanctuary. This prompted a question, "Why had the Roman Catholic congregation gone into decline while their Pentecostal church had grown so large and rather quickly?" He relayed three factors. One, the Roman Catholic priest, a U.S. citizen, lived with an order of priests in a house located at a considerable distance from the village. Two, their Pentecostal minister is a Guatemalan, raised in a nearby village, now living in their village. Three, the Pentecostal congregation had been apolitical during the recent disastrous civil war, a blood bath in which many villagers were killed. The mayor claimed the

Roman Catholic priest identified with the guerrillas, exposing the membership to the death-squads. By living a considerable distance from the village, and with his U.S. passport, he was separated from the atrocities. Apparently, becoming a member of the Pentecostal church was a safe place for one's family and one's self, separated from the violent conflict between the government forces and the guerillas.

Later in the day, we were introduced to a young graduate student. She was living temporarily in the area, gathering data for her PhD thesis focused on the religious, economic, and cultural changes now evident in the area. She concurred with the mayor's three points. She added another: the Pentecostal minister maintains a steady insistence that drunkenness cannot be tolerated in the life of the Christian. Wives, for many years maltreated by their husbands, were empowered to confront their husbands, demanding that they abandon all alcohol. The sign of sobriety was for this congregation a sign of membership, which in their case, appeared to be effective. The graduate student did indicate that, in her research, it was difficult for her to obtain hard data as to what extent the sobriety had occurred and how long it was effective. However, she was sure the challenge to sobriety drew women and eventually many of their husbands to the church.

The experience reminded me of the words that I once found written on the wall in the office of a remote medical clinic in rural India: *Go to the people. Live with them, love them, start with what they know, build on what they have. When the task is finished the people will say: "We did it ourselves."* The experience in the highlands of Guatemala and the writing on the wall in India support several points that I have been making in this writing. One is the necessity that pastoral leaders identify with their community's culture and identify personally with those among whom they are in ministry. This in no way suggests approval of all aspects of their culture. However, unless there is a significant degree of identity with the people in any community in which one is called to serve, there can be little success.

Regarding the issues related to the violent civil war in Guatemala, it is not for us who sit at some distance from the events, at least in these pages, to judge who was right in that tragic period of Guatemala's history. What we can learn is this: a Christian, especially Christian leaders, who identify with an issue of justice and publically oppose an injustice, cannot live beyond the reach of the attacks on those who support the issue. Bonhoeffer is an example of one who left the comfort of New York City and a teaching position at Union Theological Seminary for a hurried return to his homeland as war clearly became inescapable in Germany. He hurriedly returned home, knowing he could not dodge his place of responsibility, his credibility; his Christian witness would only succeed if he remained in the throes of the struggle.

Missing in the above two illustrations, the Guatemalan village and the sign on the wall, are the faith conviction and the public expressions of Christians that identifies their primary motivation. To be sure, in the end it is far better for those who have been aided to recognize that they, the receivers of service, ultimately achieved responsible change, and that Christian caregivers can quietly step aside. The limelight needs to shine on the accomplishment of the people. Yet while Christian ministry must surely be directed at an identified need, Christians ought not to assume that the context of such ministry calls for proselytizing or that there should be an avoidance of witness to one's faith. In such situations, Christians surely ought to be transparent and, where appropriate, give a genuine witness to Christ as the center of one's life and ministry. In this, Bonhoeffer was an outstanding example for all of us.

Ministry in a Conflicted Culture

An empowering of people is often obvious when the caregiver is genuinely down among them, listening for their particular needs and helping each in their struggles for survival, listening to their specific calls for help. The same can be said of fellow Christians in the workplace and the marketplace, in the home, and in their political affairs within the community. For authentic growth and responsible change there is a need for openness and genuine interchange about those things most important in one's life. Being open in one's relationships is troubling for some. Many, and that at times may include some of us, are not sure whether they or we really want to become involved, whether one is even able to share personal concerns and troubled feelings. Many lack courage to express their primary values in life, their hopes, and their fears. They may also simply suffer from apathy and uncertainty. Many will, all too often, give signals that they expect their pastor to do his or her "thing" and to be left alone. At other times, they will emotionally protest if decisions are made without them being included in the decision process, or if they are not brought into the flow of information. Realizing the existence of this (at times) perplexing problem and an ambivalent attitude on the part of some, one can conclude that this is not the time to take the risk of changing one's leadership and personally to be more open and expect others to do the same. Ambiguity today within many people is a reality we must recognize, but we are not alone in this dilemma. Sensitive leadership in many fields beyond the church today is confronted with similar difficulties and challenges. However, significant change, indeed affecting others, will usually only occur when leadership takes the initiative, when one demonstrates authentic openness, willing to listen and personally willing to change when appropriate.

The demands and fast pace chosen or forced upon many Christians today would appear to stand in the way of working toward the paradigm that I have suggested in these pages. The gospel, however, challenges us to a reconsideration of our priorities and our values. Over time, with an effective installation of a different leadership style and different relations, and an increased focus on ministry in daily life, a positive response ought to be noticeable, giving strength to continued efforts. In any case, a primary factor needs consideration: a decisive cultural shift among many people today. In many relationships there will be those who will no longer be content simply to follow the leader. Unlike the past, many today are uncomfortable with or even suspicious of those in authority. Thus leaders need flexibility and the ability to meet people where they are. We need to recognize those who for various reasons (some hidden) are either incapable or unwilling to open up and engage an issue. We need an awareness that many are uncertain of the expectations of their leaders, especially when and how they wish to experience a new quality of relationship and an increased openness within their church. To assist these people, leaders need to find the means for freeing them, allowing them to be more open and expressive of their mind and convictions. Certainly we dare not condemn those who tend to be withdrawn or who would appear introverted by nature.

For pastoral relations to change, the pastor must *usually* initiate the process, and it may not *initially* be time consuming. The same may be said of leadership in the home or of any other vocation. In addition, in many situations, especially if the pastor takes the initiative, one ought to expect an immediate sense of appreciation. When a pastor known to be somewhat authoritarian gives genuine evidence of wanting to understand another person's perspective, especially in moments of disagreement, the individual may genuinely indicate appreciation for the pastor's sensitivity. Likewise, asking simple, honest questions such as, "With changes in the economy, in what way has your work become more difficult?" or, speaking to a student, "Which courses are you enjoying this semester?" Or, "Tell me about that football game last week." Such questions may appear somewhat trivial but may be quite productive in initiating substantive relations. One may be surprised to discover how good it feels to a person who has never before been approached by one's pastor regarding his or her everyday activities. However, for such an interchange to be effective, the conversations must be congruent with the prayers and sermons in the Sunday worship, along with various educational opportunities within the congregation. The pastor's question regarding one's work or any other similar questions must be integral to the whole life of the congregation and cannot be isolated. When isolated from a larger understanding, it may be seen as an intrusion into one's personal life. I trust the pages of this book have given a variety of suggestions that might be pursued to advance a more bottom-up approach, reaching for greater openness and trust among all. Other insights are surely available to each of us as we explore this important matter further. Various educational and leadership training centers are available for those open to advancing and improving the quality of a congregation's communications and gaining a greater ability to share ministry. For major change to occur, there needs to be simultaneous recognition of and practice of openness at all levels of the church—from bishops and staff to pastors and church councils.

An ecumenical program, begun 40 years ago and continuing to grow in importance across the United States, is the Stephen Ministry.[6] Pastors wanting and willing to initiate a significant congregational change—that is, toward a powerful model of shared ministry within their congregation—may want to explore this program. Following Kenneth Haugk's ordination and his obtaining a PhD in clinical psychology, he began his calling as a pastor of a congregation. However he soon realized that he had insufficient time to meet the many and varied pastoral needs of the membership. So he began organizing and training a selected group of congregants into what he initially called "a pastoral care team ministry." The congregation recognized both the quality and the commitment of those trained. The membership was invited to request a Stephen

---

6. See www.stephenministries.org/ for more information.

Minister or to refer anyone whom they felt would benefit from a regular visit. The pastor in turn would assign a team member to relate to the person asking for service. An example: Following the death of her husband and now living alone, and following the pastor's care of her during the intense period of morning, the widow was asked if she would welcome a regular visit by a Stephen Minister for the weeks ahead. She did and not only did she feel cared for, but the pastor also could feel good, knowing a lonely member was being regularly visited by a trained, caring Stephen Minister. The program has experienced tremendous growth. Annually it draws hundreds for week-long training events of pastors and team leaders who return to their congregations, there to recruit and train others. Training focuses on several strategic areas: listening skills, avoidance of being judgmental, strict confidentiality, and regular accountability in their visits and relationships, all enveloped in a clearly and specifically understood Christian ministry. The Stephen Ministry team gathers regularly with their pastor in support of each other, discussing specific cases in order to improve their service without breaking confidentiality. Since its beginning, over 10,000 congregations have participated in the Stephen Ministry training program, representing some 150 church bodies in the US and abroad. The establishment of a Stephen Ministry may be for some pastors an initial "ice breaker" in moving toward a greater shared ministry within a parish. However, churches who succeed in the development of a fine working pastoral team ministry should never assume that such constitutes the whole of shared ministry. It may, however, be a major and significant initiation of breaking with the past and setting a new and appropriate congregational understanding of our common ministry, ultimately all the people sharing a ministry anchored in baptism through their unique vocations.

There Is Comfort and Strength in Knowing That All Are Called by Christ

I recall early in my career how several of my seasoned, pastoral mentors valued the fact that they had a divine call to serve as a pastor. That awareness, they felt, was a tremendous support as they encountered difficulties within their ministry, especially as some within the congregation sought to thwart the cutting edge of the gospel. I was impressed by the strength they derived from their awareness that their calling was truly God's will. They found strength in the fact that they were indeed called by Christ to the office of public ministry and that Christ stood beside them and worked with them in their pastoral struggles.

In no way do I wish to minimize the spiritual support ordained pastors have in knowing Christ is present in their ministry, and that God gives strength to pastors in their callings. However, we seem often to have failed to transfer the same awareness to the people, the baptized, in their daily life. Should we not also assert that God has a hand in the manner by which we all arrive at our various places along the Christian way? Each of us should know and share with others that we have divine callings as parent, as worker, and as citizen. And when things become difficult, it is important that we find renewed strength in the assurance that God is a present help as we struggle for what is right, fair, and honest and work creatively toward something fresh. To be sure, when all is going well or in moments of discouragement, it is important to be reminded that in our various endeavors at work or wherever, God seeks through us to create the new, refresh the old, and realize genuine co-creativity with God for the good of all. Not only does God will integrity in our various vocations; God also expects creativity, reshaping the old into something better, perhaps something new. The people, as well as the pastor, have a right to claim a divine call and to experience the spiritual strength, growth, and creativity that come from their call by God in their respective areas of service. This awareness should lead to fresh energy in our specific situations of responsibility. In each struggle and in every situation—parent, professional, laborer, student—we should be assured by our church and by our fellow Christians of God's presence and God's will and find support in Christian communities in our struggles for faithfulness in witness and service.

Signs and Symbols of an Inverted Church

Chapter 1 gave indicators (page 10) of an organization that is inverted. However, what public signs identify one as a man or woman of Christian faith, dedicated to a life of ministry for others? The church as community and each of us as a disciple of Christ surely are signs of God's effective work through us as we serve in ministry. The stole is often recognized as a public sign of those carrying out their calling as the ordained. Stoles are those colorful creations worn by pastors that signal the season of the church year and give lively expression to the liturgical attire. In most churches, stoles are worn only by the ordained. Worship assistants, acolytes, and cross bearers are not seen wearing the stole. Many pastors, following a long tradition, will hang a stole about their neck when serving Holy Communion to the sick in the hospital or on a home call. This is also the practice by some military chaplains serving communion in the field. The stole indeed serves as a public sign of the ministry of the ordained when conducting the orders of the office, public services of word and sacrament.

But is it the exclusive sign of the ordained? What are its origins?[7] Often the stole is given to a newly ordained pastor in an ordination service accompanied by words of Jesus as recorded by Matthew: "Take my yoke upon you, and learn from me; for I am gentle and humble in heart, and you will find rest for your souls. For my yoke is easy, and my burden is light" (Matt 11:29–30). To be sure, this is an excellent text for a sermon at the ordination or installation of a pastor. However, bishops and pastors, when preaching from this text, will—or certainly should—direct the symbols of the yoke (stole) to all believing Christians. Consider this: "You, dear Christian, have been given the yoke of Christ through your baptism as has your pastor. We are all called to carry out our various ministries, in Christ's name, by being joined to a large and great team, drawn together by the Spirit, living and serving in unity, all moving in the same direction as Christ calls us forward in faith. In truth we all wear the stole, a symbol of our being yoked to Christ and to one another through Christ." Nothing in the Matthew text or preceding verses would suggest that this instruction was directed merely to The Twelve or intended for only a few. Clearly it is addressed to "all you that are weary and are carrying heavy burdens" (Matt 11:28). So we can say again that the pastor in his or her calling as the public servant of Christ embodies publicly everything that Christians are and ought to be and to do in our respective situations.[8] Thus the stole/yoke, worn by the pastor in public worship or when giving private communion, signals that the authority of the means of grace rests in the word spoken by the pastor, shared by each of us in faith, given in our baptism. The witness of the ordained in

---

7. In my search for the origin of the stole, I have found nothing conclusive or definitive, though there are many explanations.

8. One might think the one exception is the consecration of the eucharistic elements in Holy Communion. It would be hard to find a biblical passage that orders this practice. The common explanation is that the ordained pastor is the public sign of the local Christian community's unity in Christ.

preaching as well as the witness of every Christian is directly tied to our incorporation into the risen Christ, to whom all Christians are yoked.[9]

Christian Faith Is Never Private

Jim Wallis, editor of *Sojourners* magazine and a popular evangelical Christian writer, with a strong commitment to social justice, frequently reminds his readers that Christian faith is "personal but never private."[10] We dare not suggest that the baptized community should live their lives privately, as though their life was "hidden under a basket." The call to "let your light shine" (Matt 5:16) is certainly addressed to all believers, not merely to the ordained. What are the public signs of each and all of us as servants of Christ in our common and respective ministries? Perhaps the most public place for the Christian family is the living room, the place where guests, neighbors, and family gather and share some of the richness of their lives. Should there not be symbols of the family commitment to Christ in our living room?

In making many home calls as a pastor, I have only occasionally seen signs or art objects witnessing to the family's identity in Christ. We need to inform one another of those Christian artists today who might enable us to place before our guests and extended family what is the heart and center of our living, a pictorial sign that we are members of the body of Christ, a lively servant of God. I have mentioned before that, while serving in Cairo my primary means of transportation was the taxi. Christianity in Egypt is oppressed, and Christians are discriminated against in public. After sharing my few clumsy Arabic words with a taxi driver, he would look me in the eye and ask in English, "Are you Christian?" With my yes, the driver would pull up his sleeve (if he were Christian and many taxi drivers were), revealing a tattooed cross above his wrist. While it had to be hidden in their Muslim country, it was a strong witness. Surely in a free and open society, any symbol or sign of

---

9. Only recently, I discovered that two of my grandchildren, in their first communion classes (Grace Lutheran Church, River Forest, Illinois), were given a white stole several weeks before their first communion. Their assignment was to design symbols that reminded them of their baptism, and of their Christian life and service. These were attached to their stole/yoke, which they later would wear in the worship service of their first communion.

10. Wallis, *Call to Conversion*.

our faith ought ultimately to be a reflection of our public witness to the faith as we minister, each in our own unique manner.

Keeping Faith Connected to the Struggle for Justice while Recognizing the Distinction

We have attempted in this book to be up-front on a historic problem hounding Lutherans and many Protestants since the Reformation, namely, the charge that Christians are socially and politically apathetic, lacking a sound biblical social ethic. Today, many among us may still have difficulty relating faith to issues of injustice and corruption. Because some may be offended, many avoid the effort. There is also often a reverse side to this historic problem. These are the occasions when bishops and pastors from the pulpit engage political or social problems without any connection to the gospel, and the people are left to assume there is no connection between Christian faith and ethics or human, social, and political problems. Confronting a social, political crisis in the community or nation, the pastor too easily assumes that now is the time to be up-front, to let the congregation and the community understand fully the injustice of what is happening—whether others agree or not. "This is where I stand!" This indeed may be very heroic, yet such moments of declaration need to be intimately connected to the gospel—indeed, law and gospel—but never hidden from the other nor spoken without compassion for all sides. Moral nerve must be intimately connected to the realty of faith. Through the gospel the Spirit generates the nerve and courage to stand strong in the struggle for justice. At the same time, we ought never to deliver judgments against an injustice without concern for those who perpetrate the problem. We need the discipline of faith keeping us from being vindictive. In various expressions of Christian witness, the distinction between the two subjects, which we have discussed in this book, is continually important: One is the authentic and certain conviction centered in Christ and in his Word, identified by faith; and the other is the strong commitment and moral courage in the struggle for issues of justice generated through faith, while avoiding absolutes regarding solutions. How we frame the issues is very important. One can surely be absolute in insisting that God does not want anyone to go hungry, while civilly debating and disagreeing on solutions to eliminate poverty. Some Christians may feel strongly on a particular public policy being debated in a political process, but one cannot be absolute that the proposal is going to achieve what is proposed. We may want to go all out in support of a specific political solution to a particular social problem, but we should always be open for re-evaluation and reconsideration. The latter are not signs of weakness but signs of strength.

Christian faith calls us to a degree of restlessness when confronted with oppressive social and political conditions in our midst. When we pray in the Lord's Prayer, "Thy Kingdom come, Thy will be done on earth as is in heaven," we surely ought to come away from such praying with a restlessness that compels us to further God's will among us, to seek greater clarity in engaging the issues, to be instruments of God indeed, and to truly do God's will in the struggle for justice. Henri Nouwen reminds us that this restlessness of engaging injustices and struggling for justice in our daily lives is a sign of being Christian. He writes: "You are Christian only so long as you look forward to a new world, so long as you constantly pose critical questions to the society you live in, so long as you emphasize the need of conversion both for yourself and for the world, so long as you in no way let yourself become established in a situation of seeming calm, so long as you stay unsatisfied with the *status quo* and keep saying that a new world is yet to come."[11]

However, Nouwen's very important reminder calls for a balancing message from Jaroslav Pelikan expressed in his classic essay "Divine Justification and Human Justice": "The true advancement of social *justitia* [social justice, according to Luther] came not from the idealist who seeks to establish the kingdom of God on earth, nor yet from the cynic who signs an armistice with a morally ambiguous *status quo*, but from the faith-full realist who seeks to move society from the *status quo* of where it is to the ultimate goal of where it ought to be by taking one step at a time toward the proximate goal of where it can be."[12] We can apply these words to our congregational goals and activities, as well as to all our social and political endeavors at work, in the family, and wherever we find ourselves—called by the Holy Spirit and shaped by faith in Christ.

Two sentences—one from our Lord and the other from St. Paul—and words from a Christian hymn summarize our entire effort in this work. Jesus: "Whoever wishes to become great among you must be your servant" (Mark 10:43). St. Paul: "Let the same mind be in you that was

11. Nouwen, *With Open Hands*, 126.
12. Pelikan, *The Christian Intellectual*, 102.

in Christ Jesus, who . . . emptied himself . . . And being found in human form, he humbled himself" (Philippians 2:5–8). And in faith and in prayer we sing, "Then let the servant church arise, a caring church that longs to be a partner in Christ's sacrifice, and clothed in Christ's humanity . . . We have no mission but to serve in full obedience to our Lord; to care for all, without reserve, and spread his liberating word."[13]

---

13. Green, "The Church of Christ."

Bibliography

Bailey, Kenneth E. *The Cross and the Prodigal: The 15th Chapter of Luke, Seen through the Eyes of Middle Eastern Peasants.* St. Louis: Concordia, 1973.
Billing, Einar. *Our Calling.* Translated by Conrad Bergendoff. Rock Island, IL: Augustana Book Concern, 1947.
Bonhoeffer, Dietrich. *The Cost of Discipleship.* Rev. ed. New York: Macmillan, 1963.
———. *Ethics.* 1955. Reprint. New York: Simon & Schuster, 1995.
———. *Letters and Papers from Prison.* Enl. ed. Edited by Eberhard Bethge. New York: Macmillan, 1971.
———. *Life Together.* San Francisco: Harper, 1954.
The Book of Common Prayer and Administration of the Sacraments and Other Rites and Ceremonies of the Church. Greenwich, CT: Seabury, 1979.
Boston Globe. *Betrayal: The Crisis in the Catholic Church.* Boston: Little, Brown, 2002.
Cahill, Thomas. "The Peaceful Crusader." *New York Times*, December 25, 2006.
Carey, Benedict, "Evidence That Little Touches Do Mean So Much." *New York Times*, February 22, 2010.
Christian Century, September 5, 2006.
Collins, Jim. *Good to Great: Why Some Companies Make the Leap—and Others Don't.* New York: HarperBusiness, 2001.
Context (June 2007) Part B.
Crumley, James. "Dear Partners." *LCA Partners* 6 (December 1984/January 1985) 5–6.
Dahill, Lisa E. "Jesus for You: A Feminist Reading of Bonhoeffer's Christology." *Currents in Theology and Mission* 34 (2007) 251–59.
Doberstein, John W., editor. *Minister's Prayer Book: An Order of Prayers and Readings.* Philadelphia: Fortress, 1986.
Drexler, Madeline. "18 Stethoscopes, 1 Heart Murmur, and Many Missed Connections." *New York Times*, February 28, 2011.
Dunn, James D. G. *Unity and Diversity in the New Testament: An Inquiry into the Character of Earliest Christianity.* Philadelphia: Westminster, 1977.
Evangelical Lutheran Worship. Pew ed. Minneapolis: Augsburg Fortress, 2006.
Forell, George W. *Faith Active in Love: An Investigation of the Principles Underlying Luther's Social Ethics.* New York: American Press, 1954.
Forell, George W., and William H. Lazareth, editors. *Crisis in Marriage.* Philadelphia: Fortress, 1978.
Goetting, Paul. "Openness and Trust in Congregational and Synodical Leadership." *Currents in Theology and Mission* 33 (August 2006) 304–12.

Green, Fred Pratt. "The Church of Christ, in Every Age." In *Evangelical Lutheran Worship*, hymn #729. Minneapolis: Augsburg Fortress, 2006.
Haugk, Kenneth C. *Antagonists in the Church: How to Identify and Deal with Destructive Conflict*. Minneapolis: Augsburg, 1988.
Heschel, Susannah. *The Aryan Jesus: Christian Theologians and the Bible in Nazi Germany*. Princeton: Princeton University Press, 2008.
Kraemer, Hendrik. *A Theology of the Laity*. Philadelphia: Westminster, 1958.
Krentz, Edgar. "The Egalitarian Church of Matthew." *Currents in Theology and Mission* 4 (December 1977) 333–41.
Kronman, Anthony T. *Education's End: Why Our Colleges and Universities Have Given Up on the Meaning of Life*. New Haven: Yale University Press, 2007.
Lazareth, William H. *Christians in Society: Luther, the Bible, and Social Ethics*. Minneapolis: Fortress, 2001.
Levitt, Steven D., and Stephen J. Dubner. "Unbelievable Stories about Apathy and Altruism." *New York Times*, October 16, 2009.
Likert, Rensis, and Jane Gibson Likert. *New Patterns of Management*. New York: McGraw-Hill, 1961.
———. *New Ways of Managing Conflict*. New York: McGraw-Hill, 1976.
Lull, Timothy F., editor. *Martin Luther's Basic Theological Writings*. 2nd ed. Minneapolis: Fortress, 2005.
Luther, Martin. *D. Martin Luthers Werke: Kritische Gesamtausgabe*. Weimar: Böhlau, 1888.
———. *Luther's Works*. American ed. 55 vols. Edited by Jaroslav Pelikan and Helmut T. Lehman. Philadelphia: Muhlenberg and Fortress, and St. Louis: Concordia, 1955–86.
———. "Small Catechism of Martin Luther." In *Evangelical Lutheran Worship*, 1160–67. Minneapolis: Augsburg Fortress, 2006.
Lutheran Partners, July/August 2007.
"Lutherans Take Office in 111th U.S. Congress." *The Lutheran* (January 8, 2009). No pages. Online: http://www.thelutheran.org/blog/index.cfm?person_id=1408&blog_id=1102
Lutze, Karl E. *Awakening to Equality: A White Pastor at the Dawn of Civil Rights*. Columbia: University of Missouri Press, 2006.
Marius, Richard. *Martin Luther: The Christian between God and Death*. Cambridge: Harvard University Press, 1999.
Marty, Martin E. *Baptism*. Philadelphia: Muhlenberg, 1962.
———. *Martin Luther*. New York: Viking Penguin, 2004.
Mead, Walter Russell. "God's Country?" *Foreign Affairs* 85 (September/October 2006) 24–43
Miller, Clair Cain. "Social Networks a Lifeline for the Chronically Ill." *New York Times*, March 24, 2010.
Morton, James P. "Clergy: School for a New Creation." *Time Magazine*, November 19, 1965.
Niwagila, Wilson. "Gracious Spirit, Heed Our Pleading." Translated by Howard S. Olson. In *Evangelical Lutheran Worship*, Hymn #401. Minneapolis: Augsburg Fortress, 2006.
Nouwen, Henri J. M. *With Open Hands*. Photography by Ron P. van den Bosch and Theo Robert. Notre Dame, IN: Ave Maria, 1972.

---. *The Wounded Healer: Ministry in Contemporary Society*. Garden City, NY: Image, 1979.

"Ordination (with Installation at Ordination)." In *Evangelical Lutheran Worship Occasional Services for the Assembly*, 187–99. Minneapolis: Augsburg Fortress, 2009.

Ozment, Steven A. *Mighty Fortress: A New History of the German People*. New York: HarperCollins, 2005.

Pelikan, Jaroslav. *The Christian Intellectual*. New York: Harper & Row, 1965.

Rosin, Hanna. "Did Christianity Cause the Crash?" *The Atlantic* (December 2009) 38–46.

Smith, Christian et al. "Who Gives?" *The Christian Century* (October 7, 2008) 26–29.

Tannenbaum, Robert, and Warren H. Schmidt. "How to Choose a Leadership Pattern." *Harvard Business Review* 36 (March–April 1958) 95–101.

Uchitelle, Louis. "Gilded Paychecks: Lure of Great Wealth Affects Career Choices." *New York Times*, November 27, 2006.

Volz, Carl A. *Pastoral Life and Practice in the Early Church*. Minneapolis: Augsburg, 1990.

Wallis, Jim. *The Call to Conversion: Why Faith Is Always Personal but Never Private*. New York: HarperSanFrancisco, 2005.

Weinstein, Rhona S. *Reaching Higher: The Power of Expectations in Schooling*. Cambridge: Harvard University Press, 2002.

Wendebourg, Dorothea. Review of *Priesthood, Pastors, Bishops* by Timothy J. Wengert. *Lutheran Quarterly* (November 2, 2009) 348–51.

Wengert, Timothy J. *Priesthood, Pastors, Bishops: Public Ministry for the Reformation and Today*. Minneapolis: Fortress, 2008.

Wingren, Gustaf. *Luther on Vocation*. Philadelphia: Muhlenberg, 1957.

Wittwer, Tanya. "The Authority of Scripture, Women's Ordination, and the Lutheran Church of Australia." *Journal of Lutheran Ethics* (December 2009). Online: http://www.elca.org/What-We-Believe/Social-Issues/Journal-of-Lutheran-Ethics/Issues/December-2009/The-Authority-of-Scripture-Womens-Ordination-and-the-Lutheran-Church-of-Australia.aspx.

Younger, George D. *From New Creation to Urban Crisis: A History of Action Training Ministries, 1962–1975*. Chicago: Center for the Scientific Study of Religion, 1987.

Zernike, Kate. "Making College 'Relevant.'" *New York Times*, December 29, 2010.

www.ingramcontent.com/pod-product-compliance
Lightning Source LLC
Chambersburg PA
CBHW031726230426
43669CB00007B/262